WITHDRAWN BY THE
UNIVERSITY OF MICHIGAN

PURSUING MAJORITIES

CONGRESSIONAL STUDIES SERIES
Ronald M. Peters, Jr., General Editor

PURSUING MAJORITIES

Congressional Campaign Committees in American Politics

ROBIN KOLODNY

UNIVERSITY OF OKLAHOMA PRESS : NORMAN

Published with the assistance of the National Endowment for the Humanities, a federal agency which supports the study of such fields as history, philosophy, literature, and language.

Library of Congress Cataloging-in-Publication Data

Kolodny, Robin, 1964–
    Pursuing majorities: congressional campaign committees in American politics / by Robin Kolodny.
      p.   cm. — (Congressional studies series; 1)
    Includes bibliographical references and index.
    1. Campaign management—United States—History.
2. Campaign funds—United States—History.   3. Electioneering—United States—History.   I. Title. II. Series.
JK2281.K65   1998
324.7'0973 —dc21   98-9412
    ISBN 0-8061-3069-5 (cloth)   CIP
    ISBN 0-8061-3070-9 (paper)

Pursuing Majorities: Congressional Campaign Committees in American Politics is Volume 1 in the Congressional Studies Series.

The paper in this book meets the guidelines for permanence and durability of the Committee on Production Guidelines for Book Longevity of the Council on Library Resources, Inc. ∞

Copyright © 1998 by the University of Oklahoma Press, Norman, Publishing Division of the University. All rights reserved. Manufactured in the U.S.A.

1 2 3 4 5 6 7 8 9 10

CONTENTS

List of Figures and Tables	vii
Preface	ix
Acknowledgments	xv
List of Abbreviations	2
1. Separate Elections in a Separated System	3
2. Congressional Campaign Committees in the House of Representatives, 1866–1920	15
3. The Senate Campaign Committees, 1919–1972	68
4. The House Campaign Committees, 1922–1972	99
5. Campaign Finance Reform and the Congressional Campaign Committees	124
6. Leadership and the Organization of the Congressional Party: Where Does the Congressional Campaign Committee Chair Fit In?	156
7. The Contract with America and the National Republican Congressional Committee: Innovation or Adaptation?	197
Appendix. Tables A.1–A.20	217
Notes	241
Bibliography	275
Index	287

FIGURES AND TABLES

Figures

1	Leadership in the House	161
2	Leadership in the Senate	165

Tables

5.1	Coordinated Expenditure Limits for Campaigns for the House of Representatives	140
6.1	Average Careers for CCC Chairs	172
6.2	CCC Chairs Who Rose in Leadership Ranks	178
6.3	CCC Chairs Who Were Unsuccessful Leadership Contestants	180
A.1	Election Results, 1866–1996	218
A.2	Democratic Congressional Campaign Committee Chairs	222
A.3	National Republican Congressional Committee Chairs	223
A.4	Democratic Senatorial Campaign Committee Chairs	224
A.5	National Republican Senatorial Committee Chairs	225
A.6	RNC Contributions	226

A.7	RNC Expenditures	226
A.8	NRSC Contributions	228
A.9	NRSC Expenditures	228
A.10	NRCC Contributions	230
A.11	NRCC Expenditures	230
A.12	DNC Contributions	232
A.13	DNC Expenditures	232
A.14	DSCC Contributions	234
A.15	DSCC Expenditures	234
A.16	DCCC Contributions	236
A.17	DCCC Expenditures	236
A.18	Average Campaign Disbursements, Democrats	238
A.19	Average Campaign Disbursements, Republicans	238
A.20	Consumer Price Index Conversion Factors	239

PREFACE

ON SEPTEMBER 27, 1994, more than three hundred Republican candidates for the U.S. House of Representatives assembled on the steps of the Capitol to announce the creation and endorsement of a document known as the Contract with America—a ten-point program that Republican candidates, both incumbents and challengers, promised to enact if the voters made them the majority party. Although the 1994 elections may have indicated approval of a conservative agenda, the Contract itself was given little attention throughout the general election campaign. The Contract did allow challengers to capitalize on a popular national agenda for use in local races. Therefore, it was a critical campaign tool for House Republicans to attain their first majority in more than forty years.

The Contract with America was the culmination of a cooperative effort by the House Republican Conference, the Republican National Committee (RNC), and the National Republican Congressional Committee (NRCC). This effort began after the 1992 elections, which brought about changes in both those politicians who were elected and the strategic outlook they held for future elections. George Bush lost the presidency, which left the Republican National Committee without a clear leader or mission; House minority leader Bob Michel (R-IL) announced his intention not to seek reelection in 1994, creating a future vacancy in the House Republican Conference's top leadership position; and NRCC chair Guy Vander Jagt (R-MI) lost his bid for the Republican primary nomination for his own congressional seat, creating a vacancy for the 1994 election cycle. With the defeat of President George Bush, an open contest ensued for the vacant position of Republican National Committee chair, and Haley Barbour of Mississippi emerged the victor. With Michel's retirement announcement, minority whip Newt Gingrich (R-GA) had locked up the party leader's contest more than a year early. The day after Guy Vander Jagt lost his primary, Rep. Bill Paxon (R-NY) contacted supporters about launching a bid to chair the NRCC, a post he won without contest. Barbour, Gingrich, and Paxon proceeded to define their relationship for the conduct of the 1994 elections.

The close alliance that followed was possible for both structural and political reasons. On the structural side, the 1994 elections were midterm congressional contests with no presidential race involved. They took place under the first unified Democratic rule since 1980. Also, a large number of vulnerable first-term Democratic members were up for reelection. On the political side, the NRCC was in debt and needed help (which it got from the RNC) and new RNC chair Haley Barbour, NRCC chair Bill Paxon, and whip Newt Gingrich forged a collegial working relationship (which included an invitation to Barbour to attend House leadership meetings, an invitation that was rescinded in 1995). Together, these factors accounted for the specific working relationship that gave birth to the Contract with America.

Each election cycle contains a different set of variables that the congressional campaign committees (CCCs) evaluate to realize one outcome: majority status for the congressional party in question. The NRCC protected a majority after 1994, which meant they subsequently adopted a strategy to maintain current officeholders instead of aggressively backing nonincumbent candidates. In 1996 the RNC focused on the presidential race, trying to expel the Democratic incumbent. The NRCC did not present a Contract '96 to retain their majority. Compared to their 1994 effort, the RNC provided negligible funds for congressional races. In the 1996 election cycle, the two committees were also competitors for fund-raising resources.

The above example illustrates many of the points of this book, which is an analysis and history of the four congressional campaign committees—the National Republican Congressional Committee, the Democratic Congressional Campaign Committee (DCCC), the National Republican Senatorial Committee (NRSC), and the Democratic Senatorial Campaign Committee (DSCC)—from their inception in the mid-1860s to the present day. The CCCs are led by representatives or senators and work to help their party become or remain the majority in their chamber of Congress. A strategy pursued by any one of the CCCs will depend on the current definition of the institutional party interest in the chamber. Structural variables that shape this common interest include whether or not the congressional party is in the majority, the presence or absence of a presidential election, the dominant campaign techniques of the time, and the public evaluation of the political parties. Political variables may include the relationship of the national committee leaders to congressional leaders and the individual abilities of CCC heads.

This book makes the argument that such considerations are now and have always been at the heart of how CCCs conduct their business. The CCCs have always sought institutional party goals (specifically the attainment or retainment of majority status) based on an assessment of the above factors. Therefore, this book deals with two major themes: reconstructing the history of the CCCs to show their campaign activities in historical political context and illustrating the relationship of the CCCs to the leadership of their congressional party rather than the national party overall.

But this book is about more than the histories of these four institutions. It illustrates the inadequacy of political parties in America as remedies for the divisive effects of separation of powers in a presidential political system. This is not a new theme: many have illustrated the drawbacks of separation of powers in the making of public policy and on institutional reputation. However, this study uncovers the depth and permanence of institutional divisions within political parties by exposing the persistent tension in the electoral strategies pursued by the congressional parties and their affiliated presidential party.

I first began investigating the CCCs because although they are present on party organizational charts, there are allegations that they do nothing that results in material electoral gains. I wondered why they existed and for how long. Following a new institutionalist approach, I looked into the CCCs' origins and development. Not only did contemporary staff have no idea when their organizations began, they had little institutional memory extending back more than two or three election cycles. Worse, the CCCs did not keep any archival files. It did not take long to discover that such an omission was *deliberate*: all the CCCs engaged in illegal or unethical campaign practices, and before the Federal Election Campaign Act (FECA) they were not consistently asked to make public reports of their activities. CCC executive directors thus either destroyed old files or simply threw them out when they relocated to new offices (which was frequent before the mid-1970s). Scholars of the two national party committees have confronted similar difficulties, though secondary sources documenting RNC and DNC activities are more common than those documenting CCC activity.

If the CCCs had been mere appendages to the party organizations (as some earlier literature implies), this would have been a short research project. However, since one of my central hypotheses is that CCCs are integral parts of the congressional party in government, I turned my attention to the individuals who chaired the CCCs over time and sought information on CCC activity from their personal congressional papers. I gambled that although executive directors were afraid of subpoenas (as a few explicitly told me in explaining their systematic destruction of CCC records), members of Congress were interested in their historical legacy. For the most part, I was right. The historical chapters contain my findings. I want to caution readers that I do not consider these chapters to be complete or definitive. Not all CCC chairs could be accurately identified, and gaps therefore exist in the appendix tables listing CCC chairs. Even when chairs could be identified, information on their tenure was not always available. I have visited or received material from twenty-five archives, 90 percent of them papers of members of Congress. Fortunately, many archives contained material concerning preceding or succeeding CCCs or the opponent's CCC. I have interviewed former CCC staff and chairs when possible. Other sources include contemporary journalistic accounts and secondary sources. This book will almost certainly frustrate both historians and political scientists as it does not completely fulfill the needs of either. Historians will lament the wide focus of the study (1866–1996) and the necessarily brief description of the context in which CCCs conducted their activities. Political scientists will lament the imprecise information archival sources yield. I do not see this study as the end of inquiry but rather as the beginning, and hope that other scholars will flesh out the skeleton I have constructed.

The plan of the book is as follows. Chapter 1 presents the theoretical argument, showing how the separation of powers impedes any meaningful integration of political institutions (such as the presidency and Congress) through political parties. Here I discuss how the congressional parties need not necessarily clash with the presidential parties to have a separate and distinct mission. Chapter 2 presents a history of the two House CCCs, from the creation of the NRCC in 1866 and the DCCC in about 1868 until the formation of the Senate CCCs in 1919. Chapter 3 presents a history of the senatorial committees from 1919 to 1974, and chapter 4 presents a history of the House committees in the same period. Chapter 5 discusses the implications of campaign finance reform for CCC fund-raising and the current services provided by the CCCs. The activities of the CCCs from 1974 to 1996 are discussed in this context. Chapter 6 details the connection between the internal activities of the congressional parties and the CCCs by demonstrating the relationship among CCC chairs, leadership ambition, and the goals of the congressional party. Chapter 7 returns to the Contract with America and shows how changes in campaign philosophies about an aggressive quest for electoral majorities have altered the campaign committees' practices and considers some implications of this study.

ACKNOWLEDGMENTS

THIS PROJECT BEGAN its long journey as my doctoral dissertation at The Johns Hopkins University under the direction of Professor Richard Katz and Professor Robert Peabody. Both encouraged me to push on despite the apparent dead ends. I am glad they did.

I have many people to thank for helping me complete this research. First, let me acknowledge the generous assistance of the Everett McKinley Dirksen Congressional Leadership Research Center's 1990 Congressional Research Grant which was critical to the conduct of the archival research. John Kornacki, then the Dirksen Center's director and now the chief of the Legislative Resource Center of the U.S. House of Representatives, was especially helpful when I visited the center to use their congressional archives. Over the years, he listened to my progress and my frustration over the uneven state of congressional archives around the country. I owe much to the archivists at the twenty-five archives from which I collected data; they are the unsung heroes of historical congressional research. Without the detailed knowledge many of them have of their collections, much valuable information would have been missed. The names of those who helped are too numerous to recount here; the bibliography contains a complete list of the archives I visited. I would also like to thank all those who granted me interviews; those who agreed to be cited are listed in the bibliography. I am also grateful to all those who helped me identify appropriate interviewees, especially Kathleen Havey, Ronald Lefrançois, and Margo Nousen who were staff members to Rep. Nancy Johnson (R-CT) while I was an American Political Science Association (APSA) Congressional Fellow in that office in 1995. I also owe a special debt to Representative Johnson for relating her experience with the NRCC and helping me witness NRCC activities firsthand.

A number of scholars also assisted the growth of this project, perhaps none more than Paul Herrnson. I became acquainted with Paul while I was still a graduate student, and his encouragement throughout is much appreciated. Although I do not agree with all of Paul's arguments concerning the CCCs, he has consistently applauded my efforts to draw more attention to the role the CCCs play in U.S. politics. Another scholar of CCCs, Diana Dwyre, has read most of this work in one form or another and has been a constant source of encouragement and thoughtful criticism. We have collaborated recently on CCC/NC relationships, and this collaboration has been invaluable to the revision of this book. Anthony Gierzynski and David Menefee-Libey were kind enough to share with me their dissertations on state legislative campaign committees and the three Democratic party organizations since the 1960s, respectively. Stephen Hess let me sit in his office at the Brookings Institution and rifle through his files on his own staff experience at the NRCC. Brooks Jackson, then with the *Wall Street Journal*, was kind enough to talk to me about his book *Honest Graft* and gave me names and telephone numbers of potential interviewees on this topic. Gary Mucciaroni read most of the dissertation and gave helpful suggestions for its revision. David Mayhew read a conference paper from this project years ago and provided thoughtful comments and bibliographic references. Gary Jacobson and David Rohde also read a conference paper from this project, and both have been supportive of my efforts over the years. Janine

Holc read the manuscript several times; her thoughts, suggestions, and friendship have been critical to the success of this project. I also owe special thanks to my colleagues at Temple University, especially Richard Deeg, Barbara Ferman, Bernard Mennis, Lynn Miller, Gary Mucciaroni, Joseph Schwartz, and Sandra Suarez, for their willingness to let me prattle on about my argument and for their overall support. Bernard Mennis arranged for me to make a presentation to the department during the first round of revisions which proved especially helpful in producing the final product. I also owe a debt of gratitude to David Farrell, Ralph Goldman, Susan Webb Hammond, Linda Kowalcky, Michael Moore, Thomas Little, Daniel Shea, Sue Thomas, Carolyn Thompson, and John Kenneth White for their indulgence in CCC discussions and for their assistance over the years.

One of the more significant debts I owe is to the three individuals who read the manuscript for the University of Oklahoma Press: John J. Pitney, Jr., Ronald M. Peters, Jr., and Steven S. Smith. This book is considerably stronger because of their thoughtful comments. Ron Peters's comments were especially valuable for their thoroughness and specificity. Many others at the University of Oklahoma Press deserve special thanks, especially Kimberly Wiar, senior editor, who was always patient with my numerous questions and with me in general. Alice Stanton skillfully supervised the book's production, and Sheila Berg greatly improved its clarity.

I would like to single out two individuals who were critical to this book's development: the Honorable Anthony Coelho and the Honorable Guy Vander Jagt. Both granted me personal and candid interviews. More important, if not for their extraordinary efforts at the helm of the DCCC and NRCC respectively, no one in the academic community would give the CCCs any serious consideration.

Finally, I owe more than I can say to the two people to whom I dedicate this book: my mother, Sondra Koch, and my husband, Glen Gaddy. My mother has been a constant source of encouragement in my academic career. I thank her for her support and for starting "the box" with copies of all my academic efforts. I cannot thank my husband enough for his contribution to this project. Not only has he competed with the CCCs for my attention throughout the majority of our courtship and all of our married life to date, he has rolled up his sleeves and helped me with the nitty gritty: sifting through archives, doing my bidding in libraries, making sense of computer spreadsheets, helping to sort through the mountain of materials I accumulated, and reading each and every version of the manuscript. It would not have been possible to finish this book without Glen's love and assistance.

PURSUING MAJORITIES

ABBREVIATIONS

CCC	congressional campaign committee
COLA	cost of living adjustment
COS	Conservative Opportunity Society
DCC	Democratic Congressional Committee
DCCC	Democratic Congressional Campaign Committee
DNC	Democratic National Committee
DSCC	Democratic Senatorial Campaign Committee
FEC	Federal Election Commission
FECA	Federal Election Campaign Act
IRP	Incumbent Review Panel
LCC	legislative campaign committee
NC	national committee
NRCC	National Republican Congressional Committee
NRSC	National Republican Senatorial Committee
PAC	political action committee
RCC	Republican Congressional Committee
RNC	Republican National Committee
RNFC	Republican National Finance Committee
VAP	voting age population

CHAPTER 1

SEPARATE ELECTIONS IN A SEPARATED SYSTEM

CONGRESSIONAL CAMPAIGN COMMITTEES were formed to prevent the full integration of the institutions of the presidency and Congress through the device of political parties. That is, members of Congress came to see that their political situation was of only secondary concern to presidential candidates of their party, and they invented CCCs to prevent the presidential party from dictating their electoral strategy. The reason for this change was the tacit acknowledgment that the partisans in Congress could not control the actions of the president, who since the 1840s had acted in the capacity of party head. While formal party organizations at the national level emerged in the 1840s for the express purpose of coordinating the nomination of the presidential candidate, congressional campaigns were still considered local or state affairs. No explicit organizational apparatus was established for candidates to the House of Representatives within the Democratic National Committee (DNC) or later the Republican National Committee (RNC), the national party organizations created to coordinate the presidential nomination and to campaign for the party's full slate of candidates.[1] Instead, the party's presidential nominee and the party's national convention (at first in consultation with members of Congress) set the tone, theme, and general issues for the upcoming campaign.[2]

The idea that political parties would serve the interests of the presidential campaign and that those interests would unite others elected under that party label was relatively short-lived. In 1866 Republicans in the House of Representatives created a separate organization to pursue their institutional interests in the upcoming midterm congressional elections *in direct opposition* to the articulated campaign themes of their party's president. (See chapter 2 for a discussion of the specific circumstances of the break around 1866.) Congressional Republicans recognized a difference of interests between the individuals in Congress who considered themselves duly elected members of the Republican party (each having a definition of Republican policies) and a president who considered himself the sole articulator of Republican party values. It is this difference of interests between those elected to represent the people in their localities and the one elected to represent the people as a nation, embedded in the constitutional structure itself, that cannot be reconciled by the device of political party.[3]

The creation of a separate electoral organization by Republicans in the House of Representatives (soon followed by the creation of a like organization by House Democrats) for their institutional interests exclusive of the president or presidential candidate is a significant facet of American politics. Indeed, David Truman and James MacGregor Burns have argued that the congressional party has an identity distinct from the presidential party.[4] It is possible, as others have argued,[5] to describe "party" in the American context as meaning little more than a general approach to governmental issues rather than an explicit statement of policies. Thus individual officeholders or voters make choices about party affiliation based on their interpretation of this approach.

A "common approach" does not necessarily mean common interests. In this sense, I argue that *institutional party interest*, which is shared by co-partisans in the same elected institution, is a dynamic term. That is, members of the House or Senate prefer to serve in the majority party, which controls the organization of the chamber. All members of Congress who affiliate with the same political party want to see that party attain majority status regardless of the situation of their party's presidential candidate. The political party literature often overlooks this distinct goal. According to political party theory, all affiliates of a political party want to control all facets of government.[6] At the national level, that means parties should seek to control the presidency, the Senate, and the House of Representatives concurrently. The expectation is that total control of national institutions will result in clear policy outcomes. Instead, we have many examples of periods in which unified government has not necessarily produced harmony.[7] Indeed, during these periods of unified party rule, the president tends to dominate, a situation that rarely pleases most of his co-partisan elected officeholders in Congress, especially during midterm election years. Therefore, the specific parameters of institutional party interest and the strategies for achieving it are subject to renegotiation after each election cycle.

If political party platforms (those written at the national conventions that nominate the presidential candidate) were dispassionate documents untainted by the personality of a presidential nominee (which they clearly are not), then perhaps we could see how officeholders of the three elected institutions might be able to put aside their divergent institutional interests and personal differences to pass an agenda. This is the case in most European party systems, where the agendas are determined prior to the selection of candidates (and not as a result of that selection). In the American system, individual candidate's interests play a central role in politics. It is, at times, remarkable that any party feeling exists at all. Thus institutional party interest is the maximization of the electoral security of all party-nominated elected officials in a particular governmental institution (i.e., House of Representatives, state senate, city council) with minimal costs for any one of them. There is a natural tendency for all party-nominated candidates for a similar office to help one another (their potential future colleagues) so that all of them may benefit (by being in a majority) without any individual believing his or her own interests must suffer.

At this point institutional party interest must be clarified further. Though the congressional parties have divergent interests from the presidential party, the congressional parties' interests are further subdivided by chamber. The collective electoral interests of the House parties are quite different from the Senate parties. For one thing, the House has the potential to reconstitute itself wholly every two years, a scenario the Senate does not face. House parties are necessarily more concerned with the national electoral landscape than the senatorial parties, which though facing a potential change in party control every two years, find only one-third (or 34 out of 100 at most) of their membership affected by electoral concerns in any given two-year cycle. Another difference is the magnitude of races each chamber's party considers. Knowing that the House parties are constantly concerned with 435 races explains why their approach to elections has been more systematic, and less idiosyncratic, than the Senate parties' approach to their 34 races per cycle.

The problem for all congressional partisans, though, is the nature of the presidency. If you are a member of Congress, either you share the same party label as the president or you do not. If the president is of your party, he may be powerful or a lame duck. Your party in Congress may or may not be in the majority, which is more meaningful to a president than simple common party affiliation (i.e., the president tends not to work as closely with the minority party even if it is his own). All these factors account for the changing relationship between presidential and congressional candidates which depends largely on the current partisan control of the White House and both chambers of Congress. One thing is clear: members of congressional parties are not well served by identifying their interests exclusively with those of their affiliated presidential party.

Such institutional party interest, in this case the interests of each of the parties in the House and Senate, does not necessarily clash with the interests of the presidential party. The initial presumption of each chamber's partisans is that their main goal is to retain or acquire majority status. Whether that goal can be achieved by cooperating or coordinating with the presidential party is another matter entirely. Again, the congressional and presidential party organizations are not necessarily at odds, though they may be. It does mean that institutional party interest for the congressional parties is subject to redefinition after each election cycle. That a redefinition takes place is the most consistent element in the relationship of the CCCs with the national committees (NCs). Since the CCCs exist to pursue majority status, they are the designated agents representing the congressional parties in election planning at the national level. At times, for example, when there is a popular presidential candidate, cooperation and integration between some or all of the CCCs and the NCs may benefit the congressional and presidential parties. At other times, when there is no incumbent president or presidential election, the activities, interests, and wishes of the NCs (which between presidential elections are often working on statewide races) may be considered irrelevant by the CCCs. All six national party organizations (the two NCs and the four CCCs) assess their position after each election and alter their strategies for achieving their institutional goals. The odd-numbered "off-year" after each election presents the maximum opportunity for political, organizational, and fundraising innovation for all six party committees. This is important for understanding the behavior of party organizations, the CCCs in particular.

Given that congressional parties formed the CCCs and that their collective party interests are reexamined after every election, it is no surprise that CCCs are commanded by congressional party leaders, not the president or the chair of the NC. The highest formal party leaders in the four congressional parties have a significant role in selecting members and chairs of the CCCs (who are themselves senators or representatives).[8] Moreover, many congressional party leaders are active in their CCCs, some to the point of making decisions about CCC activities (bypassing the CCC chairs). In recent years the CCC chair has been a more visible part of the leadership circle.

The relationship between congressional leaders and the CCCs differs from the relationship of presidents or presidential candidates to the NCs. Congressional leaders, of course, have their own campaign organizations for their individual reelection campaigns. They cannot (or would not if it were possible) graft their campaign organizations onto the CCC, which is precisely what presidential candidates do to their party's NC once they win the presidency. At that point the national committee becomes the incumbent president's reelection committee (or, if the president is in his second term, a committee to improve the environment for the nomination of the president's preferred successor). The CCC pursues majority status for the congressional party, which means assisting a number of campaigns, but not any one campaign in particular.[9]

Congressional leaders seek majority status in their particular chamber. They have constructed the CCCs so that incumbent members may contribute to the effort of maximizing the number of future incumbents.[10] If enough incumbents win, a majority will result, making all members of that majority more able to achieve real power in their chamber. This incentive allows members to link their separate, though simultaneous, election campaigns. In an important sense the CCCs create an institutional interest out of the collection of individual members' interests, making the pursuit of an institutional party interest possible. The CCC structure contains only chamber partisans and staff. This is a starkly different construction from that of the NCs, which focus primarily on their presidential candidate and secondarily on governors and state legislatures. NCs include among their members state party officials and supporters of the last presidential nominee. They will lead the efforts of the next nomination season culminating in the national convention. NC chairs and officers are not members of the executive branch and have no institutional capacity to influence governmental decisions. This is in stark contrast to the relationship between CCCs and their constituency, since the candidates (primarily incumbent members of Congress) they serve also compose their board of directors. The CCCs' relationship to the constituency they serve is so fundamentally different from the NCs' relationship to their constituency that it is inaccurate to describe the CCCs as parts of larger unitary party organizations.

Unlike the national committees, the CCCs have two facets that address the congressional party's collective interest: internal (party leadership) and external (campaigning). The two are so intertwined that it is impossible to imagine the CCCs servicing only one. I begin my examination with the external facet. As mentioned above, the principal goal of the CCCs is majority status in their chamber. However, since members of Congress run individual campaigns for their seats,[11] and since the winning of majority status depends on winning many seats without regard for the particular individuals who occupy them, why would members support the idea of a CCC at all? Because since 1866 the CCCs have provided an important economy of scale for incumbents and challengers regarding Washington resources.[12] The exact forms of these Washington resources have changed over time, but they can be defined as any electoral benefit that is more easily obtained in Washington, D.C., than in the local congressional district. Over the history of the CCCs, Washington resources have included a centrally administered speakers' bureau, the production of campaign literature with national themes, and, more recently, media services designed to foster members' communications with their districts while they are in the capital.[13] This is an extension of David Mayhew's argument that Congress is institutionally organized to further the election of its members. Reelection, unlike committee assignments and leadership positions, is a common goal pursued by all members individually and simultaneously but not in competition with one another. It is in the interest of all members to pool resources as efficiently as possible. The reelection goal can be furthered by Congress's institutional structure. Universal goods such as office space, staff, committee work (which can provide individual members with opportunities for self-promotion in their districts), and the ability to oppose party initiatives without retribution allow members to have maximum opportunities for electoral success with minimal costs.[14] The role of CCCs as service organizations primarily for incumbents of the congressional party follows this line of reasoning.

The CCCs are less equipped to tell candidates how to assess the political climate in their local districts. Indeed, all four CCCs have consistently refused to become involved formally in primary politics, although there have been exceptions under extraordinary political circumstances.[15] The prohibition on pre-primary endorsements has forced the CCCs to focus on general election assistance, so unlike state legislative campaign committees (LCCs), the CCCs have seldom found themselves working against state or local party organizations.[16] Because the focus of the CCCs' external activities has always been and remains on facilitating the distribution of national, or Washington-oriented, goods to individual candidates, there is little supplanting of other party organizations at either the state, local, or national level.[17]

The rationale for this focus is straightforward: Why should each member of the same institutional party develop the same contacts and garner the same information in a competitive manner when an agent, the CCC, can acquire it for them without any significant loss of benefit?[18] Using a contemporary example, without a CCC each member or nonincumbent candidate would contact several hundred political action committees (PACs), campaign consultants, pollsters, media experts, legal counsel for Federal Election Commission (FEC) matters, and, upon arrival in Washington, D.C., potential staff members and fund-raisers. Each individual would spend considerable time doing this, and most individuals would contact the same Washington sources. By allowing the CCC to make these "transactional" contacts,[19] candidates get the information they need efficiently and in minimal competition with one another.[20] The only candidates who do not benefit from this arrangement are those who are least likely to win their races, since they are least likely to receive substantial services from the CCC. This is perfectly consistent with the CCCs' goal of achieving majority status. Washington resources, which are not infinite, should focus on the most viable candidacies.

Though the example provided above is a modern one, the task of centralizing national campaign resources has remained consistent since the founding of the CCCs. Thus a corollary of the argument that CCCs work toward achieving congressional majorities is that they have historically provided Washington resources, even when these resources were not as visible as they are today. This finding contradicts several assertions that the CCCs were moribund, and have come alive only in the last twenty years.[21] In fact, a central assertion of this book is that CCCs have consistently served the external needs of the congressional party—but through a changing array of services. Significant alterations in CCC campaign activity occurred in response to changes in the congressional campaign environment. When a significant structural change took place, such as a change in campaign laws or an advance in technology, CCCs had to redefine what activities would serve the collective party interest.

CCCs do not serve this collective action problem perfectly in two respects. First, they cannot secure real power for themselves because they cannot bind their clientele to them. That is, candidates can and do duplicate CCC services by making contacts with the Washington community themselves. The actions of individual candidates are the subject of a large literature in political science and remain separate from our central concern. Second, CCCs are pulled constantly between pursuing majorities and protecting incumbents. These goals do not necessarily conflict, as they may be the same if the congressional party defends a majority; then protecting incumbents is tantamount to preserving a majority. But when a congressional party holds a minority, the pursuit of a majority demands committing resources to nonincumbent candidates. At the same time, incumbents must be maintained or the majority goal may prove elusive. The problem is that CCCs traditionally have insufficient resources to allocate to all incumbent and nonincumbent candidates (except, perhaps, for the senatorial Republicans in the 1980s and 1990s whose resources exceeded their legal authority to fund all current races). When priorities have to be made, logic dictates that candidates, regardless of incumbency status, be allocated resources based on the likely closeness (competitiveness) of the race and the probability that increased resources would bring about a victory.[22] But if this means ranking nonincumbent candidates ahead of incumbent candidates, CCCs might be unable to pursue a majority efficiently because of complaints by incumbents. Although all incumbents prefer to be in a majority, they also prefer to keep their seats (whether they serve as part of a majority or a minority). Since incumbents are known to feel electorally insecure (whether or not that belief has any rational basis),[23] they have the ability to coerce a CCC to put incumbent protection ahead of majority pursuit. Because CCCs are operated by incumbents for the benefit of incumbents, there is no reliable recourse for such inefficiency. Of course, the counter-argument is that elections are so uncertain that one can never guarantee that a safe incumbent is truly "safe." So congressional parties struggle internally to determine the maximal common strategy.

These choices spill over into the governing side of the congressional party. CCCs have served an important internal purpose. Specifically, the position of CCC chair has allowed members interested in leadership positions to demonstrate their talents to key party leaders and the party's membership generally. This is because campaigning has always been considered important for governing. Early in the history of CCCs, chairing a CCC was tantamount to a major leadership position. Important politicians held these posts in an era before the growth of the congressional leadership structure. In more recent times, chairing a CCC or performing a sizable amount of fund-raising for a CCC gives a member high prestige among his colleagues, which could lead to future rewards. This leadership connection is explicitly linked to the election needs of the party in Congress, but this relationship has its limits: the success or failure of CCC chairs is not assessed in terms of number of seats won or lost. Though a big win can never hurt a CCC chair's career, the electoral outcome is less important than the chair's perceived efforts. This is because members know that CCCs are inherently limited in what they can do to win individual elections. Their focus is on Washington resources, and very often local dynamics or national political trends that are far beyond the control of CCCs will have the greatest impact on electoral outcomes.

As stated earlier, key party leaders have a significant role in determining CCC chairs. The hypothesis here is that one of two things occurs: either leaders choose (or endorse for election) CCC chairs who hold similar beliefs and interests or leaders choose CCC chairs who have leadership potential and provide them with a venue for proving their abilities. (See chapter 6 for the career paths of former CCC chairs.) The incentive structure for CCC chairs can differ very much by chamber. Specifically, the flatness of the Senate leadership hierarchy means that Senate CCC chairs may desire two other equally important rewards for their service: high-quality committee assignments and fund-raising contacts for potential presidential bids. Though House CCC chairs may also have these goals in mind, they tend to have many more opportunities for advancement in the leadership ladder and try to parlay their experiences accordingly. The discussion here has been about chairs of CCCs and not the full committee membership because chairs have always had the greatest influence on the policies and staff of CCCs. The committee has only an advisory function.

The histories of the CCCs teach us much about American politics, political parties, and Congress. Our system calls for separation of powers and separate election of our leaders. We have long hoped that political parties would remedy the ensuing confusion. However, CCCs show that politicians' self-interests, fostered by such a separated system, interfere with any serious effort at creating such a unifying force. Though political scientists have long observed the tensions between the presidential and congressional wings of political parties, this study shows that if there had been any chance at true party unity across institutions, it was eliminated long ago. The CCCs not only enabled the congressional party to take care of its interests separately from the presidential party, they aided the internal development of the congressional party by providing it with a means to conceive of governing with or without the cooperation of the president.

CHAPTER 2

CONGRESSIONAL CAMPAIGN COMMITTEES IN THE HOUSE OF REPRESENTATIVES, 1866–1920

HERE WE EXPLORE THE ORIGINS of the congressional campaign committees for the House of Representatives and trace their development until 1920. The year 1920 is a watermark because it represents the first election in which all U.S. senators were directly elected.[1] Until 1919 only the congressional parties in the House had a need for electoral services, and senators, who were generally appointed to their positions by state legislatures, felt that they should direct the activities of the congressional parties in both houses. Therefore, the early CCCs are devoted exclusively to the Washington-based campaign activities of the House committees. The relationship of these activities to the leadership of the congressional parties began to emerge in this period as the formation of the CCCs accompanied the beginning of careerism and leadership development in Congress.

The first CCC, the National Republican Congressional Committee,[2] emerged in the context of presidential/congressional conflict. Once established, CCCs settled into their long-term role as Washington resource providers for House candidates. The CCCs first provided services for an "army style" of campaigning, which then were supplemented with additional services as the nature of campaigning changed. Using Robert J. Dinkin's delineations of campaigning in America,[3] we find that political campaigns were in transition from the army style to the "merchandised style."

The army style employed mass mobilization techniques such as marching societies and public speakers paraded in front of mass demonstrations. CCCs supplied national speakers for use in these public events. As newspapers became more available, political literature became more important. The campaign committees responded by acquiring the means to produce and distribute literature to their candidates. These two key activities were the focus of CCCs until the 1920s, when the advent of radio technology again transformed congressional campaigns.

The establishment of CCCs coincided with the institutionalization of congressional careers. Members began serving more terms by the end of the nineteenth century and seniority became an important internal norm in the House.[4] The congressional committee system became more central to the growing work of Congress, and as the number of issues increased, the management of legislative business became more important. There is very little development of congressional leadership until 1910, when the overthrow of Speaker Joseph Cannon drew attention to the distribution of power in the House. However, CCCs were headed by prominent politicians known for their oratorical and organizational talents. After their busy origins, the CCCs converted to short-term full-time operations, normally becoming active in the last six months of an election year and remaining dormant in off-years. During this period, normally characterized by Republican dominance of the presidency, there was a great deal of electoral volatility at the congressional level. In this uncertain environment, CCCs became entrenched as service organizations for incumbent members of Congress, with little outreach to challenger candidates. This is the beginning of CCC attempts to pursue majorities through direct assistance to candidates.

Origins: The NRCC

According to James G. March and Johan P. Olsen, the origins of institutions do matter.[5] Therefore, the circumstances surrounding the creation of the first CCC are critical. The Union Congressional Committee (now known as the National Republican Congressional Committee) emerged as a deliberate counter to the political activities of Republican president Andrew Johnson for the conduct of the midterm elections of 1866. It took an extreme set of circumstances to develop a new political organization, but its drama lays bare the fundamental differences between the congressional and presidential perspectives on elections and party goals. First, we must explore the setting for the beginning of the Johnson administration and the animosity between the congressional Republicans and the president. Next, we must ask why the congressional Republicans viewed these differences as persistent enough to warrant a continued institutional presence (the retention of the Republican congressional campaign committee) beyond the Johnson presidency.

On April 15, 1865, Americans were in shock over the assassination of Abraham Lincoln. Just ten days before, the Southern armies surrendered at Appomattox Courthouse, ending the bloody Civil War. Now the president whose election sparked the war and whose leadership brought about the peace lay dying. As Lincoln drew his last breath, the awesome task of reuniting the war-torn states had not even begun. Reconstruction would be left to Andrew Johnson, Lincoln's vice president and a Southerner. This was indeed an ironic twist, for Johnson's presence on the ticket in 1864 had been a concession to loyal Southerners by Lincoln and was not an expression of general Republican party sentiment. Under these trying conditions, Andrew Johnson assumed the presidency.

Not much was known of Johnson at the time, in part because of the scant public exposure vice presidents received in the nineteenth century. The "Radical" Republicans, a faction led by northwestern Republicans who were persistent and vocal critics of the South, initially were enthusiastic about the Johnson presidency. The Radicals believed that the nation should be recast in the Northern image and therefore championed a strong, centrally guided reunion of the country. Their interpretation of

Reconstruction, which referred to the public policy of reconstructing the Union, was quite literal: the Southern states would have to undergo a radical change of their social and political structures to be reintegrated into the nation. The Northerners viewed this as an appropriate punishment for those who lost, and started, the war. The more moderate lawmakers (Northern Democrats and conservative Republicans) favored a far less punishing policy of Reconstruction, in the hope of putting the divisive effects of the war behind them. However, the Radicals had seen some evidence of Lincoln's willingness to accommodate Southern concerns over the manner of Reconstruction before his death. So despite Lincoln's assassination, there was much optimism about the potential for Radical Reconstruction in a Johnson administration. Sen. Zachariah Chandler of Michigan, a leading Radical, said of Johnson ten days after he assumed the presidency: "He is as radical as I am and as fully up to the mark, if he has good men around him. There will be no danger in the future."[6] But within two years Chandler would work tirelessly for Johnson's impeachment.

The Radical Republicans came to disagree with Johnson on a number of matters, but the disputes can be reduced to a major policy difference and a major procedural difference. On the policy of Reconstruction, scope was the major sticking point. Essentially, what should the Southern states have to do to be considered full members of the Union? The president favored mild requirements: a loyalty oath taken by a majority of whites for the authorization of congressional and state elections (because they had seceded, the Southern states had not been represented in Congress); abolition of slavery by these new Southern governments; and repudiation of Confederate debts. The new president had few demands for the protection of black rights.[7]

The Radicals, by contrast, favored a massive restructuring of Southern society. Their plan included dissolution of Southern plantations; redistribution of plantation land among blacks and poor whites; denial of the right to vote to leading Confederates and provision of full enfranchisement to blacks; and the establishment of public education.[8] The Fourteenth Amendment to the Constitution, adopted in 1868, contains the Radicals' more successful provisions. The president's positions and the Radicals' proposals were the extreme interpretations; most conservative Democrats and moderate Republicans favored proposals in between.

In addition, Johnson and the Radicals differed on who would direct Reconstruction policy, the president or the Congress. The Radicals hoped that Johnson would prove more cooperative than Lincoln, who had articulated a plan of presidential Reconstruction, but this hope did not last. Shortly after his inauguration, Johnson announced his plan. According to Kenneth M. Stampp, "He did not propose to call Congress into special session, or to delay Reconstruction until December when Congress would meet in regular session. Rather, he would start and finish it in the seven months before Congress assembled and then present Congress with a *fait accompli*."[9] Thus the dispute was not only ideological but also institutional.

For a variety of reasons, but mostly because of the exigencies of war, Abraham Lincoln dominated the national government during his presidency. This was possible in part because of the mission of the Republican party—to destroy the "Slave Power" in the South. With Lincoln at its head, the Republican party had a focused mission—to win the war. With the war over and Lincoln dead, the Republicans needed a new crusade. In a sense, then, the Radicals' quest for control of Reconstruction reflects a search for an expanded mission. Because Andrew Johnson would not or could not lead the Republican party in the Lincoln manner, the direction of the party was withdrawn from him. Leadership was taken over by congressional Republicans who had played important roles in the war, although not necessarily in a representative capacity. Many of the Republican party's leaders in the 1860s and 1870s had been military officers in the Union armies. Once the war ended, they were sent to Congress to continue the crusade. This explains in part why the Congress came to greater dominance in the federal structure, marking the beginning of a long-term trend.

The State of the Party System in 1866

The institutional struggle for power between the president and Congress is endemic to the American political system. Our early presidents (with the exception of Thomas Jefferson) saw their role as adviser and general overseer of the nation, leaving substantive policy decisions to the Congress. This early national period was also the era of the congressional "King Caucus," the presidential nominating mechanism before 1832. The members of Congress of each of the leading political parties would decide among themselves who the presidential candidate would be. Not surprisingly, the president would then heed the wishes of his party colleagues in Congress who had placed him in office. The purpose of King Caucus was to ensure that congressional partisans had a like-minded partisan in the White House.[10] The reelection of President Andrew Jackson in 1832 saw the birth of the nominating convention and, concomitantly, mass-based political parties. This expanded participation gave the president a power base independent of the Congress.[11] In the 1840s and 1850s presidential supremacy waned, as the country grew in size and presidents became overwhelmed by the complex problems of sectionalism. At the same time, the Congress grew as well: by 1868 there were 72 senators and 243 House members, up from 34 senators and 142 House members in 1800. The development of the party system along the lines of the sectional issues of slavery and economic differentiation (industrial vs. agrarian) enhanced divisions within the Congress and between the Congress and the president immediately before the Civil War.

By the time Lincoln's election prompted the secession of the Southern states, Congress had adapted to some of these political changes. Henry Clay, who became Speaker of the House when the position was mostly ceremonial, instituted the congressional committee system in about 1811. Under his leadership, the speakership became a position of great power and influence. The Civil War suspended congressional development; but once the political order was reestablished, Congress resumed its relatively autonomous operation and struggled with the White House for power.

Two observers of late-nineteenth-century congressional power offer different interpretations of this struggle. According to George Rothwell Brown, internal congressional structures enabled the House Republicans to control the chamber effectively when their supposed party leader (Andrew Johnson) failed them. Brown believes that Congress's strong role in Reconstruction was not only appropriate for institutional relations but also necessary for responsible public policy.[12] Woodrow Wilson, however, saw the actions of Congress during this period as tyrannical, and potentially harmful.[13] There is some truth to both these assessments. As Brown says, it is impossible to imagine that either the Fourteenth or the Fifteenth Amendment to the Constitution would have been adopted if the Congress had not dominated the national political process.[14] Their success in these measures contributed to the decline of the presidency from 1866 to 1896. However, it was also the case that congressional leaders, once they determined that they could not achieve many of their goals without the cooperation of the president, did what they could to undermine his power (specifically by attempting to impeach Johnson) and control the political machinery that had been created largely for the president's use.

Because senators were still selected mostly by state legislatures, instead of by the people directly, they tended to be powerful political figures in the states. Personal machine-like operations were a necessary prerequisite to senatorial selection because the state legislators had to know that senators could deliver material goods to the state. Consequently, as David Rothman writes, "senators themselves enjoyed political preeminence, exercising significant authority over events in the state legislature, the House of Representatives, and national conventions."[15] Rothman's analysis of the post–Civil War Senate emphasizes the dominating role of senators in national politics as political party organizations began to develop. Insulated from the "whims" of the electorate, senators could maintain extensive patronage programs rather than cultivate constituency relationships. This helps to explain why the Senate was both dominant and corrupt. House members, by contrast, had to deal with electoral volatility and local customs, which encouraged rotation of congressional officeholders and discouraged careerism in the House until just after the Civil War.[16] The unique role of senators also accounts for the strengthening of the congressional party. Because of their political power within the states, senators usually had some control over the fate of representatives' careers. In addition, the Senate was sufficiently prestigious to attract ambitious representatives and to entice incumbent senators to seek reelection. The only other career attraction for senators, according to Rothman, was a cabinet post, but in the postbellum era this no longer translated into a presidential stepping-stone. Instead, service in the cabinet identified one too closely with the individual incumbent president.[17] Taken together, these factors encouraged a strong congressional party presence, dominated by the Senate, and at times opposed to the executive party establishment. This explains the early dominance of CCCs by senators rather than House members. By 1920, when direct election of senators was universal, senators established their separate collective campaign organizations (the senatorial campaign committees) and relinquished their dominant position in House campaign politics.

Early Activities of Congressional Campaign Committees, 1866–1890

There is confusion surrounding the creation of the first congressional campaign committee, in part because CCCs emerged shortly after the presidential party organizations and in part because we know little about the congressional campaign process in the nineteenth century. Richard Abbott asserts that the Republican congressional campaign committee was created in 1860, but most other scholars put the date at 1866.[18] Hugh Bone explains this confusion:

> The origin of the congressional committees remains somewhat obscure. Simeon Fess [political scientist of the early twentieth century and one time chairman of the NRCC] sees their birth in a committee of correspondence appointed during the presidency of James Madison. The *Democratic Manual* attributes the origin of the Democratic Committee to a joint House-Senate committee formed in 1842 to publish a "declaration of principles for General Harrison's administration." If these dates are accepted, then the Democratic congressional committee was formed before the national committee, which was officially organized in 1848. In 1860 and 1864 the Republicans in Congress used a joint campaign committee to assist their House candidates.[19]

It does seem, however, that the activities undertaken by the Republican campaign committee in 1866 and beyond were different from those undertaken by a correspondence committee. In fact, Abbott concedes this, saying that the Republican National Committee that year was headed by a Johnson supporter, making the Republican Congressional Committee (RCC) far more important in 1866.[20] But whatever arrangement existed prior to 1866 was superseded by the activities of the Republican CCC in that year.

In describing the activities of the early CCCs, we must consider what campaigning consisted of in this era. Oratory and printed literature were the predominant methods of disseminating political information and mobilizing voters.[21] What the RCC could do was orchestrate appearances of prominent speakers at local political events and produce literature to be distributed by local party or candidate organizations.

In 1866 the Republican Congressional Committee worked to elect Northern Republicans to the House of Representatives and engaged in party-building activities in the South in order to influence the new constitutions being written there for Southern states seeking readmission to the Union. The Union party's congressional committee, and more specifically, the Union Congressional Executive Committee (a subset of the full committee that oversaw the day-to-day operations), acted as the extragovernmental political arm of the Radical Republicans in Congress.[22] The Union RCC's first chair was Rep. Robert Cumming Schenck of Ohio. Schenck was a professor, attorney, member of the Ohio house of representatives, and a Whig member of Congress from 1843 to 1851. He served as a general in the Civil War and therefore was highly visible after the war. During Schenck's chairmanship the committee secretary, Thomas Tullock (who was a professional staffer, not a member of Congress), directed the vast organizational effort in the South for the adoption of "good" state constitutions.[23] Schenck's specific involvement in committee activities is unclear, but he was ambitious. While chairing the Union RCC Schenck also considered a run for the Senate, and his papers show evidence of his prominence in Ohio politics. Throughout the 40th and 41st Congresses (during and after his chairmanship), Schenck chaired the Ways and Means Committee. As Garrison Nelson argues, this was an important role in the early development of formal congressional party leadership. Nelson "regard[s] the Chairmen of both Ways and Means and Appropriations as exercising the role of floor leadership for the majority party" and goes on to say that "this dual identification [would] be maintained through 1899."[24] Schenck was tapped to head the committee because of his already high national profile, though his reputation had its limits as he was not reelected to Congress in 1870. After his defeat, Schenck did not again seek elective office.

Schenck's affiliation with the Radicals was critical to his selection as chair of the campaign committee. Evidence of the Radical bent of the committee is found in a fund-raising appeal circulated by the Executive Committee, dated March 1, 1866:

> It is clear that before such restoration of the right of representation can safely take place, Congress which alone has the constitutional

power to decide, must be satisfied of the loyal and fit condition of the States that have been in rebellion to resume their former and full relations to the Union: otherwise, we shall lose all we have contended for in the late war.

The issues involved in the coming election of Representatives to Congress are as important and vital as those which entered into the contest with Great Britain for our independence, and are the logical sequences of those in which our revolutionary fathers struggled when they were inaugurating a truly Republican Government.[25]

The Union RCC circulated 638,945 copies of speeches and raised $19,984 by the end of October 1866.[26] This is an impressive showing for any political organization in this period, but all the more so as the committee was making its debut. Also, as suggested by the fund-raising letter, the committee's activities were separate from those of the president's organization, which is remarkable given that President Johnson put great personal energy into these midterm campaigns. At the same time that the committee was distributing speeches and sending speakers around the country (especially to the South) advocating a strict congressional Reconstruction, Johnson was on his infamous "swing around the circle" speaking tour, defending his actions and plan for presidential Reconstruction.[27]

Despite the success of the committee in organizational matters, its success in affecting electoral outcomes is less clear, a matter that has plagued CCCs up to the present day. Although it would appear that the Radicals met with success in the 1866 elections, the evidence related to CCC activity is circumstantial. There was an increase in the number of Republican members in the House (from 102 to 149), though this may have had more to do with local forces than with a national "radicalization" of the Republican party. Term limits, a tradition in many communities, had been an institution in antebellum America, and to a great extent such limits were still the practice in the North, although they would soon disappear. The common practice of term limits, seen as part of a philosophy of rotation in office to minimize corruption for the benefit of the community, is believed to be the reason for electoral turnover in these midterm contests.[28]

The committee's focus in the 1867 elections for Southern constitutional conventions and subsequent selection of officeholders is impressive and consistent with the notion that CCCs work for the security of majorities. The readmission of the solidly Democratic South posed a direct threat to Republican majority interests. The manner and substance of Southern Reconstruction thus mattered a great deal. Since the North was solidly for Union causes, the Radicals did not believe that the bulk of their work needed to occur there. If the Radicals could not achieve a program of congressional Reconstruction at the national level, they would circumvent both the president and the national constitutional structure by confronting these issues directly at the state level. This explains why the congressional committee was continuously active throughout 1867 and early 1868 for the individual struggles in the Southern states over black enfranchisement, Southern state readmission, and constitution making.[29]

In fall 1867 the unreconstructed Southern states held elections to decide whether to hold constitutional conventions as stipulated in the congressional Reconstruction Acts.[30] The Union RCC became involved with the mechanics of these elections, monitoring voter registration (to make sure that black Republicans were being registered properly), maintaining timetables of the elections in each state, and responding to calls for campaign support. An RCC fund-raising circular recounted their activities:

> During the few months that have elapsed since the reconstruction acts were passed, this Committee has been earnestly at work. . . . [T]he Committee has sent several hundred thousand suitable documents through the South. It has employed over seventy active and intelligent speakers and organizers, who have been at work in the unreconstructed States, and to a limited extent in Tennessee. Both white and colored men have been and are now employed. . . . [I]n many localities, funds have been raised to defray the expenses of local agents, and much work accomplished.[31]

The distribution of reprinted speeches and other propaganda was a central activity of the Union RCC.[32] These materials reminded prospective voters that the Republican party stood for the principles of freedom and equality fought for in the war and encouraged Southern whites and blacks to join their cause. What became a strength of the committee at this time was the coordination of speakers. In early committee records there are extensive lists of speakers, classified by state and race (black or white). There is also correspondence from speakers in the field to Secretary Tullock reporting on their location, audience, and reception as well as the prospects for Republican party organization in those areas. Significantly, these letters were mostly from black Republican ministers, whose literacy, oratorical skills, and credibility were high.[33] The symbolic value of these black ministers, who were now affiliated with black-organized churches rather than white-organized churches,[34] and the rhetoric surrounding black enfranchisement fit the Radical agenda well. News from blacks in the South about the prospects for a reconstructed society did much for party building in both the North and the South. An announcement by the Massachusetts Reconstruction Association demonstrates this point:

> Gen. R. C. Schenck, Chairman of that Committee [Union Republican Congressional Committee], will be present and will fully explain the methods by which they are endeavoring to organize the loyal voters of the Southern States, and to counteract the efforts which are being persistently made to intimidate the freedmen, and to prevent them from registering. . . . We append a letter from one of the agents of the Committee, who is now at work. He is a colored preacher, and he asks only to be paid a sum sufficient to meet his expenses while in the field.[35]

The campaign in the fall of 1867 did result in the production of state constitutions that eliminated property requirements and racial restrictions from voting and officeholding privileges. Next, however, came the elections for the ratification of those constitutions.

After sending literature and speakers throughout the South in the fall, the congressional committee would try to do the same for the ratification elections scheduled for the spring of 1868. A fund-raising circular explained:

> The campaign will be most spirited, requiring much effort and activity, and involving a considerable expenditure of money. The rebels are united in organized opposition to the Constitutions, and from recent advices, we learn they are possessed of ample means and will resort to every method possible to defeat those instruments. The struggle will, no doubt, be intense and very proscriptive on their part. They were divided during the campaign for the Convention, but their most desperate efforts will be made against the work of those bodies.[36]

Yet support from the North was not as forthcoming in the spring elections. There are several explanations. The Republicans did not receive the same commanding lead in the North in the state elections of 1867 as they had previously. Consequently, after the fall elections in 1867, many Republicans began to focus on party-building needs in the North rather than the South, hampering fund-raising for the Southern spring elections. Second, there was a Northern sentiment that Reconstruction was taking too long. In Abbott's words, "The Civil War had been over for almost three years; Northern voters were increasingly eager to have the Union restored; and Democrats were accusing the Republicans of continually delaying the process."[37]

Added to this impatience was the distraction of impeachment proceedings against President Andrew Johnson in December 1867. The desire to punish Johnson and put the messy business of Reconstruction behind them contributed to the Northerners' lack of sustained interest in the constitution-ratifying elections of 1868. This attitude would impair the work of the RCC, which was still attempting to fulfill the original conception of congressional Reconstruction. After the new Southern state constitutions were ratified, elections were held for the state legislatures and various other statewide offices.

The military governments were rescinded (though the military retained a presence), and the new civil governments were installed. This was the beginning of the so-called Radical Rule that lasted until 1877.[38]

THE REGULAR ELECTION OF 1868 AND BEYOND

Attention now turned to the business of electing congressmen for the newly reconstructed states in 1868. Also in 1868, a new president would be elected. Preparations for the fall campaign reflected uncertainty about the new order in the South. Not until the summer of 1868 did the state legislatures of the newly reconstructed states convert from military rule to civilian rule, giving them little time to implement new constitutions before the Southern Republicans would have to campaign for the national elections. The Republican party organizations had to deal with this Southern disarray as well as the task of ensuring Northern support for the Republican party presidential candidate, Gen. Ulysses S. Grant.

The RCC's centennial history lists Sen. Edwin Morgan of New York as the next chairman of the committee in 1868,[39] but there is some question in the Schenck papers as to his involvement. That collection contains documents with the signatures of both Schenck and Morgan as officers of the Union RCC for their respective chambers.[40] Perhaps both played a role in the 1868 elections. If we take the RCC's publication at its word, Morgan should be considered the official chair.

Morgan was active in the business and banking communities in New York before he served in the state senate and then as governor of New York from 1859 to 1862. He became a U.S. senator in 1862. Morgan also chaired the Republican National Committee in 1856–64 and 1872–76. He has been cited as the first national chairman of the Republican party.[41] Morgan was wealthy and became instrumental in Republican fund-raising and organization. His institutional ties to the party were strong enough to retain him as the RCC chair when he failed to be reelected to the Senate in 1868. While in the Senate he was the first in a series of senators to wield substantial influence over the congressional party organization in both chambers.

In the fall of 1868 the national party organizations commenced campaign activities, but with a difference. The nomination of Grant for the presidency was evidence that the Radicals had gained control of the entire Republican party. Originally an ally of Johnson, Grant became a Radical when pushed out of Johnson's inner circle. The Radicals' choice of Grant shows their insecurity about keeping power, since they realized that a popular military hero had a better chance of retaining the national following of the Republican party than a "pure" Radical.[42] There was no longer a division between the Republican candidate for the presidency and the Radical Republicans running for Congress; in fact, congressional Radicals had a major role in selecting the presidential candidate. Consequently, the Union RCC did not need to run against the Republican National Committee as it had in 1866–67. It could cooperate with the RNC, or even merge with it. However, after the flurry of activity by the Union RCC between 1866 and 1868, an apparatus designed for congressional district politics was already in place. Also, because of the Republican party's fragile hold on the South (and nervousness about the stability of the North), it made more sense to expand the congressional committee's operations rather than consolidate them with the presidential committee. This point marks the early entrenchment of institutional party organization. It is also a clear example of how the congressional Republicans reassessed their strategic position after the 1866 elections. With Johnson politically emasculated and Grant the likely nominee, cooperation with the RNC was the logical choice for the RCC in the 1868 elections.

During the 1868 elections the Union RNC was concerned with the party's fate in the North. Their resources came from wealthy individuals there and went to political organizations in the same areas. The RNC raised over $200,000. The RCC, because of its general mission and its extensive organization for the previous two years, was primarily involved in Southern contests. Also, an additional fifty-one congressional seats were up in the 1868 election, the bulk of these from the newly readmitted Southern states.[43] The RCC continued to raise funds from assessments of Republican federal officeholders,[44] which applied to members of Congress and those who had patronage positions. They raised $46,000 in this manner, about one-fourth of the amount raised by the RNC. The practice of assessing members of Congress for CCC funds continues in the present day. In the 1860s assessments averaged about $50 per member and extended to employees of the Senate, House, and Capitol Police.[45] Through most of this period, members' assessments provided a stable level of funding for the RCC that would ensure its continued operations. Because of its presidential focus, the RNC would have much wider fluctuations in its fund-raising capacity.

Starting with the 1868 election, the RCC regularized its campaign activities for national elections using the techniques employed for the state constitutional elections: printed speeches and traveling speakers. The offices of the RCC in Washington, D.C., served as the coordination center. Requests came to the committee, and documents or speakers were deployed accordingly.[46] Many of the documents were meant to be public addresses to illiterate black voters. For this constituency, the RCC also distributed metallic badges featuring pictures of Grant and his vice presidential running mate, Rep. Schuyler Colfax.[47] It was the RCC, not the RNC, that had the responsibility for producing printed matter for the general presidential campaign (in addition to reproducing congressmen's speeches), a practice that continued until the 1880s. The RCC would also reproduce the party platform and a biography of the presidential candidate, all of which would be distributed free to local party workers, courtesy of the congressional frank.[48] When available, cash also went to local organizations for rallies and general expenses.

The primary focus of CCC activity, however, was the speakers. As Michael McGerr explains, the pre– and post–Civil War eras were times of high individual political participation. Partisanship was considered a public attribute until the early

1890s. This is substantiated by the formation of local partisan clubs and marching companies that mounted mass public demonstrations emphasizing symbolism and mirroring war-related tactics, a true "campaign." McGerr describes marching companies for both parties in the North:

> While most companies marched on foot and carried torches, others equipped themselves as "Engineer Corps" or as "Pioneer Corps" with battle axes to clear the way—symbolically—for parades. Some companies borrowed a cannon or two and became "Artillery"; some brandished fireworks as "Flambeau Corps"; many rode on horseback as "Cavalry." Most companies . . . attracted young men ranging in age from the mid-teens to the mid-thirties. . . . As veterans of the Civil War age, the parties organized the old soldiers in companies of their own.[49]

These local organizations formed and operated with little direction from Washington. CCCs encouraged such public and promotional activity and supplied money and speakers when they could.

Up until the 1890s Republican speakers out on the hustings used exaggerated symbols of Republican chivalry displayed during the Civil War. Dinkin explains some of the appeal of these symbols:

> To maintain themselves in power, Republicans often turned to the technique of "waving the bloody shirt." This meant placing the entire blame for secession and the Civil War on the Democrats and insisting that they were still politically untrustworthy. (The term specifically referred to an incident in the House of Representatives where a northern congressman held up the bloodstained shirt of an Ohio carpetbagger who had been brutally attacked in Mississippi in 1866.) In numerous campaigns Republicans would fan partisanship by raising the specter of former Confederates regaining governmental control.[50]

The speakers who waved the bloody shirt were war veterans. Although each town had its own war heroes, these larger-than-life heroes attracted large numbers of people. The scheduling of appearances by prominent Civil War heroes was where the RCC was particularly useful. It provided a communications network between the Civil War veterans who now called themselves Republicans and the local clubs and marching societies. As McGerr notes, these were the most fruitful unions:

> The appearance of a party hero from another state, with an escort of local marching companies, filled halls and "opera houses." Unable to find seats inside, thousands of people often stood in the streets to hear orators speak from make-shift platforms. Away from the cities, all-day rallies highlighted the campaign. In the morning, farmers formed their wagons in procession and drove to the county seat to watch a parade, perhaps eat a free lunch, listen to an afternoon of speeches from visiting party leaders, and then applaud a torchlight parade at night.[51]

The RCC continued to perform similar functions through the next decade. In fact, it had become the major party presence in the nation's capital. Whereas the RCC had offices in Washington, D.C., the RNC was headquartered in New York, an arrangement that would remain well into the twentieth century. In 1872 the RCC was listed in the convention proceedings of the Republican National Committee for the first time. This was the same year in which the RCC began to publish *The Republic*, a monthly magazine about the committee's activities that eventually became the RCC's *Newsletter*.[52] Beginning in 1872 the RCC was chaired by Sen. Zachariah Chandler of Michigan. Chandler assured the committee's place as a viable organization for congressional campaigning and was also essential to the early organization of the Republican party (serving as one of the RNC's early chairs).[53] As a prominent Radical, Chandler promoted congressional Reconstruction and the impeachment of Andrew Johnson. During and after the election of 1868 he became an intimate associate of President Grant. Chandler, an entrenched patronage politician, used his access to Grant to secure spoils for himself and to assure electoral success for his compatriots.[54] He also took advantage of Grant's popularity for the midterm election of 1870[55] and supported Grant for renomination in 1872. He headed the RCC during both cycles, and under his leadership the RCC became increasingly active in the publication and dissemination of campaign literature. Chandler was up for reelection in 1874 and did not head the committee then. He lost his seat but was named secretary of the interior by President Grant in 1875. Chandler returned to his old position as chair of the RNC in 1876 and was charged with running the presidential campaign of Rutherford B. Hayes. He returned to the Senate in 1878 and served there until his death in 1879. Chandler's chairmanship gave the committee staying power, as he was one of the more powerful Radical politicians of the era.

The Democrats apparently formed their own congressional committee, the Congressional Executive Committee, for the 1868 elections, but there is no detailed description of its activities.[56] Rep. Samuel Randall of Pennsylvania apparently chaired the Democratic Congressional Committee (DCC) for the 1870 and 1872 elections. Randall had served in the state senate before the Civil War and then fought with the Union Army during the Civil War. He distributed literature to candidates for the 1870 midterm elections, mostly from speeches appearing in the *Congressional Record* on issues such as the economy, the tariff, corruption in the Grant administration, and naturalization.[57] After his tenure at the DCC, Randall became chair of the Appropriations Committee when the Democrats regained control of the House in 1874 and was elected Speaker of the House in the following Congress. Randall had high visibility before and after his involvement at the committee.

From 1866 to 1874 the Republicans held the majority in the House. In 1874 the Democrats gained control. Growing dissatisfaction with corruption in the Grant administration foreshadowed Republican losses in 1874, but few expected the House to return to Democratic rule (the Senate remained Republican).[58] Sen. John Logan of Illinois, who chaired the committee in 1874, oversaw the RCC's first big loss. Logan achieved great military fame as a Civil

War general who had been a Democrat before the war and became a Republican afterward, making him a great Republican hero. He began his career in Congress in the House in 1866; he was elected to the Senate in 1870. Although Logan did not head the RCC until 1874, he was an RCC stump speaker in 1868, 1872, and 1876. Logan's military reputation preceded him, and he drew great crowds.[59] After the 1874 cycle Logan remained an active stump speaker for Republican campaigns, although he lost his own Senate seat in 1877. He did return to the Senate in 1879, where he remained until his death in 1886. In 1884 he was selected as the Republican party's vice presidential nominee with presidential nominee James G. Blaine, though the Democrats captured the White House in 1884 for the first time since the Civil War.

Sen. Simon Cameron of Pennsylvania chaired the RCC for the 1876 cycle, and in contrast to his predecessor Logan, he was an insider politician without a national following. Cameron had been president of two railroad companies, U.S. senator before the Civil War, Lincoln's secretary of war during the war, and senator again after the war. During his long career he established a formidable political machine in Pennsylvania.[60] His leadership of the RCC came at the end of his career, and in a patrician manner he orchestrated a smooth coordinated effort between the congressional and national committees with his fellow Radical and former RCC chair, Zachariah Chandler, at the helm of the RNC. The 1876 election was not an overwhelming success at either level for the Republicans, as Republican candidate Hayes won the presidency by one controversial electoral vote and the congressional Republicans, although increasing their numbers by thirty, still found themselves a minority.

Cameron was the last senator to head the RCC. Only House members chaired the RCC after 1878. No explanation was found for this shift, but the period coincides with the rise of greater seniority in the House. Rep. Jay Hubbell (R-MI), first elected to Congress in 1872, was the next chair. Little is known about Hubbell other than that he served as a prosecuting attorney during the Civil War and immediately prior to his election to

Congress. Hubbell was chair of the committee for three cycles: 1878, 1880, and 1882. He did not seek reelection to the House in 1882. It was after Hubbell's chairmanship that the committee was said to have gone into "hibernation."[61]

The Republicans regained control of the House in the 1880 election. Sen. William Wallace of Pennsylvania chaired the DCC in 1880. He had served in the state senate before his election to the U.S. Senate in 1874. Wallace lost his own reelection (reappointment) in 1880, a year in which the Republicans regained the House and the two parties had a deadlock in the Senate.

In 1882 the RCC produced its first issue book, the *Republican Campaign Textbook*, which included facts and figures on governmental activity as well as propaganda for campaign use. The contents included such items as "The Tariff" and "The National Banks" but also "Corruption of Democratic Party" and "Bounties for Treason."[62] It appears that the RCC and the RNC shared the responsibility for printing this book, the RCC doing this (for the most part) until 1910 and the RNC resuming fulltime production until 1940. The RCC has published issue books since 1882, and continues to do so today. This marks the addition of another function best performed at the national level: the synthesis of information on national issues for use at the local level. The Republicans again lost control of the House in 1882. They did not regain control until 1888. But, as the RCC publication states, "although the committee continued during this period, its activities were curtailed and historical research turns up no evidence of the election of a chairman or secretary."[63]

LESSONS FROM THE CCCS' FOUNDING

The period from 1866 to 1890 marked a great transition in the formation of American political identity and the development of party organizations. We find that the Republican party in Congress quickly adapted to the increasing differentiation between the national partisan governmental institutions. The Republican party focused on capturing the presidency in 1860 and then on the conduct of the Civil War. The Radical

Republicans developed a power base within Congress when faced with Andrew Johnson, a postwar, non-Radical leader, in the White House. To use Congress as an effective power base, the Republicans needed institutional autonomy, which they achieved through the creation of the CCCs as independent electoral organizations and the gradual development of formal leadership within Congress. Indeed, the congressional Republicans' attempt to impeach President Johnson shows that an independent congressional party was maturing. The fact that after 1874 the United States was under divided control of the branches (see appendix table A.1) also shows that the concept of unified party rule of government was threatened.

As soon as Johnson left the presidency Republicans in Congress reevaluated their relationship with the presidential arm of the party. Grant was not only more acceptable as a presidential candidate, he could be dominated by congressional Republicans. Still, despite cordial relations with the RNC, the RCC remained a separate organization. Though the congressional Republicans largely captured the RNC after Johnson's departure, they did not eliminate the organization for duplication of effort. Congressional Republicans still did not want to entrust their national campaign planning to the presidential organization, or they believed having two organizations would maximize resources through separate efforts.[64] Also interesting is the emergence of a DCC in this period, despite the lack of Democratic presidents needing a counterweight. Most likely, Democrats wanted to limit the Republicans' resource advantage and copied their structures.

The individuals who headed the committees had strong backgrounds in government and firm commitments to the principles of party—especially Republican party—organization. The institutionalization of congressional careers had not yet been achieved, and the idea of repeated reelection to either national chamber was only beginning to be accepted. In addition, there were few formal structures within Congress to satisfy individual ambitions. Thus prominent legislators sought power in the new party structures at all levels—local, state, congressional, and presidential. The fact that such prominent individuals ran the CCCs shows the strong commitment by congressional Republicans to making a viable separate campaign organization. Not enough is known about the Democrats in this period to draw any reliable conclusions about their origins. As the congressional party matured first in campaigning and next in internal differentiation, the campaign committees assumed a larger role in the life of the congressional parties.

Early CCC Adaptation, 1890–1908: Beyond the Civil War

The post–Civil War era, which exemplified the spectacular display, or army style, of campaigning, eventually gave way to a more candidate-centered, educational style.[65] The presidential campaign of 1888, won by Civil War general Benjamin Harrison, was the last clear army-style campaign dominated by images of the glorious war. By the 1890s this symbolic partisanship began to wane. The war's traumatic impact had been displaced by the equally traumatic impact of industrialization and urbanization. The country began to turn increasingly toward national rather than local solutions to persistent problems. As the Republicans convinced the people of the need for national authority in the conduct of the war and the subsequent reconstruction of the South, they would now have to suffer the consequences of increasing popular demands on the national authority to care for individuals in a rapidly changing society. Citizens now required more information about events, problems, and proposed solutions. Newspapers became more accessible and available. Campaign activity gradually changed from spectacular popular displays to journalistic accounts of issues and candidate positions.

Congress also experienced profound changes, as the House and Senate became more differentiated. The House began to institutionalize and developed centralized leadership. The Senate underwent a rocky transition from state legislative appointment to popular elections, which changed its character. The institutionalization of Congress began about this time. Nelson Polsby writes that congressional institutionalization involves three characteristics: (1) the organization must be "well bounded," or differentiated from its environment; (2) it is complex, with widely acknowledged divisions of labor; and (3) it uses universalistic rather than particularistic criteria to perform its work.[66] Polsby argues that the U.S. House of Representatives began to show such characteristics in the 1890s and was fully experiencing the process of institutionalization by 1899. He uses a number of measures to indicate these changes, most of which also confirm the rise of careerism in the House. These include a decline in the percentage of first-term members compared to returning members, an increase in the number of terms served by incumbents, and the number of years Speakers of the House served in Congress before their election to that position. Representatives were seeking reelection in significantly higher numbers.

In the wake of congressional Reconstruction, the congressional parties began to appreciate the great political potential for initiative in the expanding realms of national issues. Although they had easily dictated terms to presidents (especially after Andrew Johnson), this could not be long sustained without a clear congressional spokesman.[67] According to George Rothwell Brown, congressmen were forced to find a solution:

> A new conception of the speakership was born. The office which carried with it responsibility for orderly party government was strengthened, and as the power of the leadership was enhanced the ability of the House to function smoothly and effectively grew very greatly. The period which witnessed the rise of the speakership to its supreme height was characterized by the enactment of constructive legislation incident to and essential to the remarkable economic development of the nation which followed the close of the Civil War.[68]

The Speakers of the 1870s and 1880s adopted a number of procedures that centralized control of legislative activity in their office. In the 1890s Speaker Thomas Reed (R-ME) further expanded the power of the office.[69] This control was continued by Speaker Joseph Cannon (R-IL), who ascended to that post after David Henderson's (R-IA) brief tenure. Reed strengthened the procedural authority of the Rules Committee and solidified the Speaker's control of it.[70] He also began to recognize members who wished to speak on the floor out of order, ending the minority's long-term practice of denying a quorum for voting purposes by refusing to answer the roll call (Reed began to count the physical bodies in the room), and increased the retaliatory powers of the caucus. Reed's (and subsequently Cannon's) use of the caucus demonstrated the most intense party discipline the House witnessed yet. As Brown explains, "Those who rebelled against being bound by caucus action were marked and punished, for the Speaker not only had the power to appoint Members of the House to places on committees, but he [Reed] had the power of removal, and this power the strongest of these party leaders did not hesitate to use."[71]

Such control made the Speaker a virtual coequal with the president. During the reigns of both Reed and Cannon, it was clear that either man could make life easy or difficult for the presidents with whom they served. In fact, President William McKinley was once Speaker Reed's protégé. Moreover, the major economic issues facing the nation had been dealt with by the congressional parties long before the presidential candidates proclaimed their economic policies. Given the high efficiency of the party caucus system in the House, it is easy to see why the Speaker and his congressional party would be respected as autonomous entities.

But the stature of the Senate did not match the stature of the House. Although at the turn of the century the Senate did have the strong leadership of William Allison (R-IA) and Nelson Aldrich (R-RI), it suffered from the perception that it was an elitist institution. In the wake of the Populist and Progressive movements, much had been made of the election of Senators by state legislatures. Because the House was popularly elected, it was now the more "legitimate" branch, the one closest to the people. But there were other, more serious problems with the Senate's indirect election system, making this issue the subject of debate for more than eighty years before the Seventeenth Amendment was ratified.[72]

Among the difficulties with senatorial appointments were deadlocks in selecting senators (sometimes lasting for months or even years, leaving seats unfilled); "stampeded" elections (the victories of last-minute entrants); bribery and corruption; vacancies (sometimes as many as one per year due to failure of the legislature to make a selection before a predetermined adjournment); misrepresentation (minority candidates elected because of factional battles); and interference with regular state legislative work.[73] These issues, combined with examples of western states adopting senatorial primaries that functioned as direct elections, tarnished the Senate's image. The congressional party in the House cultivated an identity separate from the senatorial party as the latter became more like their House brethren. In the late 1860s and 1870s the Senate's membership increased, it moved into its modern chamber, it adopted procedural rules similar to those of the House, and the nature of its business became more technical.[74] Significantly, after 1890 no senator chaired either party's CCC in the House. Senators would form their own organizations as a result of the Seventeenth Amendment requiring their direct election.

CCC ACTIVITY, 1890–1908

As campaigning shifted from oratory to literature with the growth of the press, CCCs adapted their practices. Frank Luther Mott finds a 222 percent increase in the aggregate circulation of American daily papers between 1870 and 1890 while the country's population growth was only 63 percent.[75] As speakers were employed in fewer numbers, the production of campaign pamphlets and issue books increased. Also, the committees were investigating ways to obtain more press attention. Both parties had active organizations for the 1890 midterm election. President Benjamin Harrison, a Republican, wanted to keep a

Republican majority in the House and arranged for his longtime associate, James Clarkson, to work with the RCC that year. Clarkson kept the president abreast of the committee's activities for the 1890 campaign, which consisted mostly of the preparation of briefing "textbooks" for Republican speakers and editors.[76] Contemporary journalistic accounts, though, were adamant about the absence of presidential influence in the 1890 elections. Instead, the congressional party was thought to be in control. According to the *New York Times*,

> The fight is for the retention of control and for the aggrandizement of [Speaker] Reed. It is a committee that is electing the Congress and preparing the way for the nomination of the next Republican candidate for President. There is no Harrison in it anywhere. All that the committee boasts about as having been accomplished is attributed to the Speaker. The victory will be one for Reed, not Harrison. Whatever expenditure is incurred, and whatever effort may be put forth, will be for the development of Reed as the leader of the Republican party and his elevation to the head of the ticket in 1892.[77]

In this same article the DCC is described as engaging in similar activities, but at a less frenetic pace. Faced with meager financial resources, the DCC was relying on a "reprobation of Tom Reed,"[78] which, as it turns out, was precisely what they got. Reed's professed hopes to achieve the Republican presidential nomination in 1892 were never realized. The Democrats regained control of the House in 1890 and retained it in 1892 when Democrat Grover Cleveland regained the presidency.

Rep. J. J. Belden (R-NY) chaired the RCC in 1890. It is not known how long he served. Belden was elected to Congress in 1886, so he may have headed the committee for the 1888 election as well. He did not run for reelection to Congress in 1894. Belden presided over one of the worst losses the House Republicans have ever witnessed, falling from a 17-seat majority of 173 to a minority of only 88. During his tenure the press was full of speculation about who actually controlled the RCC—

Belden as a representative of Speaker Reed or James Clarkson as a representative of President Harrison.[79] Though it appeared that Reed controlled the organization, Harrison, in a sense, controlled the election campaign. Harrison's highly unpopular policies regarding the McKinley Tariff probably cost the Republicans their majority in the House.

With the Democrats in control of both the presidency and Congress after 1890, Republican hegemony appeared to be over. Fortunately for the Republican party's political fortunes, the nation then faced a deep agrarian recession in 1893. As this political opportunity unfolded, the RCC gained renewed strength, anticipating the eventual return to Republican control of the House. The politics of business now replaced the politics of war and slavery. The recession of 1893 forced consideration of currency reform, an issue that pitted western agrarians against eastern nationalists. The national government was also asked to regulate the business community for excesses against individuals and communities. Antitrust and antimonopoly discussions became common. Another societal change was the solidification of the middle class. As Robert Wiebe explains, the movement for public education helped to create a solution to the problem of declining agrarianism: individuals could now become professionals—teachers, doctors, lawyers, social workers—by virtue of universally available education. Now people were needed for the white-collar jobs of the emerging modern corporations. Wiebe refers to this as the "scientific-industrial society,"[80] "scientific" referring to advances in the hard sciences (such as the understanding of how bacteria are transmitted and cause infectious diseases) and the "natural science" of social Darwinism.

These changes affected political activity in profound ways. No longer content with emotional attachments to the party of war or peace, the electorate demanded more knowledge of the candidates and the issues. Politicians responded by shifting to an educational style of campaigning. A more professionally oriented electorate demanded politicians who would respond to their requests for information. Rather than appeal to the electorate through flowery oratory, politicians began to rely on written materials. This movement began with the production of pamphlets but eventually centered on the use of newspapers. This move toward newspaper-based appeals was hardly reserved to the political realm. Rather, it reflected a shift in the social focus of the nation. Business, through advertising and control of editorial content, found newspapers a convenient venue for their interests.[81] Commercial advertising and political campaigning began to follow similar courses.

These changes forced candidates to have more contact with the public. First, they would have to convince individuals of the soundness of their stands rather than count on straight partisan voting (especially with the temporary presence of strong third parties). Second, campaign appearances were newsworthy, giving candidates more press coverage. In fact, McGerr reports that "the [political] parties often appeared to stage public meetings, not mainly for their effect on the immediate audience as in the past, but in order to get the text of speeches printed in the papers."[82] The revolution in communications, industry, and urbanization altered the form of political dialogue.

At about this time the Republicans created the Literary Bureau, which centralized the literature production needs of the RCC (and the national committee during presidential years) and was staffed by professional writers who produced pamphlets, leaflets, handbills, issue textbooks, and candidate biographies.[83] This organization surpassed the Speaker's Bureau in prominence because of the increased demand for written materials by the more literate electorate. It also became the workhorse of the infamous election of 1896.

The person responsible for forming the Literary Bureau was Rep. Joseph Weeks Babcock (R-WI). Babcock was first elected to the House in 1892, when the Republicans were a small minority, and took over the RCC for the 1894 elections. He remained chair for six election cycles. The Republicans gained 120 seats in the 1894 election and became the majority party, which they remained for the rest of Babcock's tenure at the RCC. Babcock was close to William McKinley, who in 1894 was still governor of Ohio but was often mentioned as a possible presidential nominee for 1896. With the development of the Literary Bureau, the RCC underwent great organizational transition during Babcock's tenure.

Sen. Charles J. Faulkner of West Virginia chaired the DCC during the 1894 campaign, though he may have also chaired the committee at other times in the 1890s. Faulkner served as a judge before his election to the Senate in 1887, where he served two full terms before his retirement in 1899. However, the DCC's specific activities in the 1890s remain obscure as a result of a lack of obtainable documentation.

A pronounced change in congressional campaigning resulted from the historic campaign of 1896. The Democratic presidential nominee, William Jennings Bryan (a representative from Nebraska), undertook the largest personal speaking tour of any candidate in American history.[84] His opponent was Republican presidential nominee William McKinley, who chose to receive the people on his "front porch." McKinley employed Mark Hanna, one of America's most brilliant campaign tacticians. Hanna managed McKinley's candidacy first, then acted in the interests of the Republican party as head of the RNC. While candidate Bryan was speaking, Hanna was producing massive volumes of documents on McKinley's behalf, using the RCC as a Washington headquarters (the national committee had its offices in New York and Chicago and had no permanent headquarters in Washington, D.C.).[85] Both parties used speakers extensively and distributed massive amounts of literature and campaign buttons nationwide. At the end of the campaign, the Republicans had regained the presidency and retained control of Congress (although their lead in the House was reduced by forty seats).

Rep. James Richardson (D-TN), a former Confederate Civil War major, headed the DCC in the 1898 and 1900 election cycles. The Democrats gained 29 seats in the House after the 1898 elections and lost 10 during the 1900 elections, remaining in the minority both times. Despite this tepid success, Richardson was made minority leader immediately after the 1900 elections. In 1900 the RCC had an office in Chicago, and in 1902 a New York office was opened.[86] Although neither office was permanent, Chairman Babcock could develop support for the RCC outside of Washington, D.C. (although there, as always, the bulk of RCC business was carried out). Babcock also broadened the RCC's base by implementing a "Southern strategy" for the 1904 elections. The strategy was to contest every Southern congressional district so as to keep Southern political leaders occupied with fighting off Republican candidacies, thereby keeping Southern Democratic activity out of the North. The Republicans raised their margin in that campaign to one of the highest ever—250 to 136.[87] Babcock retired from Congress after his RCC tenure, before the 1906 elections. He cited failing health and died three years after his departure from the chamber.

The emphasis on printed campaign literature continued through the turn of the century. After 1904 the congressional committees scaled down their production of literature in favor of encouraging the press to use this material for news stories since this would result in a much wider circulation of their appeals.[88] The CCCs had been moving toward this approach for a while, demonstrated by members making a habit of reading campaign speeches on the floor of the House or Senate so that they could be reprinted from the *Congressional Record* and sent to newspapers under the congressional frank. Newspapers had acquired great authority, and their widespread circulation made them logical venues for campaign messages. Between 1892 and 1914 the number of daily newspapers grew from 1,650 to 2,250 and average circulation doubled.[89] The election year of 1904 held another interesting twist for the RCC. Joseph Cannon, who had just become Speaker of the House in 1903, conducted an extensive lecture tour for the RCC. No doubt, Cannon also stumped for President Theodore Roosevelt, but the tour was nevertheless modeled on the congressional district as a unit instead of a general national appeal. A scrapbook compiled during the journey emphasizes some of the tour's unique aspects.

> In August, 1904, the Republican National Congressional Committee, under the direction of the Hon. Joseph W. Babcock, of Wisconsin, Chairman, . . . formulated a campaign tour for Hon. Joseph G. Cannon, the Speaker of the House of Representatives. By September 1st an itinerary was agreed upon, embracing a circuit of fifteen States of the Republic from Nebraska to Rhode Island, and about sixty points designated at which the Speaker should make addresses. The original schedule covered nearly all of the so-called doubtful Congressional Districts of the North, within a territory that could be expeditiously reached. A private car was placed at the disposal of the Speaker, sufficiently commodious to accommodate such other speakers as might accompany the party, the Speaker's secretary, a stenographer, a gentleman in charge of the car, and such newspaper men as might be assigned to duties in connection with the trip.
>
> It is a noteworthy fact that every Congressional district which he visited, with the single exception of one in Rhode Island, was carried by the Republicans at the election following, and the one that was lost was by the narrowest margin.[90]

Perhaps this was an attempt to revive the dying art of oratory. Whether Cannon's tour had a role in the forty-three-seat electoral gain in the House is impossible to gauge, but it almost certainly did not reproduce the crowds known to the military heroes of the late nineteenth century. Indeed, the parades and spectacular displays had all but disappeared by then.[91] However, this does give clear evidence of the extent of leadership involvement in campaign committee affairs at this early date. That Cannon, a national political figure rather than a war celebrity, undertook such a labor-intensive tour shows that the RCC continued to provide national political resources to local candidates.

The DCC continued to schedule speakers for local congressional district tours and to produce literature for use in campaigns. Rep. James Matthews Griggs (D-GA), first elected to the House in 1896, chaired the committee for the 1902, 1904, and 1906 elections. During this period we find the first evidence of the evolving importance of the DCC chairmanship. Rep. Henry De La Warr Flood (D-VA), who eventually chaired the DCC in 1920, attempted to win this post for the 1906 election cycle. In a letter to a political friend in Virginia, Flood explains why the position was attractive to him and what needed to be done to secure it:

> Several members of Congress are anxious to become chairman of the Congressional Campaign Committee. The outlook for Democratic success has encouraged them to wish to accept this position. It will be necessary, therefore, for my friends to take some steps to aid me. Very little has been done along this line. I want you to get Mr. Ellyson to write to a few members of the National Committee. He can give me such a send-off as he sees fit. I want him to write to the members of the National Committee from a few states and get them to write to the Congressional committeemen from their states.[92]

Flood implies some glory attached to chairing the Democratic Congressional Campaign Committee in a year in which it would likely see Democratic gains in the House.[93] However, in a closed vote Griggs was chosen head of the DCCC instead of Flood.[94] The Democrats gained 28 seats in 1906 but were still the minority party in the House by 58 seats. Flood's interpretation of the DCCC chairmanship as a position of some potential power is justified because of the successes achieved by the previous DCCC chair, Richardson (see table A.3). Griggs became the ranking member of the Ways and Means Committee shortly after the 1906 election, a position that was known to produce successors to the floor leader position in the Democratic party (in fact, Griggs was replacing former Ways and Means ranking member John Sharp Williams, who had become minority leader). According to a local Georgia newspaper, Griggs's promotion resulted from his DCCC activity: "The promotion of Judge Griggs, says a Washington dispatch, is understood to be in the nature of a reward for managing the campaign which resulted in the reduction of the republican majority from 114 to 63."[95] Both known chairmen of the DCCC in this era provide a strong case for the centrality of the CCC chair in the early development of party leadership. The emphasis on the position accompanied increased activity on the part of the DCCC. In 1906, for example, the committee produced the *Democratic Campaign Book: Congressional Election*, which it distributed to all Democratic congressional candidates with the following message attached: "The price of this book is twenty-five (25) cents—hardly more than the cost of printing. If you have not remitted please do so at once. If you will enclose us one dollar ($1) we will send you, in addition to this book, copies of all campaign literature published by us."[96] The book contained statements of the party's position on a variety of issues, especially the tariff (the most controversial issue of the time) and Roosevelt's foreign policy. The appendixes also included the listing "Yea and Nay Votes on Party Questions" for the candidates' use.[97] Though the Democrats gained twenty-eight seats in the 1906 elections, they remained a minority in the House until 1910.

In 1906 the RCC was headed by James Schoolcraft Sherman (R-NY), who had served as RCC vice chairman in the previous cycle. Sherman was first elected to Congress in 1886, lost his seat in the 1890 midterm elections, and regained it in 1892. Under his chairmanship, the Republicans remained the majority party in the House but lost seats from the 1904 high of 250. Sherman was chairman for the 1906 elections and then for some or all of the 1908 elections. His role at the RCC is difficult to ascertain, as he became the vice presidential running mate of William Howard Taft in the summer of 1908. Since the Taft/Sherman ticket won, Sherman left Congress for the executive branch where he remained until his death in 1912.

CCCs at the Turn of the Century

As Congress developed into a more powerful institution and congressional careers became more coveted, congressional campaigning became a full-time commitment for both candidates and party organizations. Consequently, we begin to see CCC chairs, such as Babcock and Griggs, serving for long tenures. Although the internal hierarchy of the congressional party had not been firmly established, the evidence indicates that leadership of the campaign committees played an important role. That the CCCs survived the generation of its founders is also significant. If the CCCs were of no value, then they would have disappeared. Finally, the cooperation we see between the two CCCs and their "cousins," the national committees, is significant. Rather than overtly try to incorporate the CCCs under their direct control, the national committees used the CCCs as a resource, particularly as their base in Washington, D.C., and for the production of campaign material. This is a tacit acknowledgment of CCC autonomy in this era, though this spirit of cooperation would not be a consistent component of CCC/NC relations.

Challenges to CCC Autonomy, 1908–1920

The Progressive movement transformed politics in the United States during the first quarter of the twentieth century. The argument for closer relationships between government and the people necessitated another change in candidates' style of campaigning. A more literate population demanded information regarding candidates for office rather than mere symbolic appeals. Progressive attitudes, especially the emphasis on the protection of individual rights over business interests, entered our modern culture. President Theodore Roosevelt adopted many Progressive policies during his presidency and therefore expected that the rest of the Republican party would continue to absorb progressivism. To this end, he indicated that William Howard Taft would be an appropriate successor to the presidency in 1908. Taft was duly nominated and elected, but he then adopted a rather conservative line. After Roosevelt returned from an extended trip abroad in 1910, he discovered that the Taft administration had strayed from his original conception of

Republican policy positions and indicated that he would run for the presidency against Taft in 1912. Because of the split in Republican ranks, the Democrats under Woodrow Wilson's leadership captured the presidency in 1912. The Republican split had already allowed the Democrats to gain control of the House of Representatives (Democratic control of the Senate was to follow in 1912). These events accompanied tremendous turmoil in the internal development of Congress.

From 1903 to 1910 Speaker Cannon ruled the House of Representatives with a firm hand. Alongside an accumulated tradition of rules vesting powers in the Speakership was the jovial personality of Cannon himself, making the situation seem like a benign dictatorship. "Uncle Joe" became the symbol of a rigid oligarchy in the House (a situation he helped to create), which ultimately succumbed to the Progressive movement. In 1910 the House itself had changed from when Speaker Thomas Reed ruled it in the late 1880s and early 1890s. According to Samuel Kernell, membership stabilized in the House from the 1860s through the 1920s. As a result of longer tenure (or careerism), a culture of personal ambition developed which called for a wide array of opportunities for individual power. This conflicted with a hierarchical norm of party governance, which required strong leaders and obedient followers. Three forces changed the nature of congressional service: declining party competition for congressional seats, increasing attractiveness of the House as a career, and the decline of local district norms requiring frequent rotation of officeholders.[98] Partly as a result of the 1896 partisan realignment, the electoral bases of the parties became more clearly delineated. Therefore, incumbent congressmen had more reason to believe that they could return to office under the party's label. Contemporary ballot reform movements also focused attention on the individual congressional candidate's fortunes, as they forced voters to pay closer attention to the individual names on the ballot (an "office block" format that presented candidates for each office replaced the "party bloc" format that presented each party's nominees for each office) than they would with straight-party administered ballots.

As the national government gained power and prestige, more politicians chose to make their careers in Congress. Further, local attitudes changed to make congressional careerism possible. This was partly due to pressure from incumbent representatives themselves to change the system of frequent rotation for House seats. The change from district nominating caucuses to direct primaries also contributed to individual attachments between voters and politicians, which enabled careerism to flourish. In addition, in 1911 Congress capped the size of its membership at the current level of 435. Although the action was taken partly because of considerations of space and order, the cap also made congressional seats more scarce. Since the number of seats could no longer grow with the population, congressional seats would carry more responsibility and prestige.

As congressmen wanted to serve more terms, they also desired more power in the chamber. As it was, the leadership structure initially allowed for powerful positions within the chamber (namely, committee chairmanships) to be appointed by the Speaker. Partisan and personal loyalty were the major criteria for access to power.[99] The frustration that more senior members felt in this situation was instrumental in the overthrow of Speaker Cannon in March 1910. Conventional wisdom holds that the deposing of Cannon was prompted by the burgeoning Progressive movement. The Progressives pushed for broad political, economic, and social reforms, but some observers believe that Cannon's overthrow had less to do with these lofty issues and more to do with frustrated careerists. Cannon's near-absolute power rested on three major controls: "his power to refuse recognition on the floor of the House; his membership on, and appointment of the Rules Committee; and his power to appoint all committee members and chairmen."[100] The Republican Insurgents (as they were called) aimed their attack primarily at the Rules Committee whose membership they succeeded in expanding and whose appointment powers were given to the caucus rather than the Speaker.[101] In selecting the Rules Committee as their target, the Insurgents could damage Cannon's control without destroying the power of Congress itself. At least one historian sees the 1910 overthrow as an expression of increasing frustration from a more powerful House membership instead of a function of the general Progressive movement in the country at large; in fact, many of the Insurgents did not consider themselves Progressives.[102]

Following the ouster of Cannon, the House leadership structure began to flourish. Party leadership would no longer consist of one internal legislative leader and one external campaign leader. With the Speaker denied absolute control, other structures within the House achieved prominence. Since the early 1880s both parties had recognized floor leaders: the chair of the Ways and Means Committee for the majority party and the losing nominee in the race for Speaker for the minority party. By 1899 both parties also appointed formal whips. Traditionally, these positions had been controlled by the Speaker (or the de facto minority leader). Instead of abolishing these positions after Cannon's ouster, the House filled them by election rather than appointment, dispersing power more widely within the congressional parties.

Congressional reforms moved quickly once the Democrats achieved a majority in the 1910 midterm elections. Especially important was the Democratic Caucus, the formal organization of all Democratic members of the House, which now controlled the selection of the majority leader. In 1911 Oscar Underwood (D-AL) became the first majority leader elected by a party caucus.[103] From 1911 to 1933 the Democratic Caucus gained strength because of its enforcement of binding powers on members.[104] In this way the Democratic leadership retained many of the powers that the Republicans exercised under Cannon, but without the autocratic taint.[105] Of course, certain norms were transformed, such as the adoption of the seniority principle for the determination of committee chairmen rather than strict leader preference. Also, committee work itself became more specialized, placing a value on expertise and experience within the House (which often accompanied seniority).[106] With Woodrow Wilson's election to the presidency in 1912, the Democrats in Congress enjoyed unified government from 1913 to 1918, when the Republicans recaptured control of the House. The new leadership structure had become so institutionalized that the new Republican majority adopted similar structures. The Republicans created their own Committee on Committees in 1917 (which performed some of the policy functions of the Democratic caucus) and instituted their first elective whip in 1919. Also in 1919, the Republicans separated the positions of Ways and Means chair and majority leader. The structures for modern leadership institutions were set by the 1920s. However, they were still fairly new constructs without well-established patterns of leadership succession or recruitment. With the creation of new positions, the choice of individuals who would lead the CCCs would be adjusted.

CCC Activity, 1910–1920

Although popular election of senators began in 1914, the CCCs were still unified across chambers until 1919. After 1908 the Republicans completed several successful national elections, including the smooth transition of the presidency from Roosevelt to Taft. Republican dominance would not last, especially given the events within Congress in 1910. The revolt in the House against Speaker Cannon was widely publicized. Together with the Republican party split by Roosevelt and Taft in August 1910, the party's midterm performance was poor. According to John Baker, "The congressional Republicans, without the pull of Theodore Roosevelt's magic and beset by strong public concern over the question of business domination of government, faced a campaign certain to center strongly on the issue of the tariff and Cannonism. Indeed, the Democratic platform of 1908 had already raised the Cannon issue, and the Payne-Aldrich tariff was widely indicted as a Republican breach of faith."[107]

The specific activities of the CCCs from 1910 to 1916 are not well known. During this period the split within the Republican party was mirrored within the NRCC[108] and internal division prevented a consensus on party-oriented activities.[109] Rep. William Brown McKinley (R-IL) (no relation to President McKinley) headed the NRCC for the 1910 and 1912 election cycles. Of course, in 1910 the Republicans lost control of the House in the wake of the overthrow of Speaker Cannon. In 1912 the Republicans lost even more ground (35 more seats) in the wake of the Taft/Roosevelt split at the presidential level. McKinley lost his own seat in the 1912 election. This did not mean the end of his political career, however, as McKinley returned to the House after the 1914 election (where he remained for three more terms) and was elected to the U.S. Senate in 1920.

James Tilghman Lloyd of Missouri chaired the DCCC for the 1908, 1910, and 1912 election cycles. Lloyd served as House minority whip from 1901 to 1909, concurrent with his first term as chairman of the DCCC. The Democrats' expectation that their electoral prospects would improve after Theodore Roosevelt vacated the presidency (which they did) may explain why they looked to a senior party leader to run the congressional campaigns in the following years. Lloyd did not seek reelection in 1916.

Although the split in Republican ranks endured after 1912, discussions of the CCCs' role increased in 1913 after the adoption of the Seventeenth Amendment. In this era there were many attempts at cooperation between the national, senatorial, and congressional party organizations. In 1913 both parties' national and congressional committees announced plans to run the 1914 midterm campaigns "jointly." The incentive for cooperation for both parties was clear. The Democrats controlled the White House and had to protect a large majority in the House and a bare majority in the Senate. With Wilson still popular, cooperation among Democrats seemed reasonable. The Republicans, who were marginalized and had no incumbent in the White House, also felt cooperation would be beneficial. The Democrats created a liaison committee consisting of five national committee members and five members of Congress (two senators and three representatives), although it was made clear that responsibilities for the campaign would be split between the two organizations.[110] About the same time that the Democrats had determined their organizational stance for the 1914 campaign, the Republicans were deciding whether to hold a special midterm national party convention. At issue were the questions of representation on the national committee and the arrangement between the national committee and the congressional committee. According to the *New York Times*, "After a brief debate the committee adopted a motion providing that the National Committee, while co-operating with the Congressional Committee with regard to campaign management, should not combine with the Congressional Committee, and that there should be no joint financial agency."[111]

Minutes of an NRCC Executive Committee meeting in early 1914 indicate the scope of committee operations. The NRCC had become more diversified and remained rather independent of the RNC. The committee authorized the appointment of numerous regional treasurers and also issued a formal appeal for senators and representatives to serve as speakers. The committee also approved the purchase of machinery for in-house production of campaign materials. Subcommittees to create a campaign textbook and a women's bureau were also authorized.[112] The organization retained the Speaker's Bureau, which had been its original focus, and continued work on the campaign textbook, which had been produced since the 1880s. The focus in this campaign, however, was again the publicity bureau and its ongoing relationship with the press. The NRCC issued press releases containing information on Congress in general and on specific members (at their request), which were then mailed to selected individual voters and newspapers. This service was so well received that the NRCC was soon producing 20,000 news sheets a day, with a total of 1,100,000 pieces of mail for the election cycle. It was during this 1914 election cycle that the NRCC first started compiling voting records on Democratic members of Congress for use by Republican opponents, a service that has continued to the present.[113] The Republicans increased their House membership by forty-six seats in this election, although they remained in the minority.

There was a genuine struggle for the NRCC chair for the 1914 election cycle between a Taft Republican and a Roosevelt Republican. Rather than see the party split once again, the Taft candidate withdrew, allowing Frank Woods of Iowa to become chair.[114] Under Woods's direction the House Republicans achieved steady gains, winning 66 additional seats in 1914 (from 127 to 193, still a minority) and besting the Democratic total by 6 seats after the 1916 election.[115] Although electoral gains were steady under Woods's control, he did not have a positive experience overall. During his tenure NRCC fund-raising agents engaged in questionable activities that resulted in extensive investigations (conducted by the NRCC itself) and ultimately a temporary suspension of the NRCC's ability to raise funds autonomously. Woods also faced a challenge for his position for the 1916 cycle. The Taft supporters urged the former chair, William McKinley (who vacated the NRCC chair after the 1912 election cycle), to challenge Woods, a Progressive. When it seemed that a direct attempt to defeat Woods would not succeed, the conservatives then pushed for the creation of an executive committee within the NRCC. McKinley then became its chair.[116] After the success of the Republicans in 1916, Woods was no longer challenged. In fact, he was reelected chairman in January 1918 but lost his own bid for renomination in July 1918. At first Woods did not want to relinquish the chair after his electoral loss, but in the face of strenuous political pressure, he resigned that August.[117]

At the DCCC, Rep. Frank Doremus of Michigan was chair for the 1914 and 1916 election cycles. The Democrats retained the majority in the first cycle and lost it to the Republicans in the next by six seats (though they had an organizational majority).

Doremus did not head the committee after 1916. The DCCC under Doremus's leadership in 1914 was far less organizationally diverse and much more tied to the DNC than its Republican counterpart. The Democrats' most important political spokesman in the 1914 election was President Wilson. But instead of stumping for Democratic congressional candidates, Wilson agreed to write letters of support.

> In accordance with his recent letter to Chairman Doremus of the Democratic Congressional Committee, President Wilson will not make any speeches himself, but he intends to carry on an active letter-writing campaign in several States. The President has requests before him for letters of support from Democratic candidates in all parts of the country. It was intimated at the White House today that all the Administration would support all candidates nominated in open Democratic primaries. . . . It was intimated in high Administration circles today that practically all members of the President's Cabinet would speak in the campaign.[118]

Clearly, there were close ties between the DCCC and the White House at this time, and it was expected that the White House would be active in the congressional campaign, though it is telling that Wilson did not commit to personal appearances and sent cabinet members to speak instead. The ties between the DCCC and the DNC were very close, and the two organizations merged temporarily for the elections. This arrangement seems to have been dominated by the president and the DNC, which printed pamphlets extolling Wilson's accomplishments.[119]

The elections of 1916 included a presidential race and also witnessed the first widespread use of paid advertising in political campaigns. According to McGerr, the Democrats were the innovators, using film, billboards, electric signs, and advertising panels on streetcars.[120] There was still cooperation between the DNC and DCCC; in fact, the DCCC was used to produce all campaign literature. Still, the Democratic organizations focused on Wilson's accomplishments in the domestic economy and in keeping the country out of war. Wilson was reelected, along with a Democratic Senate, but Democrats in the House had to appeal to independents elected to Congress to retain control because of their narrow margin.

On the other side, Republican organizational separation could hardly have been more complete. The NRCC's executive committee organized exceptionally early for the 1916 campaign. In a meeting on February 25, 1915, the following subcommittees were organized: Finance, Judiciary, Literature and Text Book, Newspaper Publicity, Speakers and Chautauqua.[121] Their activities remained quite distinct from the RNC's, which was working on behalf of the Republican presidential nominee, Charles Evans Hughes. In fact, one senior congressman believed that the organizational division cost Hughes the election, because the elections of individuals were given precedence by the NRCC. Ebenezer Hill (R-CT) had this to say:

> I am satisfied that either the dual organization of National and Congressional committees is a mistake, or else much more harmonious relations between the two are necessary. The great Democratic effort was made to secure the re-election of Woodrow Wilson, and the National Committee at least gave the election of individual members of Congress decidedly second place.[122]

Despite such calls for unity, the NRCC remained independent in this presidential year. The NRCC was organizationally stronger than the RNC at this time, whereas the reverse appears to have been the case for the Democrats.

The 1918 elections produced a significant Republican victory in Congress, when both chambers switched to Republican control, 237-191 in the House and 48-47-1 in the Senate. This happened while the United States was enmeshed in World War I; indeed, the election took place ten days before the armistice. The election was thus couched in terms of the performance of President Wilson and the conduct of the war effort. That the election became a referendum on the president's policies was the result of efforts on both sides. For the Republicans, opposition to Wilson could unify the party still split between Progressives and Conservatives. Democrats retained the unity of effort that had been relatively successful in the 1916 elections. According to Seward Livermore, Wilson considered his activities abroad to be the relevant issue in the elections and believed that the congressional vote would indicate support for him: "Seldom delegating authority and rarely accepting advice on important matters, Wilson assumed all responsibility for party policy and strategy as the situation dictated in the course of the campaign."[123] Unfortunately for the Democratic party, this plan failed. The unified Democratic organization raised and spent $665,000,[124] the most ever spent in a Democratic midterm election effort. The organizational initiative by the Democratic National Committee obscured the congressional effort, for the DNC chair, Vance McCormick, claimed that a congressional victory was necessary to secure the presidency for the Democrats in 1920.[125]

Scott Ferris, a congressman from Oklahoma who was well regarded by President Wilson and an advocate of the president's policies, headed the DCCC in 1918.[126] Congressional Democrats still saw Wilson as a popular figure who would help them retain their majority. Plans for the 1918 campaign started early, in June 1917, and focused on the production and distribution of campaign literature and press releases to Democratic newspapers.[127] Presumably, speakers were used, but the most important speaker of all decided against a speaking tour. Wilson's refusal to defend his policies personally was not lost on the electorate or the Republican party, especially as he had refused to stump for candidates in 1916 as well. Though the Democrats' campaign in 1918 was not successful, Chairman Ferris used his increased visibility at the DCCC to run for the Senate in 1920, a bid he lost. Some records indicate that Ferris returned to the post of DCCC chair for the 1922 election cycle, although he was not a member of Congress at that time.[128]

The Republicans, by contrast, ran a coordinated but not unified effort in 1918. As a combined financial force, the Republicans outspent the Democrats by about $10,000.[129] The RNC and the NRCC had some joint financial dealings during this campaign, but unlike the Democrats, the RNC chair, Will Hays, deferred to the NRCC chair, Simeon Fess, in the allocation of such monies. In a memorandum from Hays to Fess, which outlined district-level allocations as of October 10, 1918, Hays explains, "I am enclosing herewith a memorandum of our discussion the other day as to the amounts you thought . . . should go to the different districts and the amounts you thought you could send, and the amounts which you wanted this committee to send."[130] The two committees cooperated in the other traditional ventures, campaign literature production and employment of prominent speakers. The Republicans were more unified in their purpose: both party organizations agreed that achieving a Republican majority in Congress was critical. Discussion of the party's prospects for the presidency in 1920 are absent.

Yet the RNC and the NRCC were in a territorial war concerning fund-raising. During the summer of 1917 the NRCC held hearings concerning accusations that two agents of the campaign committee had acted improperly. A major fund-raising method used by all the party committees was extraction of large donations by individual agents who would receive a commission, based on a percentage of the total amount they collected (most professional "fund-raisers" operate on a similar principle in the 1990s). At issue was the size of the commission these agents received for collecting funds on behalf of the NRCC. The more powerful revelation was that the NRCC's agents were "obstructing" the work of the less resourceful RNC agents.[131] In other words, the NRCC was beating the RNC to the punch when it came to securing large donations. The RNC made its dissatisfaction well known, but this alone was not enough to make the committee back down. In response to a chastisement of NRCC activities by the RNC, the NRCC chair said, "I assure you that your position is correct and that our arrangement with these collectors is that they shall not interfere with regular patrons. The Congressional Committee is simply endeavoring to head off the Republican Publicity Association [the fund-raising arm of the RNC] from gathering all of the funds."[132]

This tense arrangement endured during the 1918 cycle but gave way to a more formal agreement for the 1920 cycle. Of course, a presidential election would take place that year, which enabled the RNC to argue for a superior position. An agreement between the two committees provided that the NRCC would suspend fund-raising activity if the RNC would supply them with operating funds. Further stipulations in the agreement were as follows:

> It is agreed that no publicity in bill-board or newspaper advertising will be undertaken by the Congressional Committee except in co-operation, after consultation, with the National Committee.
>
> The National Committee is empowered to use the machinery of the Congressional Committee to assist in the collection of funds under this agreement, the expense to be divided as at present.
>
> It is understood that the Congressional Committee is to retain its individuality in its organization and in the application of the funds except in the publicity items before mentioned.[133]

Curiously, this arrangement seems to be designed to assure the liquidity of the RNC rather than to rescue the NRCC from the danger of financial oblivion. This system of financing shows that despite cooperative efforts the two organizations would not merge. Fess's letter to Hays demonstrates the occasional nature of this cooperation: "It was thoroughly understood of course, that the proposed arrangement was one of convenience, for the 1920 campaign only, and that the separate status and utter independence of the two committees would in no way be effected thereby."[134] Given the Democrats' tendency toward cooperation, this statement shows significant autonomy on the part of the NRCC.

Fess, first elected to the House in 1912, was one of the first chairs to use the NRCC position to satisfy his career ambitions. He did not lobby for the post but instead emerged as the consensus choice when the party needed to replace Woods close to the general elections. Fess took over during the last days of August yet still mastered the national scene with only two months before the general election. In the 1918 election the Republicans increased their control of the House by twenty-one seats and gained control of the Senate by one seat. Fess familiarized himself with all the House districts, negotiated financial allocations with the RNC and various state parties, and became thoroughly acquainted with all the issue positions. In addition, he was an eloquent spokesman for congressional candidates in their districts. All these factors, plus Fess's general popularity, led to speculation that he could be a contender for Speaker in 1919. A contemporary Ohio newspaper said about Fess in late 1918, "Fess . . . who it will be recalled at first objected to taking the chairmanship of the National Congressional Committee . . . was persuaded to take up the work over his personal disinclination because of the prestige that his work at the head of that committee would give him—a possible candidate for speakership of the next house."[135] This is the first clear mention of the NRCC chair as a stepping-stone to higher leadership positions. Fess did not become a final candidate for Speaker in 1919 (which went to Frederick Gillett of Massachusetts), but his work as chair continued to attract national and local attention.

Fess continued as chair for the 1920 election cycle, when fellow Republican and Ohioan, Warren G. Harding, was running for the presidency. Republicans gained sixty-three seats in the House, making the outcome a 300 to 132 advantage for Republicans. The Senate received nine more Republicans, making their count 59 to 37. The success of this campaign, especially for two Ohioans, influenced Fess's next move. Although Fess was reelected chair of the NRCC for the 1922 cycle, he chose to run for the Senate instead. According to his biographer, Fess chose to run at this time because of his renown throughout the state of Ohio, much of which was a result of his leadership of the NRCC. His chairmanship figures prominently in his senatorial campaign literature—in fact, none of his other congressional work is mentioned. One pamphlet reprints an editorial with this evaluation: "He is unquestionably the most influential man in Congress, excepting such official influence as the speakership carries. . . . Mr. Fess is the only idealist who has been so devoted a realist that the credit for the overwhelming majority of his party elected to the Senate and House in 1920 was under his masterful official leadership."[136] Fess thus used his prestige at the NRCC to further his political ambitions. At first he tested the waters on ascendancy to the Speakership and once blocked, used his prestige to propel himself to the Senate. Fess was elected to the Senate in 1922 and served two terms. In his second term in the Senate Fess served as Senate Republican whip.

Henry De La Warr Flood, a member of the Flood political dynasty in Virginia, chaired the DCCC for the 1920 election cycle. Flood had lobbied for the post for the 1906 election cycle but was not successful. According to his biographer, he was encouraged to become a speaker for the DCCC in the 1906 elections by Champ Clark (an eventual Speaker of the House).[137] Flood's interest in the committee endured from 1906 to 1920. Like Fess, Flood used the campaign committee chair to raise his profile within his own state. In a letter to a party worker in his district, Flood wrote,

> I appreciate very much your interest in my Congressional campaign and also in regard to the Governorship. I have my hands full right now as Chairman of the Democratic National Campaign Committee, and as a candidate to succeed myself in the House of Representatives. I have not, therefore, made any decision in regard to the Governorship and will not do so until after the election in November.[138]

Flood was always more powerful within his home state than within Congress, and he may have been seeking leverage for the governor's mansion. However, Flood died in office in December 1921.

Conclusion: The CCCs, 1866–1920

The CCCs' origins as institutional party instruments grounded their early organizational development. When the Republican Campaign Committee formed, it focused its efforts on assisting campaigns for rewriting the constitutions of the newly reconstructed Southern states in the immediate post–Civil War era and then moved to assist congressional candidates in their elections from these areas as well as in the North. It soon became clear that members valued an organizational presence dedicated to providing them with nationally oriented campaign resources. The CCCs provided centralized resources for the use of all incumbent members and for challenger candidates once they were nominated. The CCCs began by providing speakers for their candidates. They secured the services of prominent senators, representatives, or recent military heroes and sent them to the districts of members who requested them. The CCCs then added literature production to their resource offerings. This would include reprints of speeches in the *Congressional Record* by either the incumbent member campaigning for reelection or by party leaders who would outline the themes for the campaign at hand. Later the literature production would be supplemented by early press assistance. That is, the CCCs worked with reporters to get newspaper stories printed about their individual candidates. Many of these services were consolidated in the 1880s with the first production of campaign issue books. These books contained facts and figures and suggested arguments concerning the issues of the day for candidates to use on the campaign trail. This development coincided with a shift from the army style of campaigning to the educational style, when voters demanded more information about individual candidates and their particular positions on issues. Also, in the 1910s CCCs began systematic opposition research by tracking the voting records of the opposing party's incumbents. It is especially interesting to note that CCCs simply added new services, making them more organizationally diverse. To sustain all these activities, CCCs began to develop fundraising plans beyond the traditional subscription assessed of all members. Thus by the 1920s, when separate Senate committees formed, the House committees had already developed a clear set of services to offer House candidates and had established an identity distinct from the national committees. Although NCs often attempted to dominate CCCs, especially during off-year elections when there was no presidential race, there is no clear pattern along that sole dimension. Other factors, such as the personalities of the various chairs and the position of the congressional party as a majority or minority party, mattered more.

Note what is missing in this account of early CCC activities: the lack of any concerted effort to run specific congressional campaigns. In other words, the CCCs offered a wide array of services for candidates, but these were provided mostly for the convenience of incumbent members. CCC chairs did not actively engage in candidate recruitment and often began their work only a few months before a general election. There is no mention of any attempt to give candidates particularized advice. So nothing that we can say about the CCCs' activities would clash with evidence that local parties were active in matters such as candidate recruitment, nomination, and the conduct of local campaigns. The CCCs were not created to supplant local parties but to counter the national committees' bias toward the presidency. This also explains why electoral outcomes are not necessarily attached to the other side of the CCC equation: leadership development in the House.

As the internal workings in Congress grew more complex and the development of the national party organizations became more advanced, the stories of the individual chairs of the CCCs reveal much richer information. As the leadership structure of Congress opened up, more members of Congress presented themselves as contenders for CCC chairs. Furthermore, the contests for CCC chairs also reflected internal factional battles, indicating that the individuals involved with the campaign committees believed that it *mattered* who chaired the committee. Ambitious men sought CCC chairs more and more in this era, in some cases using the position to help improve their access to other powerful leadership slots. This was mostly true for House members. Few senators of either party took on later leadership posts, probably because senatorial leadership was still undeveloped. The Republican House members who chaired the NRCC in this era either lost bids for reelection or left the House to run for the Senate. Two DCCC chairmen did take on other leadership positions. Although evidence on CCC chairs as leadership positions is scant, profiles of these individuals show that they were more committed to long-term careers in Congress than their predecessors. Perhaps the CCCs were seen as powerful in their own right, as there were few other positions of equivalent stature. Tables A.2 and A.3 present summary information regarding the careers of the NRCC and DCCC heads. Though few chairs went on to other leadership positions, they tended to be ending long careers at the time of their CCC tenures. This may indicate that the CCC position was considered a part of the developing leadership structure. Also, CCCs were not chaired by obscure members but instead by prominent individuals. In the early twentieth century we find more direct evidence that CCC chairs considered their positions to have great potential for future career moves.

CHAPTER 3

THE SENATE CAMPAIGN COMMITTEES, 1919–1972

THE SENATE CAMPAIGN COMMITTEES—the National Republican Senatorial Committee (NRSC) and the Democratic Senatorial Campaign Committee (DSCC)—had distinct needs and leadership structures. They did not separate themselves from the House committees until 1920, by which time all sitting senators had been popularly elected at least once. This, along with the tradition that senators had been a part of the House committees almost since their origins and the fact that only one-third of the Senate is up for reelection in every two-year election cycle, also accounts for the lag in establishing an active and separate organization. Given the staggered election terms for the Senate, the senatorial committees' focus is on only one-third of the country at a time. This restricted focus meant that the senatorial committees did not pursue campaign activities nearly as aggressively as the House committees and from their origins to the present day have focused much more narrowly on the channeling of funds from various contributors to specific senatorial candidates rather than on the provision of specific services. Senate candidates tended to be more experienced than House candidates and therefore required less assistance from Washington, D.C., to mount successful campaigns. Senate candidates must generally win statewide primaries before they appeal for Washington campaign assistance. Still, senators obviously thought that their campaigning needs and interest in majority status warranted their own organization.

Although congressional scholars argue that the Senate was institutionalized by the turn of the century, the direct election of senators changed the nature of the institution. For example, formal leadership posts were not well defined until this time. Floor leaders had been present since the late nineteenth century, but party whips did not exist as formal positions until 1913 for the Democrats and 1915 for the Republicans.[1] Still, it was not until much later (almost twenty years) that patterns of succession to leadership positions emerged. The House, in contrast, established patterns of succession from floor leader to Speaker soon after 1910. This is not to say, however, that the Senate did not have strong leadership—merely that this smaller body of powerful politicians with similar experience in public office required less structured leadership than the larger, less homogeneous House.

The relationship between tenure at the campaign committees and leadership succession patterns is more difficult to ascertain in the Senate. This is partly due to the informal rule that senators do not chair the committee during the cycle in which they run for reelection because they need to devote time to their own campaigns. In addition, there is natural decentralization of formal leadership in the Senate, which reflects its collegial norms: even the most junior senators have tremendous opportunities for power, making the need for leadership training grounds far less relevant. Because of the wide dispersion of power, senatorial parties have not formed hierarchical leadership structures, though the committee system is still a powerful tool. Thus the senatorial CCCs have a smaller scale of activities than the House CCCs, and there is a less direct relationship between them and Senate leadership. In the period examined here senators became prominent individual politicians whose ambitions grew in proportion to the size of their campaign efforts. Therefore, we begin to see senators use the CCC position to explore their own political prospects outside their home states for possible bids for higher position inside or outside the Senate, specifically, prominent standing committee assignments or potential presidential bids.

Campaigning in this era was firmly in the "merchandising style," whereby candidates were packaged like products.[2] However, the Senate CCCs, unlike their House counterparts, did not develop a wide range of services in response. Instead, they focused on getting money to candidates so that candidates could hire the services they needed on their own. This chapter traces the early development of the Senate CCCs through the 1970s, when campaign finance reform significantly changed the fate of all four CCCs.

Early Origins: 1919–1950

According to the NRCC's own history, the National Republican Senatorial Committee was established in 1919 "mainly through the efforts of Sen. Charles L. McNary of Oregon."[3] Though there is no description of the NRSC's activities at this time, McNary eventually became Senate minority leader (1933–44) and chairman of the Republican Conference (1933–44) as well as the Republican vice presidential nominee in 1940. The earliest information on the activities of the NRSC is for the 1922 midterm election, when Sen. Medill McCormick of Illinois served as chairman. The NRSC cooperated in a joint Speaker's Bureau (with both the NRCC and RNC) but also hired its own speakers.[4] The NRSC chairman was also in demand for his speaking services. By late October 1922 the NRSC had raised and spent in excess of $100,000. Much of this was expended through individual contributions to state parties on behalf of senatorial candidates ($3,200 on average per race). Although the NRSC gave candidates funds out of Washington, D.C., fundraising took place both there and in a Chicago office.[5] In the area of campaign services, the NRSC produced and distributed resource documents for the use of speakers and candidates during public appearances, rather than for direct press consumption as the House CCCs had. For the 1922 cycle the senatorial committee produced two major publications: *Business Day by Day* and *The Truth, the Facts, the Record*. *Business Day by Day*, which was compiled by a "nonpolitical" organization but distributed by the NRSC to senatorial candidates and state party committees, contained twenty-nine charts and accompanying explanations on various aspects of the American economy. *The Truth, the Facts, the Record* was essentially a campaign textbook, written by NRSC chair McCormick.[6] The booklet was forty-eight pages long and contained exhaustive statistics and propaganda on the issues of the day. It is clear that by 1922 the NRSC was actively assisting candidates in the conduct of their campaigns from Washington. A letter from McCormick to his successor for the 1924 campaign cycle, Sen. George Higgins Moses of New Hampshire, indicates that these activities were part of a long-term plan:

> As you know, our Committee published and paid for the text books used by the Congressional and National Committees; contributed its share to the maintenance of the Joint Speakers Bureau, and for the first time actively collaborated with the two other Committees in the campaign and pre campaign work. I understand that the other two Committees seek your collaboration for the forthcoming campaign.[7]

By alerting his successor to the NRSC's current arrangement with the NRCC and the RNC, McCormick signals that the arrangement between the campaign committees and the national committees was subject to reassessment at the start of a new election cycle.

McCormick was the son-in-law of Marc Hanna, the campaign manager for William McKinley's 1896 presidential bid. McCormick served for only the 1922 cycle, probably because he was up for reelection in 1924. McCormick gives some evidence that the NRSC chairmanship could lead to other aspirations in a letter to a supporter:

> As you know, I do not, as a rule, seek controversy nor do I run from it. When I have discharged my present duty as Secretary of the

Steering Committee for this Congress, and Chairman of the Senatorial Committee for this campaign, I can counsel with my friends as to my own course. As you know, some believe I ought to be a candidate for Governor and more of them that I ought to be a candidate for reelection to the Senate, but I think that this is not the time to anticipate the problems of '24. We have before us the issues of the campaign of this year.[8]

McCormick chose to run for reelection to the Senate in 1924 but lost.

The origins of the Democratic Senatorial Campaign Committee are also obscure, though it was probably founded by Sen. Key Pittman of Nevada. Pittman's name appears on DSCC expenditure reports in 1918,[9] but as is the case for McNary, I found no description of committee activities. The DSCC was active by 1922, with Sen. David Walsh of Massachusetts as chair. Walsh seems to have had a relatively difficult time establishing himself in the Senate. He was appointed to fill a vacancy, and immediately after his arrival in the Senate he chaired the DSCC. After his DSCC tenure Walsh stood for reelection in 1924 but was defeated. He was again appointed to the Senate in 1926 and was reelected in 1928, serving until he was again defeated in 1946.

Unfortunately, DSCC activities and chairs remain unknown for the rest of the 1920s, when the Republicans held majorities in the Senate. Sen. Millard Tydings of Maryland, first elected to the Senate in 1926, served as chairman for the 1930 cycle. He was recognized for his efforts in that campaign by his colleagues in 1932, acknowledging that the DSCC did carry on campaign activities.[10] Although the Democrats gained seats, they failed to win control of the Senate until after the 1932 elections. Tydings served in the Senate for four consecutive terms but did not serve as DSCC chairman again.

Senator Moses chaired the NRSC for the 1924 and 1930 election cycles. Moses had been a newspaper editor for almost twenty years when he entered Congress. He was a conservative

Republican, and there was some concern about his capacity for fairness in the campaigns of liberal Republicans, the first mention of ideological concerns within the CCCs. These fears appear to have been allayed, as the Republicans picked up three seats in the Senate in 1924 and Moses was elected president pro tempore of the Senate in March 1925, just after the 1924 elections.[11] When Moses became chair for the 1930 cycle, he was far more controversial. He attempted to raise and spend funds independently of the RNC (although little is known about funding practices at this time, making it difficult to evaluate how exceptional this action was).[12] He had a falling-out with President Hoover and attacked all but the most conservative members of his own party. Despite unhappiness from several Republicans concerning Moses's behavior, and talk of removing him as chair, he remained at his post.[13] Although the Republicans did control the Senate after the 1930 elections, it was by a single vote. Moses was not reelected to the Senate in 1932.

More is known about Moses than about any other NRSC chair until the 1950s. Fortunately, the records of DSCC activity during the 1930–50 period are extensive, and we do have some knowledge of several NRSC chairs in the 1930s and 1940s. Between Moses's two terms, Lawrence Phipps of Colorado served as NRSC chairman for the 1926 election cycle. First elected in 1918, Phipps served two terms in the Senate. The Republicans lost seats in the 1926 elections but still retained control of the Senate by one seat. Phipps did not hold any positions of leadership after his chairmanship and was not a candidate for reelection in 1930. After Moses's second term as NRSC chair, Sen. Henry Hatfield of West Virginia held the post for the difficult 1932 elections. Hatfield served only one term in the Senate from 1928 to 1934. Consequently, he did not hold higher leadership positions after his CCC tenure. Sen. John Townsend of Delaware chaired the NRSC for the 1936 election cycle and apparently continued through the 1948 election cycle, eight years past his 1940 electoral defeat. Townsend remained employed by the committee for nearly twenty years after that, sometimes as executive director and, it seems, sometimes as chair.

Since one individual, Col. Edwin A. Halsey, secretary of the Senate from 1928 to 1944, served as the de facto executive director of the DSCC for sixteen consecutive years,[14] we have a comprehensive view of the DSCC and its activities in his records. Each campaign cycle in this period began with a letter of inquiry from the newly elected DSCC chair to those Democratic candidates seeking Senate seats. The letter from Sen. Claude Swanson (D-VA), DSCC chair for the 1932 race, declared, "It will be very helpful if you will write to me giving me the political situation in your State; the prospects of carrying it; the funds necessary to help you in making your fight; the speakers and literature you will need; and other suggestions."[15] Despite these good intentions, the DSCC was constrained by its financial relationship with the DNC. Swanson explains the financial arrangement between the various Democratic party organizations at the time:

> The Democratic Senatorial Campaign Committee is organized to furnish information, records in Congress and literature to aid Senators in their reelection. In the year of the national [i.e., presidential] campaign, the funds are contributed to the National Committee. The Senatorial Committee has very little funds. In the off years the Senatorial and House Committees take care of the campaign. This year the National Committee has charge of the funds and I suggest that you communicate with your State Chairman concerning your financial needs. The National Committee had decided to distribute such funds as it can furnish to the State Chairmen, in order that the entire ticket may be aided.[16]

The practice of parceling funds to the state chairs, instead of to the candidates themselves, was a long-standing tradition in the Democratic party. Funds were normally earmarked for specific candidates, but ultimate spending decisions were made at the state level. The advantage of this arrangement was that funds spent directly for candidates were hidden from public view. As Swanson declared, "You will note from this that this money is to be expended at your direction, and this is possibly better than to have it sent directly to you."¹⁷ The DSCC also provided resource materials such as basic opposition research (which consisted of the voting records and lists of bills and resolutions introduced by incumbent Republican senators facing Democratic challengers) and speech materials.¹⁸ Swanson had been governor of Virginia and was originally appointed to the Senate to fill a vacancy before he led the DSCC in 1932. Under Swanson's watch the Democrats regained control of the Senate with an advantage of 59 to 36 seats. Swanson did not remain in Congress long after the 1932 election, however, as he joined the Roosevelt administration as secretary of the navy.

The DSCC continued to provide basic services (information, opposition research, and minimal funds) for the 1934 races. James Hamilton Lewis of Illinois, the first Senate Democratic whip (1913–19), was chair. At the same time Lewis was chosen to head the DSCC he was again appointed Democratic whip, a position he held past his DSCC tenure until his death in April 1939. Either the DSCC post was considered important enough that only someone with the stature of whip could execute the tasks or it was considered so trivial that Lewis could also serve in this capacity. In either event, we can say that campaigning was seen as related to governing duties. However, we may assume that after the historic elections of 1932 Democrats might still expect to have good electoral footing, which might have precluded them from establishing an extensive organization. In the fund-raising realm the DSCC had the entire financial responsibility for senatorial candidates in this off-year election, which was little appreciated by the DSCC. Executive Director Halsey informed a senator running for reelection of the contemporary realities: "I wish it were possible to send you more financial aid. The National Committee to date has not contributed one cent to our Committee. I would advise you to write to Mr. Farley [DNC chair].ʺ¹⁹ At this time the DSCC's fund-raising efforts were minimal. Also, DSCC-DNC relations appear strained, which was a frequent trend for the Democrats in off-year elections.

Sen. Joseph Guffey of Pennsylvania served as the next DSCC chair. He was first elected in 1934 and then chaired the committee for two nonconsecutive cycles, 1936 and 1942. He had been an active member of the Democratic National Committee long before his election to Congress. This national party experience combined with his reputation as a "party boss" in his home state most likely led to his selection as chair. While in the Senate Guffey played a role in House politics by backing Sam Rayburn for House majority leader in 1936. Guffey stated that he was mainly concerned with fund-raising during his two terms as chair but ideological clashes with the "Dixiecrats" led to his departure from the DSCC in 1943. Though Guffey gives the impression that he was forced out of this position, he claimed relief at not having to raise funds for conservative Democratic senators he disliked.[20] He did not hold any other formal party positions during his congressional career but was considered a man of great informal influence.

Sen. Prentiss Brown (D-MI) chaired the DSCC for the 1938 cycle. The DSCC became more sophisticated in the extent and type of services it provided in response to the increased reliance on newspaper advertising by senatorial candidates. The precise form of the DSCC's assistance in newspaper advertising is detailed by Halsey in a memorandum to all Democratic senatorial candidates:

> The Committee asks that the nominee send at his earliest convenience to the Secretary-Treasurer of the Committee a photograph of himself, a short biographical sketch and any suggestions or general information which may be helpful in the campaign program.
>
> The photograph will be used for making a drawing from which a cut and mats will be made; the biographical sketch, accompanied with the photograph, will be made into a three-column cartoon of

which the nominee will be furnished mats to be distributed to the general press of his State. The biographical material will be furnished to those desiring information about the Democratic Senatorial candidates.

The Senatorial Committee has factual information in the form of pamphlets (which can be furnished to the nominees in limited number) regarding governmental activities showing definite and substantial progress made by the New Deal under President Roosevelt.[21]

The DSCC had a staff cartoonist whose full-time job was to provide camera-ready mats using this information. This service is an example of a resource that could be provided more cheaply and easily by a central organization. In addition, the DSCC took seriously its offer to reprint speeches from the *Congressional Record* on the major issues of the day: it printed twenty-nine pamphlets and cards (postcards that discussed issues in condensed form) that were then distributed under the congressional frank of various senators, normally those who made the speeches and were up for reelection.[22]

Though the DSCC services logically helped incumbents more than challengers, the financial arrangements were discussed universally, regardless of a candidate's incumbency status. In this off-year the size and composition of the DSCC budget was uncertain, as Halsey explained to Chairman Brown:

> The Senatorial Committee has never been able to actually have a budget, from the fact that contributions have always been so uncertain. We have planned from time to time, of course, to give each candidate a certain amount of money, but have not always been able to fulfill or comply with the suggested amount.
>
> . . . We should figure at least on $2000 to each candidate and adjust the distribution as equitably as possible.[23]

At $2,000 per candidate, the DSCC would have needed a budget of approximately $64,000. This did not include the committee's normal operating expenses. For the calendar year of 1938, the

DSCC raised $45,050 and spent $39,538.[24] Thus it could not achieve its goal of direct contributions to all targeted races.

Because of his DSCC chairmanship, Brown was considered to be a Washington insider. A newspaper article published on the basis of a DSCC press release describes Brown's background and position: "Chairman Brown of the Democratic Senatorial Committee is a 'freshman' in the Senate. Prior to his election [to the Senate] in 1936, he served two terms in the House. His selection as chairman makes him a member of the Democratic high command."[25] Though Brown appeared to be amassing influence in Washington, D.C., it did not translate into local political strength and he lost his seat in 1942.

The DSCC performed similar services for the 1940 campaign.[26] The new chair, Theodore Francis Green of Rhode Island, also made many speeches. He served at the beginning of a very long Senate career, which culminated in his chairmanship of the Foreign Relations Committee. Having served first in the state House and then as governor of Rhode Island, Green had a more parochial focus. He did not become a formal leader, although he did become chair of the Committee on Privileges and Elections immediately after his DSCC tenure. During the 1942 campaign, which found Joseph Guffey as DSCC chair once again, the DSCC continued to offer the same services it had offered in 1940.[27]

The DSCC continued to provide mats and campaign literature in 1944 under its new chair, Sen. Joseph O'Mahoney of Wyoming. The committee was financially strapped, claiming an account balance of only $15,000 six weeks before the general election.[28] Perhaps this was due to the control of the DNC over the fund-raising and campaigning machinery during presidential election years. O'Mahoney did not hold any positions of formal leadership after this post.

Neither the DSCC's financial resources nor the extent of services it provided increased for the 1946 and 1948 election cycles. The Democrats lost control of both the House and the Senate in the 1946 elections after having controlled both chambers continuously since 1932. The DSCC chair, Scott Lucas (D-IL), declared that the committee did not have nearly enough money to contribute to the campaigns of every Senate candidate and in fact encouraged the channeling of contributions from individuals to candidates through the DSCC.[29] This function, sometimes called money laundering or earmarking, became the chief service the senatorial CCCs of both parties performed for members from this time (and perhaps even earlier) until campaign finance reform in the 1970s. The idea was to disguise the questionable origins of funds (from corporations, powerful individuals, etc.) by having them donated to the CCC and allocated for a particular candidate. The CCC would then make a contribution to the candidate in that amount. Responding to charges concerning this type of suspect campaign tactic by the Democrats, Lucas contrasted the resources of the DSCC with his counterpart, the NRSC: "The last two reports of the Republican Senatorial Campaign Committee show that well over $300,000 has been spent for Republican candidates for the Senate. The Democratic Senatorial Campaign Committee, according to its last two reports, has spent only a little over $42,000 for the election of Democratic Candidates."[30] Despite these meager resources, the Democrats recaptured both chambers of Congress after the 1948 election.

Lucas did not consider the DSCC chairmanship a particularly welcome assignment at the time, a sentiment he expressed to the majority leader, Alben Barkley, who appointed him in the spring of 1945:

> Sometime ago you appointed me as Chairman of the Senatorial Campaign Committee for 1946. I doubted seriously at that time that I was one to accept this chairmanship. Today I am convinced more than ever that some other Senator should take over these obligations and duties.
>
> Therefore, I respectfully request that my resignation as Chairman of this Committee be accepted, and some other Senator be appointed to take my place.[31]

Despite Lucas's wishes, Barkley prevailed on him to serve. Lucas continued as DSCC chair for the 1948 cycle and also served as

Democratic whip at the same time. After that cycle, when the Democrats regained control of Congress from the Republicans, Lucas was elevated to majority leader. He served in this post until his defeat for reelection in 1950.

The Senate CCCs, 1950–1972: Modest Work

The Senate CCCs remained modest operations in their first thirty years. Like the House CCCs, they developed literature for candidates' use, collected research materials on incumbent senators of the other party as well as potential challengers to their own incumbents, and distributed the modest funds they had available. Fund-raising for both the NRSC and the DSCC seems to have been a low priority. During presidential election years, the Senate CCCs got financial allowances from the national committees; in off-years, they relied predominantly on member assessments. The first mention of the Senate CCCs acting as money channelers appears in the late 1940s, though in all likelihood they performed this function much earlier. Below we examine the expanded services added to accommodate senators' needs for more media resources as well as their need for enhanced money channeling.

Though the response of the senatorial CCCs to the mass media age was modest compared to that of the House CCCs, they did expand their services to accommodate the greater campaigning needs of senatorial candidates. For the 1950 elections the DNC still controlled the budget of the DSCC. The new DSCC chair, Sen. Clinton Anderson of New Mexico, received approval for a $25,000 budget that consisted mainly of salaries for one part-time and four full-time staffers.[32] No extensive fund-raising efforts were conducted on behalf of senatorial candidates. Instead, the DSCC's activities focused on services that could best be provided by a Washington, D.C., bureau. The first of these was to coordinate the production of television endorsements by Vice President (and former senator) Alben Barkley for eleven competitive Senate candidates. Although the DNC had a large hand in this operation, the DSCC was the central coordinator.³³ In addition, Senator Anderson, a national spokesman by virtue of his DSCC position, served on the DNC's Speaker's Bureau for candidates on the Democratic party ticket throughout the country.³⁴

The DSCC continued to provide written materials for candidates. It tailored campaign literature for individual candidates instead of using generic appeals, as had been the practice. As one DSCC staffer writes,

> I hope you share my views that we may best help them by deviating from the customary manner of supplying identical material to all candidates. While I *have in preparation several speeches*, I do not think that such general appeals are enough. Our candidates should take advantage of local sentiment, and their speeches should be geared to the dominant interests of the voters in their own states.
>
> Besides, seasoned campaigners need only factual data and a few pungent paragraphs to incorporate into their speeches; others, less experienced, need considerable more help from us.³⁵

The last paragraph is telling as it points to one of the major differences between House and Senate candidates: experience. Most senatorial candidates needed little assistance from a national campaign organization. If they could win the party nomination in a statewide race, they normally could run a viable general election campaign. Here we see sensitivity to candidate experience and an acknowledgment that campaigns were shifting toward the individual candidate's attributes. General party appeals proved to be insufficient. Although previous DSCC staffs sent materials that promoted Democratic presidents' views, now such appeals were of marginal utility.

During this cycle we find evidence of collegial DSCC administration. Since the DSCC worked for the senatorial party's benefit, the chair and staff were sensitive to the senators' wishes. Indeed, the DSCC apparently feared taking action without the approval of its incumbent membership. This was evidenced in an appeal to all DSCC members concerning permission to print campaign literature condemning Sen. Joseph McCarthy (R-WI) on DSCC letterhead, even though such use of letterhead would not place any demands on DSCC resources:

> This copy was written at the request of Senator Tydings from material he gave me. Both Senator Tydings and Senator McMahon desire 10,000 copies each, prepared in the form of a 4-page folder, with art work.
>
> The cost is being assumed by the Senators themselves, but for obvious reasons they want the Campaign Committee imprint to appear on them instead of their own name.
>
> It is Senator Anderson's request that you read this and state whether you agree to the use of the Campaign Committee's imprint.[36]

Here, the DSCC was used as a cover, a function entirely consistent with its purpose of working for senators, directed by senators. The DSCC afforded senators protection from accountability for their own initiatives.

Senator Anderson treated the DSCC chairmanship as an opportunity for advancement in the Senate. Anderson was a former House member and secretary of agriculture under President Harry Truman. He had been in the Senate for only two years before his appointment as DSCC chair. Although the Democrats lost seats in 1950, they still controlled the Senate. Anderson clearly wished to continue in the DSCC chairmanship for the 1952 cycle. He advised the new Senate majority leader, Ernest McFarland of Arizona, of his desire to continue as DSCC chair, but this request was denied. Anderson voiced his disappointment in a letter to the DNC chair, Bill Boyle:

> I mentioned to the President [Truman] last night that I had been expecting that Senator McFarland would reorganize the committee and appoint a new chairman and he did not seem to take too cordially to the idea. He felt that you and I had gotten along well and I had enjoyed nice relationships with Mike Kirwan on the House side and that it would be well if the team stayed together. Naturally, I have no way of knowing what Senator McFarland would think about that.[37]

McFarland nevertheless replaced Anderson with Sen. Earle Clements of Kentucky. So, in Anderson's view the position was a prize, not a chore. It is also noteworthy that Anderson's assumption was that the DSCC would be reorganized between election cycles.[38]

With Clements at the helm and a presidential election on the horizon, preparations for the 1952 campaign included a plea for better coordination between the DNC and the DSCC. The DSCC feared organizational encroachment by the DNC and proceeded to make the case on a number of occasions for the continued need of separate resources for DSCC autonomy. In their 1952 campaign plan the DSCC called for coordination with the DNC in the following areas: publicity, finances, speakers, research, campaign schedules, and issues. The DSCC also argued for the retention of its three-member permanent staff along with occasional supplemental staff from members' clerk-hire allowances.[39] Because the GOP won the presidency and both chambers of Congress in 1952, there was talk of disbanding the DSCC immediately after the election. Clements argued against this idea, which was originated by the DNC.[40] Rather than disband the DSCC, arguments were made (and later adopted) that the DSCC's role should be *expanded*. Suggestions included closer coordination of the DSCC with the Senate Democratic Policy Committee, more extensive work in opposition research, watchdog responsibilities on administration activities, tracking of separate individual voting records for incumbent Republican senators, accelerated development of "publicity" media, more advance planning for speakers, and a more careful monitoring of legislative activity in committees (now that the Democrats were in the minority).[41] These plans were implemented after the 1952 election, and the DSCC became a year-round full-time operation.[42]

Clements chaired the DSCC again for the 1954 election cycle. Clements was being groomed for leadership, as evidenced by his appointment as Democratic whip in 1953, a position he held along with the DSCC chair. Although the Democrats lost control of the Senate in 1952, Clements was reappointed chair of the DSCC in 1954 by then minority leader Lyndon Johnson, who declared, "It would be difficult to find a Democratic Senator better qualified for this important position.... Senator Clements rendered outstanding service during the last Congress and his experience and his ability will be needed by the Democratic Party in the 1954 campaign."[43] This is another example of the irrelevance of actual seat gains or losses for the evaluation of the DSCC chair's performance. Clements was obviously a favorite of Johnson's, and only a senator loyal to him could assume the DSCC post at this time.

Soon after the DSCC was reorganized for the 1954 cycle Senate Democrats engaged in an extensive discussion of preparations for the 1954 campaign. A budget of $24,280 was proposed, most of which was to support the salaries of three permanent staff persons. The executive director's salary was not part of the budget (probably because he was on several members' clerk-hire allowances).[44] In a turn of policy the DNC and DSCC agreed that the DSCC should pursue its own funding sources. The DNC chair, Stephen Mitchell, gave his views on the new arrangement to Clements:

> I have agreed with you that a great deal of assistance might be available to and through the Senate Campaign Committee that would not come to the Democratic National Committee and might otherwise be lost for the candidates. Also, I think it is right and proper from every standpoint that the Senate Finance Committee [sic] should finance its activities to the extent that it is able to do so and certainly there is no possible basis for criticism of members of that Committee or the members of the Democratic National Committee for urging separate efforts to raise necessary funds.[45]

With the DNC acknowledging DSCC independence, the two committees experimented with different political relationships and entered into some joint fund-raising ventures. These fund-raisers, usually "high-dollar" dinners, were held in Washington, D.C., and the proceeds split between the two organizations.[46]

Still, most DSCC financial activity consisted of money channeling, the rerouting of earmarked funds from contributors to the appropriate recipients.[47]

Immediately following the 1954 elections, in which Democrats regained control of the Senate, the DSCC announced another function that has also continued: transitional services for freshman members. This move was partly to justify the retention of a permanent staff and partly to establish ties with new incumbents as members of the institutional party. Clements advertised these services to new members four days after the election:

> I wish to take this opportunity to assure you that the staff of the Democratic Senatorial Campaign Committee and the writer and the facilities of his office are at your service to aid you in anyway possible to make this transition smoothly. There are problems of arranging office space, securing such office staff as you may not find among your own constituents and other matters on which we will be more than glad to give aid.[48]

Thus incumbent services came full circle, providing assistance in setting up senatorial offices so that reelection needs would be maximized by the new incumbents.

When Lyndon Johnson suffered a heart attack in early 1955, Clements, who was also minority whip (also knows as assistant floor leader), took over Johnson's floor leader responsibilities. Clements did not serve as DSCC chair in 1956 because he was up for reelection. He lost that election, but Johnson wanted to keep Clements in Washington, D.C., so he appointed him executive director of the DSCC for the 1958 cycle. Clearly, the majority leader of the Senate, who had exploited the power of the DCCC when he was in the House (see chapter 4), thought the DSCC had important political power.

We have a fuller picture of the NRSC after the passage of the Legislative Reorganization Act of 1946 and the creation of the policy committees for the Senate. The Republican Conference Rules for the Senate in 1949 stipulated that "a Republican Senatorial Campaign Committee shall be appointed within 6 months after the beginning of each Congress by the Chairman of the Conference, subject to confirmation by the Conference."[49] Senator Owen Brewster of Maine chaired the committee during the 1950 cycle, when the NRSC offered minimal services. In 1951 the NRSC had a staff of five, two professionals and three clerical assistants. In addition, because they conducted extensive research on legislative issues, the Senate Policy Committee staff of twelve served as reelection staff for senators.[50] Like the DSCC, the NRSC was producing literature and conducting opposition and issue research. The Republicans gained five seats in 1950, though they still fell one short of a majority. Brewster was up for reelection in 1952 but lost.

Even with an official staff of only five, the NRSC was extremely active for the 1952 cycle. The new NRSC chair, Everett Dirksen (R-IL), planned to raise $500,000 for the NRSC's operations, based on the 1948 election figure of $493,000 (actual monies spent). By the end of 1952, however, the NRSC had raised $811,548.[51] Part of this money came from the RNC (less than 10 percent), and much of the remainder from state party committees and individual donors. For this presidential election year the RNC created the Republican National Finance Committee (RNFC) as a nationwide fund-raising operation centralizing fund-raising from state party organizations. The RNFC then apportioned its funds to the three national party committees on a percentage basis: RNC, 66.7 percent; NRSC, 7 percent; and NRCC, 26.3 percent. So the NRSC received only $72,668 from the RNFC for the 1952 cycle,[52] but its more critical financial role was to act as "agent" for the transmission of funds from specific donors to specific candidates.[53]

Though the RNC was a meager financial resource, its membership did prove helpful to the NRSC. Dirksen wrote to all RNC members in states with upcoming senatorial elections asking them to organize on behalf of the senatorial candidate in their state.[54] One reason Dirksen wanted their active cooperation was that the NRSC was limited by law to contributions of $5,000 per political committee. The NRSC would first contribute directly to the candidate's campaign committee, then if the race seemed promising, it would make a contribution to state or special committees for use on the senatorial candidate's behalf.[55] This strategy was in response to the Federal Corrupt Practices Act, which curbed expenditures of political committees but not the number of committees that could act on a candidate's behalf.

Dirksen also divided the NRSC into regions and assigned one candidate to each member of the committee (another incumbent senator not up for reelection) as his special concern, although as the chairman indicated elsewhere, the NRSC could not become involved officially until after the primaries had determined the party's nominee.[56] This "buddy system" called on incumbent Republican senators to make appearances in the candidate's state (normally for the purposes of fund-raising) and to keep an eye out for information on incumbent Democratic senators being challenged by their "buddies" that could be used to the Republican candidate's advantage.[57] Dirksen did have clear service plans for the NRSC in the form of a revised candidate handbook:

> In other years it seems to have been customary for the Senatorial Committee to send a ton of undigested data to candidates in the field and obviously they were so busy that it was impossible to go through this material and extract from it things that would be immediately useful.
>
> Knowing something about the pressure one is under when the campaign is under way, I had in mind that for 1952 I would prepare a campaign book for each candidate, which would contain not only the essential data for his state but in addition would contain a dozen well prepared articles on the important issues which could serve as the core for speeches and also for radio programs.
>
> The candidates could then modify their introductions from time to time, add whatever of local material is necessary, and so use this series of a dozen articles on speeches throughout their campaigns.[58]

Dirksen sent this explanation of his intentions to several prominent Republican journalists and scholars, hoping to obtain their submissions for such a publication. The NRSC provided other services, especially processing photographs in camera-ready formats for a variety of campaign purposes but primarily for use by newspapers in the candidate's state.[59] The NRSC also paid for part of a coordinated national media effort with the RNC and the NRCC, which included television messages by presidential candidate Dwight Eisenhower and vice presidential candidate Richard Nixon. This was largely done to assist the RNC, which was running up against expenditure limits for the 1952 presidential campaign, a favor the NRSC did not enjoy bestowing. The NRSC sent speakers out in the field for candidates, with Dirksen and Styles Bridges, the minority leader, making most of these appearances. Also, Vic Johnson, the NRSC's director of field operations, was sent to visit Senate candidates to assist the campaigns and give feedback to the Washington, D.C., office.[60] During this cycle the NRSC, the RNC, and the NRCC engaged in a joint fund-raising effort. Still, each organization continued to accept direct earmarked contributions for specific candidates.[61] The Republicans won control of the Senate in 1952 by a one-vote margin.

Dirksen remained NRSC chair for the 1954 elections. In preparation for the 1954 midterm elections, Dirksen wrote a memorandum to candidates outlining the services available to them throughout the Republican party organization and indicating those responsible for providing them: data information and material, including opposition research and legal advice—Republican Conference staff director; speakers, of the executive branch variety—chairman of the Speakers' Bureau (an "adjunct" of the RNC); campaign information, legislation, records, miscellaneous data—director of public relations, RNC; miscellaneous, including speeches by Dirksen and distribution of party and "earmarked" funds—NRSC.[62] The extent of committee activities was less than during the presidential year when the RNC was consumed with the Eisenhower campaign. Dirksen was quite happy to let the RNC handle the research and literature functions during the midterm campaign, leaving him more time for public appearances with candidates and channeling money to their campaigns. He reiterated the NRSC's earmarking function to a Senate candidate:

> From the time I became chairman in 1951 I have carefully respected the wishes of contributors who wish to render special aid to a particular candidate and have always felt that the Committee should carry out the wishes of a donor without letting it in any way affect the regular and uniform distribution of funds which the Committee seeks to make to every candidate in a campaign year. I am sure that long before November other earmarked funds in your behalf will come to the Committee and they will be transmitted as soon as vouchers can be drawn.[63]

This recycling of funds was clearly the NRSC's most important service.

After Dirksen was reelected in 1956, he was appointed to the vacant minority whip position, which he held until 1959. Dirksen's service at the NRSC helped him secure the position because his colleagues thought he worked hard at what they considered a demanding job.[64] From 1959 until his death in 1969, Dirksen served as Senate minority leader.

Sen. Barry Goldwater of Arizona took over the NRSC for the 1956, 1960, and 1962 election cycles. The NRSC continued the same activities with a few modifications. They adopted the same radio and television film production agreement that the House Republicans had been using (see chapter 4) and also continued to specialize in the production of camera-ready newspaper mats. Starting with the 1956 cycle Goldwater added an additional professional staff person to the research division of the NRSC.[65] For the 1956, 1960, and 1962 election cycles, Goldwater traveled around the country to speak on behalf of Republican senatorial candidates. Goldwater's own assessment of the post reveals much about its potential: "Five simple words tell it all—no one wanted the job. So in 1955 my GOP colleagues chose me—with only two years' experience in the Senate—to be the new chairman of the Republican Senatorial Campaign Committee. The post opened the way to the GOP presidential nomination. I had no idea of what was being set in motion."[66] Although Goldwater held no formal leadership positions in the Senate, he was an important individual in American politics generally and in the Senate in particular. The NRSC helped Goldwater to emerge as a credible candidate for the 1964 Republican presidential nomination, mostly because of the contacts he had made nationwide while conducting NRSC business. Other senators, especially in more recent years, have looked to Goldwater's example and asked to chair the NRSC because of the potential it holds for securing the presidential nomination. Goldwater could not serve as NRSC chair in 1958, as he was running for reelection. Sen. Andrew Schoeppel (R-KS) held the post for that cycle. Little is known of Schoeppel's activities or ambitions. He was reelected in 1960 but died in office early in 1962.

On the Democratic side, George Smathers of Florida became chair of the DSCC for the 1956, 1958, and 1960 electoral cycles. During his leadership there was great tension between the DSCC and the DNC. Smathers repeatedly refers to the "reactivation" of the DSCC after the Democrats lost control of the Senate in 1952, though no other evidence corroborates the idea that the DSCC had been entirely shut down.[67] The reason Smathers gave for the DSCC's reactivation was that the DNC was not in a position to give money to Democratic senatorial candidates. In fact, Smathers said the DSCC "will go out of existence when the Democratic National Committee achieves a favorable financial situation, which we hope will be soon. It has been a stop-gap committee."[68] Still, the DSCC's money operation was not a general push for funds but a money-channeling operation, just like that of the NRSC. Direct individual contributions and House-Senate dinner contributions (the annual House-Senate dinner was the major source of funds for both the DSCC and the DCCC) could be earmarked for particular candidates.[69] No provision of services is evident during Smathers's tenure.[70] He did engage in some sniping with DNC officials over party ideology. Throughout the 1950s, a significant rift was evident between the presidential and congressional wings of the Democratic party. Supporters of two-time presidential nominee Adlai Stevenson and the DNC leadership resented the accommodations by House Speaker Sam Rayburn and Senate leader Lyndon Johnson to President Eisenhower's legislative program.[71] A particularly interesting problem arose over the issue of civil rights just before the 1958 midterm elections. It seems that Paul Butler, chair of the DNC, wanted to stake out a clear position for the party, but Smathers felt that such statements by Butler would threaten the DSCC's goal of retaining a Democratic majority in the Senate:

> Certainly every knowledgeable Democrat recognizes that the issue of Civil Rights is a delicate and difficult one because of the differing background and experience of Democrats within our Party. However, I am sure you must also appreciate that it is not a general issue in the Fall elections of 1958, and in fact, takes the attention off of our fine candidates themselves. Our candidates are each running within the boundaries of his own state. Each knows best what the issues should be in his particular campaign and very properly he will pick them. What might be a good issue in New York State, might not be important at all in Arizona or West Virginia. We therefore should leave this decision to our candidates.
>
> ... For these and other reasons I therefore respectfully suggest to you as Chairman of the National Democratic Committee that for the next two weeks at least we try to avoid allowing ourselves, or for that matter—our opponents, to accentuate any division which exists in our Party. That, on the contrary, we spend our time in talking about the splendid leadership we have had within the Democratic Party. ... As you know, the only help the candidates receive is that through the Congressional Committees such as ours, and that they are able to raise for themselves in their own States. Unfortunately, the National Committee no longer makes any contributions to their campaigns.[72]

Smathers thought that the DNC was only concerned about posturing for the 1960 presidential election. His words show the concern shared by all chairs when they believe the DNC is working at purposes contrary to their own.

Like Clements, Smathers was close to the majority leader, Lyndon Johnson. Smathers used the DSCC position for his own ambitions. He was the first in a series of Democratic senators to break tradition and chair the DSCC during his own reelection year—in this case, 1956. Apparently this was not a difficulty for Johnson or Smathers. After Smathers's last cycle at the DSCC, he was elected secretary to the Democratic Conference, a position he held until his retirement from the Senate. The DSCC chair for the 1962 cycle, Vance Hartke of Indiana, did not have such leadership success and left no records of his tenure.

Sen. Thruston Morton (R-KY), who had previously served as RNC chair, chaired the NRSC for the 1964 and 1966 cycles, taking the committee controls from Barry Goldwater. Senate minority leader Everett Dirksen maintained an interest in NRSC affairs. He requested that as Morton assumed control of the NRSC a fund within the committee be earmarked for joint work by the House and Senate Republican leaders on behalf of the 1964 congressional campaigns. According to Dirksen, "The Joint Leadership meetings serve a substantial political purpose from which I very obviously derive political benefit in the form of advertising and exposure to the voters in Illinois. Under Internal Revenue rules, one can utilize contributions for a political purpose regardless of how far in the future the political contest may be."[73]

Morton's response to Dirksen reflected the typical reaction of new CCC chairs when taking over the organization. Morton claimed to have no separate account standing for this purpose, or the necessary funds to set one up:

> I don't know anything about the $5,000 that is earmarked for you in the funds of the Senatorial Campaign Committee. All I know is that I am taking over a Committee which has no assets and debts of some $40,000.
>
> However, I feel that it is up to me as Chairman of the Senatorial Committee, and I hope my good friend Bob Wilson agrees as Chair-

man of the House Committee, to see that the modest funds that are required are made available to you and [House minority leader] Charlie Halleck.[74]

Morton's references indicate that campaign operations at the NRSC were very similar in both 1964 and 1966, except that in 1964 the committee interacted with the Goldwater/Miller presidential campaign organization. According to Morton, the NRSC benefited from the assistance of the RNC's Speaker's Bureau and research staff and the coordination of appearances by Goldwater, Miller, and Republican senatorial candidates. These appearances proved to be delicate matters, as Morton felt that Goldwater's conservatism might be harmful. Therefore, he stressed the importance of voter independence while on the campaign stump and tried to remain neutral on issues pertaining directly to the Goldwater campaign.[75]

The financial relationships between the RNC and NRSC were less clearly defined, a subject of much discussion during the 1960s.[76] Morton's correspondence implies that a pooled fund-raising system was used throughout the 1950s (a continuation of the RNFC arrangement), whereby Republicans would join together to raise money and then allocate funds among the three committees (RNC, NRSC, and NRCC). However, Morton states that the campaigns of 1958 and 1960 left the general Republican party funds depleted and that from 1961 "it was pretty much every man or every committee for himself or itself."[77] He made this statement in the context of explaining why he felt the NRSC had to pursue independent fund-raising.

The services provided by the NRSC included the production of radio and television tapes for all incumbents, opposition research, photographic services, matting of photographs for newspapers and for incumbents seeking reelection, provision of a credit card to be used by senators for air travel between Washington, D.C., and their home states. These services, though, came with very low overhead: "We have only three permanent employees; we do not pay any rent; we do not use field men; we rely on other committees for research and public relations help. Our budget this year is in the area of $300,000. This is less money than is spent in most individual senatorial campaigns."[78] In later correspondence Morton referred to the campaign contribution practices of the NRSC. Morton's goal was to contribute $5,000 to each Republican incumbent running for reelection. However, he revealed that the NRSC's more significant financial contribution was to encourage donations to specific candidates directly. Morton also mentioned that recruitment of Republican challengers was believed to be the responsibility of the state parties, not of the NRSC.[79]

The most divisive issue in 1966 was the persistent problem of financial disagreements among the three Republican committees. Since Morton felt he could not rely on the RNC for sufficient funds to meet the NRSC's 1966 campaign obligations, he held a fund-raising dinner in Washington, D.C., exclusively for the benefit of the senatorial committee. The dinner was tremendously successful, raising $60,000 more than the maximum budget needed by the NRSC. Instead of sending these excess funds to the RNC for general party needs, Morton gave them to the NRCC chair, Bob Wilson (R-CA), for use in House campaigns. This action outraged RNC officials.[80] Still, Morton's generosity toward the NRCC should not be mistaken for a united Senate-House effort. A few weeks after Morton had given Wilson the excess funds, Wilson called to see if he could get a copy of the donor list used for the dinner so that the NRCC might solicit additional funds from them directly. When this request was passed on to Morton, he told his staff, "Our lists are confidential and will remain so!"[81] Morton did not seek reelection in 1968 and retired from public life.

When Sen. Warren G. Magnuson (D-WA) chaired the DSCC for the 1964 and 1966 election cycles, the DSCC still functioned primarily as a money conduit. Numerous memos from Magnuson's secretary indicate that some donors would make cash contributions to the DSCC with the understanding that this money would be donated to the appropriate senator either through a check from the DSCC or as cash delivered by Senator Magnuson's office.[82] The committee continued to cover the expenses of speakers, especially prominent senators, to make appearances on behalf of incumbents[83] and to provide "speech cards" on topical issues for Senate candidates.[84] Magnuson also made important introductions for candidates with Washington groups, as he described in a letter to a candidate: "This morning I received your letter . . . wherein you requested some advice on enlisting labor's support in your campaign. I discussed this problem with John Maguire of the Campaign Committee staff and advised him to arrange for an appointment with Mr. Al Barkin of the AFL-CIO Committee on Political Education."[85]

Magnuson struggled with the difficulties of coordinating DNC activities with both the DSCC and the DCCC. One of Magnuson's staffers expressed concern that the DNC held a large fund-raiser with senators and representatives in attendance without consulting the DSCC. A meeting was proposed between the president, DNC chair Larry O'Brien, DCCC chair Mike Kirwan, and Senator Magnuson "to try and develop some kind of policy to which the White House and [the] Committee might adhere in connection with the future of this particular type of operation." The staffer continued, "In my own opinion, I think this might be very helpful to serve as an opportunity to discuss the overall relationship of the House and Senate Committees with the National Committee, and the President, himself."[86] This does not signify a mutually cooperative effort but instead shows that the redefinition of the relationship among these three organizations was a chronic problem.

Magnuson served in the Senate until 1980, when he failed to win reelection. He did not hold another leadership position, although he chaired the Commerce Committee during and after his second cycle as chair. Magnuson also had a reputation for distinction in legislative matters, especially health care issues.

Sen. George Murphy (R-CA) headed the NRSC for the 1968 election cycle. He succeeded Thruston Morton and headed off a challenge for the position by Sen. John Tower (R-TX), who chaired the committee for the 1970 cycle.[87] Murphy was far less a maverick than Morton had been as NRSC chair, announcing in mid-1967 that he was cutting the NRSC's budget projections from $550,000 (Morton's estimate) to $400,000 at the direction of General Lucius Clay. Clay, the new head of the RNFC, was trying to recentralize the finances of all three committees and to direct as much money as possible to the RNC's presidential effort for Nixon.[88] The consequence of the reduced budget, according to Murphy, would be a reduction of services to senators not up for reelection in 1968, until alternative funds were acquired or the NRSC's other obligations could be handled under budget.[89] Murphy later clarified that the NRSC "would be able to handle television and radio [production expenses] for all Senators up to the amount of $500 per month, with the exception of those who are standing for reelection. In those cases, we will place no top limit on the expenditures for which we will reimburse."[90] Later, a limit of $8,000 per year in media expenses was imposed on members seeking reelection.[91] The travel credit cards were retained for the 1968 cycle as well. Murphy also installed an Associated Press news ticker in the NRSC offices for those senators who did not have such access.[92] In a final push to increase funds, Murphy asked senators to solicit additional contributions to the NRSC from donors in their states and localities. Though Murphy thought that repeated solicitation from the same donors was unfortunate, he dismissed it as part of the campaign process in an especially competitive election year.[93] This practice continues to the present.

Sen. Edmund Muskie (D-ME) chaired the DSCC in 1968, until he was named the vice presidential candidate on the Democratic ticket. The DSCC under Muskie remained a small organization with a staff of no more than six. They continued skeletal services such as opposition research and provision of campaign materials. The new executive director (who continued in that position into the late 1970s) was asked to clean up the financial practices of the committee. In the 1970 cycle, when Sen. Daniel Inouye (D-HI) was chair, the DSCC began to hold a "trade fair" for political consultants to show senators how their services could be useful to their future campaigns. The DSCC at this time also arranged for prominent senators not up for reelection to campaign in states with impending elections and gave each incumbent senator a $10,000 television and radio production allowance (a practice the House CCCS had offered for some time). Though there were significant fund-raising initiatives in the 1972 cycle, from 1968 to 1976, the DSCC's budget remained relatively stable, fluctuating between $600,000 and $800,000.[94]

Senate CCCs: Semidevelopment

Neither the NRSC nor the DSCC became full-service campaign organizations, as we will see was the case for the House CCCs. Instead they became efficient channelers of funds from individuals or groups to candidates. Both Senate committees interpreted the prevailing campaign finance law literally and helped candidates circumvent the law by sending money to state parties or other committees. Since the Senate CCCs acted as money channelers rather than money raisers, they seemed only mildly perturbed by the efforts of the national committees to control common financial planning until the 1960s. As the use of radio and television became more common in campaigns, the Senate CCCs did provide some modest services for candidates. One thing they did continue to provide which must be understood as a Washington resource is the services of other prominent senators as speakers, specifically CCC chairs and party leaders. Their main purpose in visiting other candidates' states is likely to be for fund-raising rather than for media exposure.

By the 1950s the congressional campaign committees were clearly linked with the leadership structures in the senatorial parties. Tables A.4 and A.5 list all the senatorial CCC chairs and their subsequent leadership positions. The CCCs had become far more useful for leadership recruitment, now that the concept of leadership had become an integral part of the operation of Congress. The CCCs also gave the leadership an additional resource to control. Republican senator Everett Dirksen and

Democratic senators James Lewis, Scott Lucas, Earle Clements, and George Smathers all realized higher leadership positions after their tenure as CCC chairmen. Also in this period, the CCCs became known as part of the leadership, not outside it. Although there were some attempts by the national committees to absorb senatorial CCC resources, none were successful, and such proposals originated from the national committees exclusively. Thus the senatorial CCCs established an autonomous position and focused on providing funds and services to their constituencies, although there was cooperation within party families.

CHAPTER 4

THE HOUSE CAMPAIGN COMMITTEES, 1922-1972

THOUGH SIMILAR CAMPAIGN INNOVATIONS APPLY to House and Senate candidates, the task of facilitating Washington-based resources was much greater for the House committees. Not only did they have a far greater number of candidates seeking reelection every two years, those candidates were generally less experienced than senatorial candidates (some had no electoral experience). Therefore, the demand for campaign services from the CCCs was greater for the House committees than for the Senate committees. A larger number of services were also provided because of the House CCCs' inability to give significant monetary assistance to so many candidates. Little evidence of earmarking is found for the House CCCs (though this does not mean it did not happen), and those funds they did raise on their own had to be allocated for many more races than was the case for the senatorial CCCs. The money role of both the House and the Senate CCCs remains modest in this period, changing only as a result of new campaign finance laws in the 1970s.

Congressional careers were now quite coveted, and highly ambitious people ran for national office. The CCCs thus had more members desiring their services and found more members wishing to cultivate the opportunities CCC chairs provided. The House also institutionalized its leadership and committee structures at this time. Both chambers, but especially the House, experienced profound changes after the passage of the Legislative Reorganization Act of 1946. This act consolidated the standing committee systems (making committee assignments more scarce and hence more powerful) and increased the number of congressional staff, which increased the stakes for both individual politicians' ambitions and majority control. Still, this created a tension for the CCCs between pursuing majorities and protecting incumbents, but the demands of incumbents usually restrained the House CCCs from aggressively pursuing nonincumbent races. Also, technological innovations rapidly changed the tools of congressional campaigns. Incumbents unfamiliar with these campaign methods became more nervous about potential opponents' activities in their home districts while they were in Washington, D.C.

House CCCs: First Decade of Separation, 1922–1932

Rep. Simeon Fess's (R-OH) decision to run for the U.S. Senate in 1922 left the NRCC without a chair. Rep. William Wood (R-IN) was elected the new NRCC chair, a post he held for six consecutive cycles. Few details are known about Wood's tenure, except that he was in danger of losing his position after the 1922 elections in which the Republicans lost seventy-five seats.[1] Despite this loss Republicans retained a majority, having 225 members instead of the previous 300. Republicans continued to hold majorities in the House throughout the 1920s until after the stock market crash of 1929. After the 1928 election, Wood became chairman of the Appropriations Committee, a position he held concurrently with the NRCC chair. Although the Republicans retained control of the House after the 1930 election (with 218 Republicans, 216 Democrats, and 1 Independent), the Democrats organized the House in the 72d Congress because of two Republican deaths between the elections and the beginning of the congressional session. As a result of the two Republican deaths, special elections were held to fill the vacancies. The Democrats won one of these seats (making the partisan split 217–217) and organized the chamber. The Republican membership shrank further to 117 (a 100-seat loss) after the 1932 election. One of those who lost his seat in 1932 was Wood.

William Oldfield of Arkansas served as DCCC chair for the 1924, 1926, and 1928 election cycles. This coincided with his service as minority whip, which lasted from 1921 until his death in 1928. Apparently the DCCC chairmanship was considered important enough to be held by the second-highest ranking party official but not enough of a burden to preclude Oldfield's other duties as whip.

Rep. Joseph Wellington Byrns (D-TN), who ultimately became Speaker of the House, chaired the DCCC from December 1928 to 1934, for the 1930, 1932, and 1934 election cycles. First elected to the House in 1908, Byrns chaired the DCCC through the stock market crash of 1929 and the elections of 1930, when the Democrats ultimately regained control of the House. Byrns corresponded with Democratic candidates for the 1930 elections, asking them to indicate what form of help they required. The most common form of help offered was publicity materials aimed for release to local press outlets. There was some modest monetary assistance for candidates, some of it coming from subscriptions from incumbents of $150 per year. Byrns also used the committee for the special elections between November 1930 and the start of the 72d Congress in 1931 that proved critical to Democratic control of the House.[2] He rose from ranking minority member to chair of the Appropriations Committee, a position he took over from his Republican counterpart, the NRCC chair, Will Wood.[3] Byrns remained chair of the DCCC for the 1932 election, when the Democrats enjoyed an overwhelming victory at all levels. One consequence of these victories was that Speaker John Nance Garner was elected vice president on the Democratic ticket with Franklin Delano Roosevelt. The Speaker position became open, and Byrns was a candidate. Although he lost to Henry Rainey, Byrns did become the majority leader for the 73d Congress, getting this post over the Democratic whip.[4]

On becoming majority leader, Byrns resigned as chair of the Appropriations Committee but remained chair of the DCCC. During the 1934 election cycle Byrns wrote a short piece for a book on congressional procedures explaining the DCCC's functions and purpose:

> The functions of this Committee are purely political, and it was created to support Democratic nominees against their opponents in their respective districts. The committee endeavors to affect election returns in accordance with the needs of the Democratic party; it attempts to aid democratic nominees to their election; and thereby, make it possible for the Democratic party to regain or retain control in the House. It is customary for this organization to take no active part in the primary campaigns.[5]

Byrns's clear view that the campaign committee should strive only for control of the House, rather than for the promotion of any party program or coordinated party strategy, speaks to the entrenchment of institutional party interest at this time, even though Byrns was an FDR loyalist. In addition to the usual provision of publicity materials, Byrns also sent a questionnaire to incumbent Democratic House members asking about their prospects for reelection. This activity, reported by the Associated Press, was notable for its attention to primary election contests, usually something the DCCC stayed out of.[6] After the primaries Byrns sent out endorsement letters for incumbents, emphasizing the political effectiveness of these members that Byrns had witnessed in his capacity as majority leader.[7] In the 1934 election Byrns presided over an increase in the Democratic majority in the House to 322 seats. Speaker Henry Rainey (D-IL) died in August 1934, but this time Byrns was the unanimous choice for Speaker, and he relinquished all his other positions. Thus the DCCC chair contributed to Byrns's ascent in the Democratic party hierarchy.

The Elections of 1932–1952:
A Move toward Professionalization

In November 1932 Franklin Delano Roosevelt was elected to the presidency, along with 313 Democrats in the House and 59 Democrats in the Senate. After the stock market crash in October 1929, President Herbert Hoover and the Republican governing apparatus seemed unwilling to respond to the deepening economic crisis. In the national elections many voters switched their preference from Republican to Democrat, resulting in Democratic political dominance of the country.[8] This realignment was evident before 1932, with the midterm congressional elections of 1930 being the first indications that something was happening to the Republican party's grip on Congress. By 1932 it was clear that the Republicans could not easily control any of the three elective sectors of government, and indeed they had to wait until 1946 to regain any of them.

In 1933 congressional Republicans believed that their electoral misfortunes were simply temporary, and they immediately began planning for the 1934 midterm elections. After the disastrous 1932 elections, in which NRCC chair Wood lost his own seat, Rep. Chester Bolton (R-OH) took over as chair. He headed the committee for the 1934 and 1936 cycles. The Democrats gained seats in the House each time. The NRCC was very active in 1936, producing 32 radio speeches by Republican congressmen that were broadcast over national networks; 1,560,000 written transcripts of these speeches (which were distributed nationally); 8 pamphlets criticizing various aspects of the New Deal (664,000 of which were distributed); a radio news column (press release service) that served 170 stations; and a cartoon service that delivered cartoons to 3,000 newspapers weekly.[9] During this cycle one finds the first mention of a field force, consisting of as many as twelve employees working in electorally marginal parts of the country. Their activities were coordinated by the Washington headquarters, which also provided opposition research.[10] Yet the Republican minority shrank further, leaving only eighty-nine of their number to serve in the 75th Congress. One of the losers in 1936 was NRCC Chair Bolton.

These were trying times for congressional Republicans, and it was difficult to imagine how things could get worse. The NRCC needed a new chair and in January 1937 Joseph Martin (R-MA) was elected unanimously. Martin had been in the House for twelve years and was the first NRCC chair from New England. His candidacy was bolstered by his experience as a newspaperman and a primary campaign organizer for 1936 Republican presidential candidate Alfred Landon.[11] When Martin assumed the NRCC chair position there were only 89 Republicans in the House. After the 1938 election there were 169 Republicans, an increase of 80 members. Although most observers expected Republican gains (due to the stalled economic growth after the initial New Deal boom and FDR's failed "court-packing" scheme), few expected gains of this magnitude.

With a new chair and an infusion of cash from the RNC (with only eighty-nine members, there was good reason to ask for and accept RNC funds), the NRCC again braced itself for the coming campaign. The projected budget for 1938 was to be the same as for 1936: $350,000. The NRCC had a staff of eight: three secretaries, two statisticians, two newspapermen, and an executive director. They were responsible for writing campaign speeches, assisting with publicity efforts (media public relations), and, of course, handling requests for contributions. It is not known if field men were again employed, but Martin toured the country speaking on behalf of candidates and evaluated local political climates.[12] Although money apparently came slowly to the NRCC,[13] their activities continued at a high level throughout the summer and fall of 1938.

Given the high expectations for Republican gains in 1938, Martin took full advantage of this opportunity to use NRCC resources to advance his bid for floor leader. At least five months before the election, Martin, aware of minority leader Bertrand Snell's plans to retire after the 75th Congress, began to approach fellow members about supporting his candidacy. Martin blatantly used his position as NRCC chair to its fullest potential, reminding members of their commitment to support him as floor leader in the same letter that promised financial support to their campaign. A response from August Andresen (R-MN) to Martin's request to current members regarding support for the leadership race gives clear evidence:

> First, I want to assure you of my wholehearted support for the majority leadership in the 76th Congress to succeed our friend Bert Snell. I say Majority Leader because I believe that we have a good chance to sweep the traditional republican north. At any event, you can count on me and I am sure that you can count on the rest of the republican congressmen from Minnesota. May be it will be Speaker for you in 1939.
> I want to thank you also for the check for educational work which will come in mighty handy.[14]

Once he had secured commitments from 80 percent of the eighty-nine Republican members, Martin waited until after the November election to solidify his commitments. After the eighty new members were elected, Martin wired all of them with campaign congratulations. Then he sent a form letter on NRCC letterhead asking for support for the minority leader position based on his experience as "Assistant Leader" and ranking minority member on Rules.[15] Though he did not explicitly reiterate his performance as NRCC chair, his selection of NRCC stationery over regular office stationery speaks volumes. Martin was elected minority leader after the 1938 election, a position he held consistently until 1959, except for the two Congresses (80th and 83d) in which he served as Speaker of the House of Representatives.

Less is known about DCCC activities during this same period. The Democratic organization was substantially less sophisticated than that of the Republicans, and commensurately less financially established. Indeed, during the 1930s and early 1940s the DCCC had been existing on funds from the DNC and on the traditional "subscriptions" of Democratic members of Congress. Although these individual contributions from members had been as much as $100 in the early 1930s, they were reduced to only $25 per person by 1940.[16] Operation of the DCCC was so lax that Lyndon Johnson (D-TX), a relatively junior congressman, was able to control the fund-raising and allocation of contribution functions of the DCCC in 1940 without being formally affiliated with the organization. Johnson, with the blessing of Speaker Sam Rayburn, arranged for the laundering of campaign monies from wealthy Texas oilmen interested in keeping Rayburn in control of the House. Johnson would arrange to have donations made to the DCCC with specific instructions as to which candidates would receive donations and in what amounts.[17] Patrick Henry Drewry (D-VA) was the disengaged chair of the DCCC from the 1936 cycle to the 1946 cycle. Drewry, elected to Congress in 1920, was a member of the Virginia Democratic machine and was more interested in local matters than national interests. This may explain why he was willing to allow Johnson to use the authority of the DCCC for his own ambitions. Drewry died in office in December 1947.

On the Republican side, Martin's election as minority leader meant that the NRCC chair position was again vacant. Rep. William Ditter (R-PA), who was elected to Congress in 1932 (a remarkable feat for a Republican), served as chair for the 1940 and 1942 cycles. He was elected to chair the committee again for the 1944 cycle but died in an airplane crash in November 1943. The NRCC kept similar arrangements in place for the 1940 and 1942 election cycles that they had under Martin, though some differences in organizational arrangement did occur for the 1944 and 1946 cycles.

Rep. Charles A. Halleck (R-IN) jumped on the opportunity to succeed Ditter at the NRCC after Ditter's death.[18] Under Halleck, the publicity and research activities of the committee expanded considerably. For the 1946 midterm elections the RNC created a liaison with the NRCC and the NRCC created a new subcommittee to perform publicity functions for individual members.

New equipment was purchased for the production of press releases for distribution to congressional districts throughout the country.[19] Republicans recaptured the House after the 1946 elections by a margin of 246 to 188, a gain of fifty-six seats. Republicans also gained control of the Senate in 1946.

Halleck, like Martin before him, took full advantage of the NRCC chair position to advance his career. He was already a member of the full NRCC and Martin, the minority leader, supported him for the post. During his reign Halleck reminded his colleagues of the assistance he had arranged.[20] When the Republicans recaptured the House of Representatives after the 1946 elections, one result was Joseph Martin's elevation to Speaker. This meant that there was a vacancy in the floor leader's position, and Halleck wasted no time announcing his candidacy. According to his biographer, Halleck's performance at the NRCC made him an obvious choice for majority leader, since he was partially credited with the party's success in recapturing the chamber.[21]

According to the NRCC's historical assessment, the origins of the modern committee can be traced to after the 1946 election. The Legislative Reorganization Act of 1946 expanded staff on all congressional standing committees. In addition, the 80th Congress was under Republican control, allowing Republicans more access to political resources. In this environment the NRCC acquired a permanent full-time staff (i.e., in both election and nonelection years).[22] They began to hire professionals, which was possible through a liberal interpretation of the clerk-hire allowance. From the time of the Legislative Reorganization Act of 1946 to the Federal Election Campaign Act and amendments of the 1970s, the House CCCs were staffed through creative applications of unused resources in individual members' clerk-hire allowances. This enabled CCC employees to receive the same employment benefits, salaries, and job security as regular congressional office staff. At this time the NRCC had a publicity division with three professional staffers and a full-time photographer to establish and supervise the committee's own in-house photo lab.[23] Despite the NRCC's increasing sophistication, the Republicans lost control of the House in the 1948 elections and did not regain it until 1952.

Rep. Leonard Hall (R-NY) served as NRCC chair for the 1948, 1950, and 1952 election cycles. Hall was first elected to Congress in 1938, the year in which the Republican membership almost doubled under Martin's NRCC reign. Although the Democrats recaptured the House after the 1948 elections, Hall had a successful NRCC tenure. Perhaps because of this President-elect Eisenhower selected Hall to be chair of the RNC. Hall left Congress shortly after the 1952 election to serve in this capacity.

Joining the Mass Media Age: 1952–1972

Leonard Hall was succeeded by Rep. Richard Simpson (R-PA), who was elected to Congress in 1936, another tough year for Republican victories. Simpson chaired the committee during the 1954, 1956, and 1958 cycles. The NRCC witnessed significant professional expansion under Simpson's watch, which aided the committee's transition into modern campaigning. Stanley Kelley, writing about public relations and politics, observed that "the present public relations departments of the Republican National Committee and the Republican Congressional Campaign Committee are, in effect, commercial public relations agencies performing political functions. While themselves offering propaganda services, they have encouraged each of their party's candidates to retain his own counsellor."[24] The description of services below confirms Kelley's contention that the conduct of political operations centered on public relations work with the media.

An NRCC pamphlet for the 1954 cycle stated that many of the campaign services described in it duplicate the material and ideas of the 1950 and 1952 campaigns, indicating that the obsession with media relations predates Simpson's reign. The services the NRCC provided to candidates included a speech kit (with "Quotable Quotes"), a weekly newsletter with recent political developments, newspaper ads (a portfolio of 24 finished ad layouts, needing only a candidate's picture and name for completion), radio spots (20 one-minute open-ended spots with time for individual lead-ins/outs), materials to produce television spots, information on the "equal time" rule for political broadcasting, and visual aids (film strips and slide shows coordinated with recorded narration).[25]

By the 1956 cycle, the NRCC had a sophisticated film production center. A memorandum from Harold Slater, public relations director, to all Republican members during January 1956 (a full ten months before the election) indicates the extent of their capabilities:

> The Committee has once again prepared a five-minute TV show for use by Members during the annual observance of Lincoln's birthday.
>
> This year the film has been prepared largely around the figure of Lincoln at the monument in Washington. Other scenes deal with additional memorials concerning Lincoln and the time he lived in Washington.
>
> The body of the film runs three and one-half minutes. A prepared 30-second opening and 30-second closing has been written for Members desiring to use them. The opening and closing has been put on teleprompter.[26]

This format was applied to a wide variety of subjects, including the development of radar, state-of-the-art military equipment, the president's office in the White House, and Fort Washington (a historic site near Washington, D.C.), all of which the NRCC considered of interest to congressional audiences. Invitations to congressmen to use the new television films were continually distributed throughout the 1956 election year.

In 1957 the NRCC announced its willingness to provide publicity assistance to members who lacked sufficient office staff to handle assembly and distribution of press releases. The committee prepared an interim speech kit for use in the 1957 off-year, which provided members with materials for speeches they might want to make at home during the congressional recess.[27] It also announced subsidized rates for the films the NRCC produced so that members could afford to use them at home. Early in 1957 the NRCC announced a practice that may have been in effect for some time: the television and radio production allowance. This allowance became a fixture of the NRCC's operations until the mid-1970s. Chairman Simpson explained:

> The Republican Congressional Committee will finance TV film and radio productions by the House Recording Facility for each Member up to $750.00.
>
> Members will be billed for the television and radio costs directly by the House Radio and TV Facility. If the bill is approved by the Member, it should then be sent to the Public Relations Office. Payment will be made by check to the Member, who in turn will send the check to the House Radio and TV Facility.[28]

The bulletin emphasized that the money could be used only for radio and television film production, but specific applications within the House facility were not restricted. (This was before the NRCC had its own in-house production facilities.) Obviously, the service was available only to incumbent members while in Washington, D.C., and the NRCC subsidy encouraged Republican members to take advantage of this perk.

By the 1958 cycle the NRCC was providing free services to members in six areas: news, especially press releases; radio-television, including production and scriptwriting; complete photographic production for use in newspapers and newsletters; art (location of printers, advice on bulk rate mailings); subject-specific research; and a campaign booklet describing various services.[29] This extensive organization was in place for the 1958 and 1960 cycles. The Republicans remained in the minority throughout this period. Simpson's promising career was cut short by his death in late 1959.

The Democrats lacked a sophisticated public relations division at this time and would not have one for years. Drewry's successor at the DCCC after the 1946 cycle was Rep. Mike Kirwan (D-OH), who served for more successive cycles than any other CCC chair.

Kirwan held his post from the 1948 election cycle until his death in July 1970. While never an activist chairman, Kirwan's twenty-two-year control of the party coffers, combined with his chairmanship of the Appropriations Subcommittee on Public Works, made him one of the most powerful men in the House for more than two decades. A former DCCC aide said that Kirwan never aspired to higher leadership positions because he already had more power than most of the other party leaders.[30] During his long tenure, the services the DCCC offered were relatively limited: photographs of candidates with the Speaker, opposition research, a flat contribution to each candidate each election cycle for travel between Washington, D.C., and the district, and coverage of other campaign-related expenses while in the district.[31] Kirwan did write a book with the DCCC treasurer, Jack Redding, entitled *How to Succeed in Politics*. This book, published in 1964, consists mostly of vignettes of individual triumphant Democratic candidacies, but it does provide a few insights into the DCCC. Kirwan indicated that the DCCC budget grew during his tenure from about $17,000 in 1952 to $250,000 in 1962. Kirwan stated that money was distributed first to swing districts of incumbents, then to challengers with the closest races (a maximum of $2,000, which he believed would be between 10 and 20 percent of the total budget necessary for an individual race).[32] The DCCC conducted most of its fund-raising through the annual House-Senate dinner. In 1964 Kirwan made it clear to all Democratic members that proceeds from the dinner would go to congressional candidates, with no share for the DNC, though it had been previous practice to provide some funds to the DNC so that in the future the DCCC could appeal to them for money.[33] Toward the end of Kirwan's tenure, the DCCC considered running a media coaching program. Robert Squier, who remains a well-established political consultant in the 1990s, gave a presentation to Democratic members concerning media services, and a decision on establishing a program was to be reached after that.[34] Meanwhile, with the exception of the 80th and 83d Congresses, Democrats continued to organize the

House.³⁵ This position of strength, needing only to defend incumbents to preserve majorities, explains much of the complacency of the DCCC under Kirwan.

As the minority party, the House Republicans sought to improve their campaign committee. Almost immediately after the death of NRCC chair Richard Simpson in 1959, a contest developed to succeed him. By this time, House Republicans had witnessed the succession of three former NRCC chairs (Martin, Halleck, and Hall) to visible, high-ranking positions, and many began to covet the post. Four congressmen, Robert (Bob) Wilson (R-CA), William Springer (R-IL), William McCulloch (R-OH), and William Miller (R-NY), emerged as contestants, making this the most competitive CCC chair contest to date. Wilson and Springer withdrew from the race, leaving McCulloch and Miller as the two serious contenders. Vice President Richard Nixon, who was then running for the presidency in 1960, preferred Miller, who had important ties in the eastern United States. Nixon's congressional service and his expressed desire to promote himself and a Republican Congress had some influence and Miller was elected NRCC chair for the 1960 cycle.

Early in 1960 Miller circulated a memo to all Republican incumbents explaining that each member was entitled to an allotment of $1,000 for publicity expenses. Later, an additional $500 was granted, for a total of $1,500. Allowed uses for these funds included production costs of radio and television public service programs at the House Recording Studio; production and mailing costs of photo mats to district newspapers; printing, mailing, and typesetting costs of newsletters, questionnaires, and other mailing pieces; and purchase of radio and television time and newspaper advertising. Bills went to the committee for direct payment to vendors. Travel expenses and payment of campaign personnel salaries were explicitly excluded items for NRCC reimbursement.³⁶ The NRCC also ran a candidates conference "to give Congressional candidates firsthand information on major issues in the campaign and guidance in the field of campaign techniques."³⁷ The conference was scheduled for late

August to early September 1960, relatively late for launching the general election campaign. After the 1960 cycle the House Republicans had increased their number by 20 seats, to 174, a good showing, although hardly close to a majority. Nevertheless, Miller was rewarded for his good work (and ostensibly his loyalty to Nixon) by being named chair of the RNC in 1961. Miller worked with NRSC chair Barry Goldwater on the $100-a-plate joint House-Senate dinner before his departure. The proceeds went to the Republican National Finance Committee of the RNC for distribution to the NRSC and the NRCC.[38]

Representative Wilson became Miller's successor in 1961 after a four-way contest. Wilson had long sought the position because of his background as an advertising executive and his leadership ambitions. The major contenders were again Bob Wilson, NRCC vice chairman William McCulloch, John Rhodes (R-AZ), and Jack Westland (R-WA).[39] The Westland candidacy faded quickly, and most sources discussed the contest as one between Wilson and McCulloch, with Rhodes gaining attention only immediately before the vote. The race reflected factional and geographic divisions within the leadership. A press release on the subject illustrates the problem:

> [Another consideration] is whether the Mid-West will continue to exercise a stranglehold on the leadership of the Republicans in the House, ignoring to a considerable extent the large East and West Coast states where the Republican Party must pick up a substantial number of House seats if it wishes to control the House of Representatives and elect a Republican Speaker. At the present time, the following Midwesterners hold the chief House Republican leadership posts: Minority Leader Charles Halleck of Indiana; Chairman of the Policy Committee, John Byrnes of Wisconsin; Chairman of the Republican Conference, Charles B. Hoeven of Iowa; Minority Whip Leslie Arends of Illinois; and Minority Leader of the Rules Committee, Clarence Brown of Ohio.[40]

Midwestern control plus Ohio's failure to meet fund-raising quotas for the party committees put a serious damper on the

McCulloch candidacy.⁴¹ Geography was also an issue for Rhodes, as Sen. Barry Goldwater was then serving as chair of the NRSC. Having both campaign committee chairmen from the same small state seemed politically unwise. Ostensibly, both chairmen would approach the same sources for funds. Despite these legitimate concerns, the Goldwater-Rhodes forces felt a need to contest the election on ideological grounds (both McCulloch and Wilson were moderate to liberal), hoping that a more conservative compromise candidate would emerge as a result.⁴² Because of his West Coast roots, his past service to the NRCC, his background as an advertising executive, and the support of the minority leader, Charles Halleck, Wilson became CCC chair for the 1962 cycle and remained at that post until just after the 1972 elections.

There is scant information about the NRCC's activities for the 1962 campaign, but we do know that it was now a full-time operation. The size of the NRCC staff varied from thirty to thirty-five between March 1961 and December 1962.⁴³ A financial report dated July 31, 1962, shows the committee had raised and spent over $600,000, although more than half covered overhead expenses.⁴⁴ These resources were obviously not considered sufficient, as Wilson approached Halleck about appropriating Republican congressional staff for campaign purposes:

> You may recall a discussion we had several weeks ago about the necessity of using them in the forthcoming Congressional campaigns. I would hope that you would notify each Minority employee to plan to make himself available to the Congressional Committee immediately after the close of this session of Congress until November. Unless they are notified early, I fear they may plan vacations right at the time we need them most. Several of these men would make good field men for us and we can use others in the Headquarters.⁴⁵

It is unclear if these employees were transferred to the NRCC payroll or remained part of the clerk-hire allowances of individual members.

Specific information on services provided by Wilson's NRCC in 1964 and 1966 is also limited, but there is substantial information on the 1968 cycle. The fund-raising relationship between the three Republican committees was still tense, though apparently cooperative. The Republican National Finance Committee still kept track of fund-raising quotas and redistributed funds, but at this time there is a more overt recognition that the three committees ought to be very careful about their associations. In planning a House-Senate Republican gala for spring 1968, the following agreement was reached:

> The Republican National Committee will receive ten per cent of the net proceeds of this Gala. . . . The House and Senate Committees have agreed to the ten per cent participation because of their awareness of the universal value of the National Committee organization programs. . . . The identity of the National Committee is being kept entirely out of the . . . Gala in order to gain full support of the Washington lobbyist group and individuals interested essentially in House and Senate incumbent support for this year.[46]

It is interesting that the RNC acknowledged its liability with the Washington community. The preference of Washington lobbyists, now represented by their political action committees, for interactions with the CCCs over the NCs is still present in the 1990s. There is further evidence that the three committees were moving away from shared or pooled fund-raising efforts. Wilson wrote to a contributor who expressed annoyance at solicitations from each of the various committees that "there is no single Republican activity which embraces all three levels," meaning House, Senate, and the presidency. Instead, Wilson argued that the responsibilities of these three committees were quite distinct.[47]

In 1968 the NRCC had a staff of fifty-four in nine divisions: administration, art, campaign, executive, field service, finance, photo, public relations, and the Booster's Club, a special fund-raising apparatus for nonincumbent Republican candidates.[48] The services the NRCC offered were extensive, with much of the emphasis on television advertising. More traditional services included the provision of prominent speakers and assistance in public relations through a Republican congressional news bureau. All Republican incumbents were invited to contact the News Bureau so that press releases could be written on the member's behalf citing praise from Washington luminaries (such as the minority leader, Gerald Ford).[49] On the television front, the NRCC hired a cameraman and rented mobile sound motion picture equipment so that members could film television news statements, programs, documentaries, and action shots of members on the job in Washington, D.C., settings. The NRCC paid for the cameraman and equipment and charged members only for the price of the film used. This cost would still be absorbed by the committee if the member had funds remaining in his public relations allocation.[50] The NRCC joined the NRSC in hiring a full-time television expert to coach House and Senate candidates for television appearances and advertising. Wilson and the NRSC chair, George Murphy, agreed to split the cost of the television coach's salary for a three-month trial period.[51]

Another interesting development was the outreach effort by the House Republican Research and Planning Committee, a recent addition to the House Republican leadership structure in 1965, to the NRCC. Charles Goodell (R-NY), the chair of this committee, wrote to Wilson offering his committee's resources for research on national issues.[52] This is further evidence of leadership interest and involvement in the winning of a Republican majority and the activities of the NRCC, and indicates less of a reliance on the RNC for research services.

For the 1970 cycle Wilson, with the new NRSC chair John Tower, retained the services of the television consultant on a half-time basis.[53] Careful attention to the marginality of individual races was now clear. The NRCC compiled a list of all marginal congressional seats (48 Democratic seats and 29 Republican seats), with marginality defined as any seat for which the incumbent received between 50 and 55 percent of the vote.[54] The committee's policy was to put no more than $10,000 into any campaign, and this maximum was guaranteed only for marginal races.⁵⁵ This distinction was now found in the public relations allocations to members. For 1969 the public relations amount was $2,000 for nonmarginal members and $3,500 for marginal and freshmen members; for 1970, $3,000 and $5,000, respectively. The committee also planned to give cash contributions of $4,000 to nonmarginal members and $7,000 to marginal and freshmen members. The NRCC expected to have additional funds available for Republican challengers running against vulnerable Democratic incumbents. Those races were entitled to $10,000 in cash, most of which came from the Booster's Club funds.⁵⁶ Other services for challengers were training films, field representatives for public relations support, and provision of telex machines at committee expense.⁵⁷

In addition to these monetary considerations, the NRCC continued to provide a high level of service with about forty-eight staff members in 1970.⁵⁸ The NRCC had an extensive field operation, separate but coordinated with the RNC's, aimed primarily at challenger races. To better serve challengers, the NRCC held a major candidate conference in June 1970.⁵⁹ To recruit candidates, the NRCC established a candidate selection committee, chaired by Rep. Ed Derwinski (R-IL) for both the 1968 and 1970 cycles. This committee was subdivided into eight regions, each chaired by a subcommittee of one or more members.⁶⁰ Similar entities exist at the NRCC in the 1990s. Also, a list of points to be discussed at a staff meeting included how the NRCC field operatives should work with local representatives of groups such as the American Medical Association, the Chamber of Commerce, and the National Association of Manufacturers for additional sources of money.⁶¹

The RNC, under the direction of Rogers C. B. Morton, attempted an integration among the three committees for the 1970 cycle. Morton led the effort to create the Republican Research Board, which would be chaired by the director of research at the RNC and would have research staff representatives from the NRCC, the NRSC, the House and Senate policy committees, and the House Research Committee. Each committee was entitled to three research staff representatives.[62] Although the RNC tried to exercise this coordinating power (again, in an off-year), it did not seem to have the same interests in coordinating fund-raising. Wilson explains his committee's growing financial independence in a letter to a contributor:

> When I took over the Committee we went hat in hand to the National Finance Committee for a few hundred thousand dollars for our total campaign effort. Through our Newsletter subscriptions we are now able to finance our entire budget of two to three million dollars, including campaign funds to incumbents amounting to anywhere from ten to fifteen thousand each Congress. Compare this to the five hundred or thousand we occasionally got every two years during the 40's and 50's.[63]

In spite of this professed independence, a Republican Majority Dinner was held in spring 1970 with the proceeds being split equally among the NRCC, the NRSC, and the RNC.[64]

Although some have believed that CCC resources were used as incentives for proper ideological behavior, Wilson shows that the CCCs' philosophy at this time was entirely utilitarian:

> Senator Tower's campaign committee and the Republican Congressional Committee of which I am chairman have the sole responsibility of keeping the Republicans we now have in Congress and electing a sufficient additional number to give our party control of both houses. As you pointed out, we have Republicans of all political philosophies in the party—as do the Democrats. But keep this in mind: The most important vote they cast at the start of each Congress is for Speaker—and they unanimously vote for a Republican for that post. If we elect 218 members next November, they will then cast their votes for Jerry Ford for Speaker and the Republicans will control the House of Representatives! This one single vote will then give us control of all the committees which, in turn, formulate the legislation which passes the Congress. I am sure you will agree that it's more important for the legislation to have a

majority Republican philosophy behind it than a Democratic one—which is the case now and will continue to be as long as the Democrats control the Congress and the committees.[65]

The NRCC's focus on majorities was clear. As is the case today, no CCC imposes an ideological litmus test on its candidates. Only winning matters.

To kick off the 1972 cycle, Wilson wrote to all Republican incumbents reminding them of NRCC services. In addition to the public relations allocation, radio and television services, news bureau, and photo and art services, the NRCC also produced several major publications, including the *Daily News Digest*, which was sent to each Republican congressional office daily with major news highlights.[66] However, the NRCC was having more difficulty raising funds because of competition from President Nixon's reelection campaign. In fact, Wilson made a formal request to the Republican National Finance Committee for a budget supplement and asked all his Republican colleagues to put pressure on the RNFC to come up with the funds. In his plea Wilson asserts that the NRCC had to retreat from an independent fund-raising position:

> For your information . . . as of July 28 the Republican National Finance Committee had raised 108% of its 1972 budget. The Congressional Committee had raised 59% of its budget. Further, we have unprecedented opportunities this year to pick up seats in the House, but we simply do not have the money to take advantage of all these opportunities based on our present cash position and projected income from now until Election Day. Therefore it is necessary to ask for a budget subsidy from the RNFC.
>
> It is interesting to note that the last time such a subsidy was given, 1966, we gained a net of 47 seats. Since that time there has been no subsidy from the RNFC to the Congressional Committee and we have raised all of our own funds.[67]

Although the NRCC was having financial trouble, it continued to channel money, as evidenced by a letter from Wilson to a congressional candidate. A check for $1,000 in earmarked money was issued by the NRCC. Wilson notified the candidate of the individual donor's identity and suggested he call to thank him. However, he cautioned the candidate not to declare the donor on his campaign disclosure forms but to indicate the NRCC as the money's source: "It [the donation] was channeled through the Committee and you must show the Committee as the donor. . . . *Do not*, and I repeat, *do not* show his name on your report form."[68]

Although the Republicans did not become the majority party during the 1960s, Wilson was never challenged during his tenure. He left the post over a rift with President Nixon after the 1972 elections, although some believe that then minority leader Gerald Ford asked Wilson to step aside. At that time, there is evidence of congressional-presidential tensions over who controlled the various party organizations. The Nixon White House was trying to force Wilson out of the NRCC (in his view), but Wilson found a face-saving solution. An article in the *San Diego Union* recounts Wilson's interpretation of events:

> "The next thing I know, the White House, not the President, is putting out the word that they're going to fire Bob Wilson. I went back to Ford and said the agreement [to resign] is off. I am not going to move out in disgrace." Sen. Bob Dole of Kansas, then chairman of Republican National Committee, was also in White House disfavor at this time and he subsequently announced: "I was fired." Ford told Wilson to do whatever he wanted to do. Wilson ran for the chairmanship again and won unanimously.[69]

Wilson was reelected in January 1973 and announced his resignation on March 15, effective the end of that month. The White House may have had some influence on the NRCC, but Wilson would not allow them to dictate the terms.

In 1970 the Democrats had their first new chair in twenty-two years. After Mike Kirwan's death in the summer of 1970, Rep. Thomas P. (Tip) O'Neill (D-MA) and Rep. Ed Edmondson (D-OK) took over the DCCC for the remainder of the 1970 cycle and continued to co-chair the committee for the 1972 cycle until Edmondson resigned to run for the U.S. Senate. O'Neill was closely affiliated with former Speaker John McCormack (D-MA) while Edmondson was new Speaker Carl Albert's (D-OK) ally. At first O'Neill and Edmondson did little more than send incumbents automatic contributions of $1,000, using most of its $382,000 budget for this purpose.[70] A postelection report from the DCCC detailed the committee's activities during the 1972 election. The staff consisted of ten people, evenly divided between basic services and photo/news media operations. The DCCC raised and spent more than $1 million, compared to the DCCC's estimate of $10 million spent by the NRCC. In terms of direct cash contributions, the DCCC gave every incumbent in a marginal or highly contested district a minimum of $3,000. Other races received contributions but had a lower priority. The committee provided a wide range of low-technology services: a speakers' bureau, research material on congressional activities (specifically legislation under consideration and floor statements by congressional leaders), color photography (a new innovation at the time), a seminar series on the new campaign finance law (FECA 1971), and a variety of events at the Democratic National Convention for members and candidates to meet with the Democratic presidential nominee and his campaign staff. The DCCC also attempted to meet with each candidate individually, either in their district or in Washington. If the candidate came to Washington, the DCCC arranged for a meeting with congressional leaders for pictures and briefings. This same report described plans under way for the 1974 cycle: campaign materials to be sent to all congressional candidates which included a Democratic campaign manual, a fact book, a communication handbook, the Democratic platform, the 1971 FECA, factual campaign information, a special report from the DNC, a handbook for Democratic candidates, a brochure for campaign specialities, and complete speech material. There is still no provision of television and radio services like those the Republicans had been providing since the early 1950s.[71] Because

Democrats had been in the majority for almost twenty years the DCCC still was not engaging in extensive services.

The House CCCs: Service Providers in the Modern Campaign Age

The congressional campaign committees broadened their services considerably in the mid-twentieth century to address the media needs of members. Because of the number of members involved, the House CCCs, especially the NRCC, offered more extensive services than their Senate counterparts. Although CCCs continued to channel money, they devoted more attention during this period to radio and television as important congressional campaign tools. The CCCs continued their press release service, photo service, and campaign literature production. The CCCs also began modest outreach to challenger and open seat candidates by employing field forces and holding conferences to familiarize candidates with modern campaign techniques and to introduce them to political consultants. Throughout this period, the CCCs continued issue and opposition research.

It is clear that the Republicans' services were more substantial and professional than those offered by the Democrats. Perhaps the Republicans' long minority status was responsible for this difference. Their only hope of achieving a majority in Congress was through the use of increasingly sophisticated campaign communication technologies. When the Democrats protected their majority status, they had only to encourage their incumbents to continue the practices that worked for them in the past. What remains unknown is how extensively candidates used the CCCs for their individual campaigns. Such information would allow us to assess the utility of the CCCs in individual elections.

Tables A.2 and A.3 summarize the career moves made or attempted by House CCC chairs. On the Republican side, we see some significant contests develop to select CCC chairs, with multiple candidates emerging to succeed Richard Simpson and William Miller. Earlier, both Joseph Martin and Charles Halleck made good political use of their CCC tenures. This is a period of particular tension for the House Republicans in their long-term minority status and explains the increased competition for the NRCC slot.

As the CCCs' scope, staff, budget, and operation increased, the role and power of its chairs increased accordingly. In addition, the scope and conduct of the CCCs became better defined. The CCCs gained permanent financial autonomy from the NCs and proved to be capable stand-alone organizations.

CHAPTER 5

CAMPAIGN FINANCE REFORM AND THE CONGRESSIONAL CAMPAIGN COMMITTEES

THE DECADE OF THE 1970s witnessed the most sweeping legislative reform movements in U.S. history: the major revision of campaign finance law and the reform of seniority and congressional committee operation in the House of Representatives. The Senate experienced significant change as well, which corresponded to changes in the alignment of political coalitions, especially along ideological lines.[1] Congressional parties were forced to respond in a variety of ways. The nature of campaigning for Congress was materially changed, especially how candidates received money, who they received money from, and how these transactions were reported. Ultimately, different types of candidates, those who could adjust to the constant fund-raising demands brought on by the new laws, were motivated to run for Congress. The laws also contained significant new provisions stipulating how political parties could operate regarding all candidates for federal office. Therefore, the CCCs had to modify their campaign activities to become significant fund-raisers.

As the previous three chapters have shown, the CCCs did not emphasize the raising and distributing of vast sums to candidates. Rather, they acted as conduits through which major contributors would channel funds or as purveyors of campaign speakers sent to local districts to help raise money directly. The

Senate CCCs saw earmarking as their major function, while supplying speakers and campaign literature as requested. The House CCCs, who were less likely to be approached to channel money by a great number of their candidates' supporters, focused more on supplying services to their candidates, especially incumbents. Along the way, the CCCs raised money, hired staff, and gave modest contributions. However, the generation and distribution of major sums was never a central function for the CCCs. Congressional candidates did not have the fund-raising constraints they now do and did not consider their personal fund-raising to be as burdensome. The CCCs became money raisers because of campaign finance reforms of the late 1960s and early 1970s.

This shift of campaign activities has been characterized as party resurgence by some,[2] but as no more than a reorganization of party functions by others.[3] In my view the shift is a predictable adjustment on the part of congressional parties to work toward the institutional goal of attaining or retaining majority status under new rules. Previous CCC activities commenced without much regard for campaign finance laws. The prevailing law, the Federal Corrupt Practices Act of 1925, placed strict limits on the raising and spending of money by political committees but no limit on the number of committees a candidate could establish. Also, there was no significant enforcement of the law. Therefore, when major reforms were enacted the CCCs were at first unprepared, but they eventually adjusted to the new legal requirements to meet members' demands. As the previous three chapters have shown CCCs did not begin in this era, nor were they entirely irrelevant. Rather, the CCCs entered the fund-raising world out of necessity, although their money donations comprise only modest proportions of candidates' campaign budgets.

Alongside the campaign finance reforms were extensive reforms in the House of Representatives (and to a lesser extent, the Senate). The connection between CCCs and the leadership became more explicit in the late 1970s to the present day.

Essentially, campaign finance reforms meant that members with great media presence and fund-raising abilities would more likely succeed at any leadership position, but the CCC chair was a special attraction for individuals with these talents. The potential for quick distinction as CCC head increased exponentially in the 1980s and 1990s. Therefore, CCC chairs' careers are geared even more toward leadership (or other ambitious goals), and in most cases contests to become CCC chair intensified. However, the distinction in incentive structures for House and Senate CCC chairs becomes more pronounced. Senate CCC chairs are now more likely to use presidential prospecting as an incentive to head a CCC than the promise of ascension within their chamber, which is generally the goal of House CCC chairs.

The Relevance of Campaign Finance

To understand the behavior of the party committees (both the CCCs and the NCs) since the late 1970s, it is important to understand how campaign finance reform affected them. The campaign finance legislation of the 1970s changed campaigning for all federal offices and changed the nature and type of services the CCCs offered, specifically in the realm of fund-raising. Only the substance of what CCCs provided to their constituency changed, not their relationship to it. The CCCs have always serviced, and continue to service, candidates' needs on a hierarchical basis: incumbents, open seat candidates, and then challengers.

Another consequence of campaign finance reform legislation was that the CCCs gained new financial autonomy, allowing even greater financial freedom from the national committees. As explained below, the major financial split between the CCCs and the NCs, when the CCCs no longer needed any monetary assistance from the NCs, did not take place until the 1980s. The important point is that changes in campaign finance laws affected all party committees profoundly. Though the party committees became more active in fund-raising after the new campaign finance laws were in place, they did not behave like revitalized parties. That is, they still did not have the same political goals or apply programmatic ideas to their activities.

The sweeping legislation of the 1970s (the FECA and its subsequent amendments) was written by an alliance of interest groups and congressional incumbents. The prevailing campaign finance law, the Federal Corrupt Practices Act of 1925 was not only unenforced but easy to circumvent as well. The immediate events that brought about campaign finance reform, a subject that had been under discussion for some time, concerned President Nixon's 1968 campaign transactions and his Watergate activities. Suspicions about presidential candidates, especially Republicans, motivated Congress to seek a broad reform of current campaign finance practices and the public accounting of these practices. Although this incarnation of major campaign reform was inspired by presidential excesses of the 1960s and early 1970s, campaign finance legislation dates back to the nineteenth century.[4] The 1968 election was particularly important for motivating extensive reforms because of serious questions that arose regarding political advertising on television. Regulation of political broadcasting was especially attractive to financially strapped Democrats who wanted an equal level of competition with richer Republicans.[5] When Nixon vetoed the proposed Political Broadcasting Act, many more congressional Democrats became champions of reform.[6] Their response was passage of the Federal Election Campaign Act of 1971. It required full, enforceable disclosure for the first time.[7] The administrators of the 1971 act were the clerk of the House for House candidates, the secretary of the Senate for Senate candidates, and the comptroller general of the General Accounting Office for presidential candidates and party and nonparty committees. An independent commission for enforcement matters was proposed but was lost in congressional committee deliberations.

During the late 1960s and early 1970s the CCCs were still limited operations, largely invisible to anyone off Capitol Hill. Until the mid-1970s the executive director and other officials of the committees (especially treasurer) were employees of either the sergeant-at-arms of the House or the secretary of the Senate. Much CCC activity also took place in the chair's congressional office, handled by the chair's personal office staff. The CCCs continued to channel earmarked funds from individuals, corporations, or labor unions (who either did not want their identities revealed or could not legally contribute directly to federal candidates) and issue a check on their bank account in the same amount to the designated member. The 1971 FECA required only disclosure, and there was nothing embarrassing in receiving contributions from the partisan organization of one's chamber. This kind of questionable earmarking activity by CCCs led a former DCCC executive director to shred all that committee's records prior to 1975.[8]

Rep. Wayne Hays (D-OH) who would later become DCCC chair for the 1974 and part of the 1976 election cycles, opposed the creation of an independent commission to oversee compliance with the new campaign finance law. Hays was chairman of the House Administration Committee, which had jurisdiction over campaign finance legislation, while the FECA reforms were working their way through Congress. Hays had leadership ambitions, and he used his control over campaign legislation as well as office space and standing committee budgets through the House Administration Committee to establish a personal power base. In 1971 he made a bid for House majority leader, but Hale Boggs (D-LA), the majority whip, emerged the winner.[9] Hays rejected creation of the FEC as an independent monitor of campaign finance practices because he wanted the House to retain control over campaign finance reporting, something he considered a sensitive aspect of Congress's internal business. In fact, Hays was willing to let the reform legislation die over the issue.[10] Even after the initial bill passed in 1971, Hays suggested "that a revision be passed transferring the supervision of the new law from the Clerk [of the House] to his Administration Committee."[11]

But the 1971 FECA did not have a great effect on the CCCs during the 1972 cycle. DCCC chair Tip O'Neill was raising money that went unreported for the DCCC's candidates,[12] and Bob Wilson was doing the same in his last term as NRCC head. The Senate committees, led by Ernest Hollings (D-SC) and Peter Dominick (R-CO), remained modest organizations engaged in similar kinds of money reallocation. But a few things unsettled these arrangements. First, President Nixon took advantage of the fact that the 1971 FECA did not take effect until April 7, 1972. The Federal Corrupt Practices Act of 1925 was repealed as of March 1, 1972. The Nixon campaign used this gap in legislation to collect and spend millions of dollars. Their indiscretions were soon discovered. Second, if this violation of the spirit of the FECA was not enough, Watergate generated intense support for further reform. As Susan King and Robert L. Peabody put it, "Only a few members of Congress had actively supported campaign finance reforms before, but now the vast majority were on record as trying in this way to restore some measure of confidence in government and its elected leaders."[13] Thus the 1974 FECA amendments were born.

The 1974 amendments provided for public financing of presidential general elections (with a system of matching funds and spending limits for presidential primary nomination campaigns which are still in effect today), greater reporting requirements supervised by an independent commission, and spending limits for congressional campaigns. In addition, contribution limits to federal candidates were placed on individuals, parties, and multicandidate committees. The Federal Election Commission was finally established, but commissioners were mostly appointed by Congress (which was later found to be unconstitutional). The FEC's governing board consisted of eight members, six of whom had full voting power and authority and two of whom were ex officio (the clerk of the House and the secretary of the Senate). Of the remaining six commissioners, two were nominated by the Speaker of the House, two by the president pro tempore of the Senate, and two by the president. Furthermore, the FEC chair would rotate among the various governors. Congress maintained a legislative veto power over

FEC decisions as well.[14] The 1974 laws also included overall spending limits for congressional campaigns, even though these campaigns received no public money.

Apart from the spending limits (which were set above the amount spent by the average contemporary campaign), congressional campaigns were conducted much as before. There was also little difference in operations at the CCCs, besides having to inform candidates of the new law's reporting requirements. Significantly, by 1973 events changed some of the principal players. The House majority leader, Hale Boggs (D-LA), disappeared in a plane over Alaska, creating a vacancy in the leadership. The majority whip, Tip O'Neill, who had also been co-chair of the DCCC in 1972, advanced to majority leader. Wayne Hays took over the DCCC position, partly as an inducement not to enter the 1973 leadership contests.[15] Now, Hays's control over campaigning was nearly complete. He still chaired the House Administration Committee. He also now controlled the DCCC, which used staff employed by the House of Representatives. The clerk of the House, who was also responsible to the House Administration Committee, oversaw campaign finance reporting. With an eye to the 1974 midterm elections, the DCCC under Hays amassed detailed information on congressional races., a function it began in the late 1960s and one that continues today as a particular strength of the CCCs.[16] The money operation at this time remained modest, partly because of spending limits imposed under the 1971 law but mostly because of the traditional lack of significant funds. The channeling function continued. The DCCC did engage in media services for members by hiring a film crew to create action footage of members at work in their offices which could later be dubbed for campaign use.[17] The DCCC also offered a series of seminars designed to introduce members to modern campaign techniques, such as polling, media use, direct mail fund-raising, and telephone banks assisted by computer indexing, and to potential vendors of these services.[18] The DCCC does not appear to have retained a large in-house staff to perform these services for candidates, preferring instead to subcontract to outside providers.

The key operatives changed for the House Republicans as well. As discussed previously, Wilson resigned as NRCC chair in 1973 and was replaced by Bob Michel (R-IL). Michel's unenviable task was to steer House Republicans through the 1974 elections, which were held under the cloud of Watergate. Michel kept many of the media-oriented services Wilson had established,[19] though he was not able to sustain an operation quite as large as Wilson's because of the difficulty of raising funds as Watergate was unfolding. The senatorial committees had their customary personnel changes, with Lloyd Bentsen (D-TX) at the DSCC and William (Bill) Brock (R-TN) at the NRSC. At the DSCC, a modest operation was maintained. Apart from the earmarking of funds, the DSCC maintained speech and issue files for senators' use. Unlike their Republican counterparts, the DSCC did not provide these materials to individual senators but instead instructed them to come to the DSCC's office, pick up the file they needed, and return it when finished.[20] Thus the DSCC had not extended services much beyond what it offered in the 1960s.

As a result of the Watergate scandal, the Democrats had significant triumphs in the 1974 midterm congressional elections, despite the spending limits. The CCCs never had to raise large amounts of money independently, since they primarily processed contributions from other sources, so the spending limits did not impose hardships on them but rather on the individual candidates.[21] Still, Democrats increased their membership by 46 seats, to 289.

The campaign finance arrangement in force for the 1974 elections was short-lived. In its hurry to write a punitive piece of legislation, Congress virtually ignored the dubious constitutionality of various facets of the law. Almost immediately after the 1974 FECA became law, Sen. James Buckley (R-NY) filed a lawsuit against Francis Valeo, secretary of the Senate. The resulting decision, *Buckley v. Valeo*, was handed down by the

Supreme Court on January 30, 1976.[22] Two major provisions of the act were found unconstitutional: mandatory spending limits (both for congressional campaigns and for independent expenditures made by individuals or groups) and the manner of appointment of the FEC. Because the FEC dispensed matching funds, the timing of the decision was particularly relevant for the presidential primary candidates. When the remedial legislation was not completed by the court-mandated date of February 29, 1976, an extension was granted to March 22, 1976. As no legislation was passed by that date, the FEC ceased to exist until May 11, 1976. At that time President Gerald Ford appointed all the governors and the FEC resumed operation.[23]

Meanwhile, the CCCs continued to give small contributions, even though spending limits for congressional races had been repealed. There was little change in the two Democratic committees, largely because of their 1974 victories. The DCCC was still led by Wayne Hays, under O'Neill's ultimate direction, until he resigned his seat in the House over a sex scandal in the summer of 1976. Speaker Carl Albert appointed James Corman (D-CA) as his replacement. Corman asked for the spot to leverage his position in the party. He wanted to chair the Ways and Means Committee and thought the DCCC would be one opportunity to get it.[24] The DSCC was taken over by J. Bennett Johnston (D-LA) for the 1976 cycle.

On the Republican side, things were different. Despite the humiliating defeat in 1974, NRCC chair Bob Michel became minority whip after Les Arends (R-IL) retired, proving that favorable electoral outcomes while chairing a CCC are not necessary to demonstrate commitment to congressional party needs and leadership talent. The NRCC chair position was now open. The candidates for the position were from different ideological wings of the party: liberal Pierre du Pont (R-DE), conservative John Rousselot (R-CA), and moderate Guy Vander Jagt (R-MI). Vander Jagt defeated Rousselot in two ballots[25] and served as NRCC chair until 1992, when he lost his congressional primary. The start of Vander Jagt's tenure marked the beginning of a significant transition for the NRCC. Vander Jagt, first elected to the House in 1968, hired Steven Stockmeyer as his first permanent executive director. Stockmeyer hired Wyatt Stewart as his principal fund-raiser and Jan Baran as his legal counsel. Both Stewart and Baran continued with the committee throughout Vander Jagt's tenure, and both became campaign consultants afterward. As this team moved to build a financial base for the NRCC, they realized that they knew little of the ever-changing FECA and its implications. Two things in particular troubled the NRCC: the $70,000 spending limit in the 1974 House elections and their understanding that the FEC considered party overhead costs to be a contribution to candidates. Given this, they made a plan to shut down the entire service function of the committee and do nothing more than give information and money to candidates with a skeleton staff of only two or three people.[26] Then, of course, the 1976 court decision (*Buckley v. Valeo*) finding that congressional spending limits were unconstitutional gave the committee new impetus. Republicans thought they might make electoral gains if they were not constrained by spending limits. Stockmeyer ended the old dual payroll system, whereby NRCC staffers (like their DCCC counterparts) were paid from congressmen's clerk-hire budgets. The NRCC also ended the practice of having the executive director be an employee of the sergeant-at-arms.[27] The NRCC was trying to become more professional. Now that spending limits had been repealed (but contribution limits on individuals, parties, and PACs remained), the context of congressional elections changed once again. With this new information Vander Jagt asked President Ford to sign a fund-raising letter for the NRCC for the 1976 congressional elections.[28] Although the letter did not have much effect on the outcome of the 1976 congressional elections (the Democrats witnessed a net gain of one seat in the House), it did bring the NRCC into the modern direct mail age.

Both the NRCC and the DCCC provided limited services to their candidates in the 1976 cycle. Each committee gave its candidates resource material for speeches (including the 1976 party convention platform and congressional committee reports) and analyses of the voting records of the members being challenged. Seminars were also held for candidates, though the NRCC's were more extensive since they had more challengers running.[29]

The NRSC was not experiencing the same energy. It was led by Bill Brock (R-TN) during the 1974 cycle and Ted Stevens (R-AK) for the 1976 elections. It had even fewer staff and less resources than the NRCC. NRSC staff remained at 1950s and 1960s levels: borrowed regular staffers from the chair's office. By the end of 1977 the NRSC had a debt of $70,000.[30]

While the CCCs were trying to regroup the FECA was once again headed for revision. After several election cycles there was pressure to simplify the reporting procedures and to encourage the role of state and local parties in the political process. Several housekeeping amendments passed in late 1979,[31] after more restrictive measures were rejected in 1978. In addition to proposing public financing of congressional elections, the Democrats (then the majority in both houses) wanted to reduce the limit of combined party spending to $15,000 per campaign ($10,000 in direct contributions and $5,000 in coordinated expenditures). Previously, party committees, defined as the national committee and state party committee at this time, were entitled to make a direct contribution of $5,000 in the primary election and $5,000 in the general election (for a potential total of $10,000 in direct contributions) plus $10,000 (plus a cost of living adjustment [COLA]) in coordinated expenditures. The congressional Democrats were becoming suspicious of the congressional Republicans' organizational changes following the Watergate elections. While the Democrats were still enjoying greater electoral success, they wanted to curtail Republican organizational and financial advances. The original 1978 FECA amendment proposals amounted to what RNC chair (and former NRSC chair) Bill Brock called a "blatant Democratic power grab and a reaction to Republican fundraising successes that threatened the survival of the party."³² Just a year earlier the Democrats passed a bill that forbade the use of government funds to pay for parties' affairs. Previously, all the CCCs had been located on federal property, which amounted to a federal subsidy for party overhead. This Democratic initiative surprised the Republicans.³³ Overall, they were upset that the Democrats tried to shut down their CCCs rather than compete with them openly. According to Nancy Sinnott Dwight, NRCC executive director in the early 1980s, "The Democrats always thought we were spending in ways that we weren't."³⁴

The NRCC was able to raise $14.1 million for the 1978 midterm elections, compared to the DCCC's $2.8 million. The NRCC was also reviving its service organization and rebounded from a staff low of thirty in 1976 to sixty in 1978. The NRCC was so well-off that Sen. Robert Packwood (R-OR), NRSC chair during the 1978 cycle, was able to borrow money so that his organization could get out of debt and attempt to reorganize itself for the 1978 elections.³⁵ In response to a number of close losses in the 1976 congressional races, the NRCC engaged in more aggressive recruitment efforts in 1977 in preparation for the 1978 cycle. It promised early support to near-winners from 1976, prompting contemporary observers to call this "a measure of Republican despair." In addition to earlier recruitment efforts, the NRCC targeted veteran Democratic members rather than just those who were recently elected. The DCCC did not perceive the NRCC tactics as any sort of threat since they still had an extensive farm team of potential candidates and virtually all of their large Watergate class was running strong.³⁶ The Republicans gained 15 seats in the House in 1978. By 1980 they had more than doubled that figure, gaining 34 seats (Senate Republicans gained 3 seats in 1978 and gained control in 1980). They had great success with general appeals for a Republican Congress using the Vander Jagt-penned theme "Vote Republican—For a Change" and getting some help from presidential candidate Ronald Reagan at the head of the ticket. Senator Packwood used the loans from the NRCC to erase the NRSC's debt and increase its staff for the 1978 cycle. Packwood launched the NRSC's first direct mail program targeted at small contributors, laying a foundation for later fund-raising successes.[37]

The DCCC and DSCC efforts immediately after the FECA was amended were considerably less ambitious than those of the Republicans. Anticipating the eventual demands for a move out of federal office space, both committees relocated to adjacent offices, which allowed some coordination and sharing of staff. Both organizations provided seminars to candidates, mostly by political consultants discussing new campaign technologies.[38] The Democrats were in a position of strength, with healthy congressional majorities and a Democratic president. DCCC chair Corman decided to concentrate donations to first- and second-term members at the full $5,000 legal contribution limit (for the general election), a policy continued from the 1976 cycle.[39] Though both organizations made significant contributions to their candidates (see tables A.14 and A.16), neither engaged in coordinated expenditures at this time. This would soon change.

Contributions and Expenditures

To understand the events of the 1980s, it is necessary to explain the legal differences between contributions and expenditures as defined by the FECA. Direct contributions to a candidate's campaign are in the form of an actual check (or cash) and are unrestricted as to candidate use. Once awarded, the giver has no control over how the funds are spent. The FECA strictly limited direct contributions so that no individual or group would "own" a candidate.[40] In other words, the legislation aimed to eliminate fat cats. Theoretically, the candidate, if elected, would feel no particular debt to any one special interest, all contributions being roughly equal. Congress did allow for another type of aid, coordinated expenditures, to be made for candidates by political parties. This was intended to strengthen the party system, which Congress thought had been weakened by the earlier laws that encouraged candidates to seek large individual contributions. So under section 441a(d) of the FECA, the national party committees and state party committees were explicitly allowed to make expenditures on behalf of candidates up to $10,000 (in 1974 dollars plus a COLA) in House elections and in varying amounts according to state voting age population (VAP) for Senate elections and at-large House districts.[41] For the parties, coordinated expenditures meant activity initiated by party committees on behalf of candidates but *with* the candidate's knowledge and consent. Unlike direct contributions to candidates, political party organizations actually spend the monies for goods and services, giving the parties total control over these funds. The party committees could make expenditures that *they* deemed important (e.g., commissioning a poll or arranging for a direct mail campaign), instead of trusting the judgment of the candidate. This was in contrast to an independent expenditure, which is money spent or activities engaged in by individuals or multicandidate committees (PACs) *without* the candidate's knowledge or consent. Because party organizations were not believed to be capable of independence from their own nominees, a separate category of coordinated expenditures was born. Recently, the Supreme Court has reconsidered the relationship between party committees and independent expenditures in the 1996 decision *Colorado Republican Federal Campaign Committee v. Federal Election Commission*. In the 1996 election cycle, the NRSC made extensive use of the new independent expenditure allowances while coordinating other financial activities with the RNC.

THE NCs, THE CCCs, AND 441A(D)

The FECA gave the national committees a significant role in the congressional committees' finances until 1982, when a Supreme Court decision officially allowed the CCCs to have a more autonomous financial role. According to the 1971 law, only the NCs and the state party committees, not the CCCs, could make coordinated expenditures on behalf of House and Senate candidates. Although the law seemingly gave the NCs legal superiority by designating them to provide coordinated expenditures, they had little incentive to exercise their power. As we have seen, the NCs have always had to raise money for the presidential campaigns, whereas the CCCs have always been asked to maximize the number of incumbents in pursuit of majority status. In the CCCs' early history the Speaker's Bureau was the critical service. Later, issue papers became important. Previously, incumbents had little problem attracting money either from individuals or from special interests; the problem was explaining the connection to their various constituencies. Therefore, the CCCs accepted this money, often in cash, and funneled it to the proper incumbent. In an era of campaign finance reform, this earmarking function was no longer acceptable since direct contribution limits applied to both individuals and parties. That meant that earmarking functions would be strictly limited and that contributions from the CCCs' own funds would be precluded as they would easily reach the legal contribution limit.

As there was now enforcement of disclosure laws, contributors could no longer remain anonymous. Also, the fact that limits on contributions to candidates were as low as $1,000 and $5,000 (from individuals and PACs, respectively) while limits on contributions to parties were much higher, at $15,000 and $20,000 (PACs and individuals), encouraged both individuals and PACs to give to the parties. So the new law hindered individuals from donating great sums to candidates while also limiting what the parties could donate directly. By designating the NCs and state parties to be the distributors of coordinated expenditures, congressional candidates were bound to feel the squeeze since the NCs and state parties did not see spending funds on congressional races as their priority. At this time the CCCs became the purveyors of information (district demographics, opposition research) and services, especially for dealing with the new law and campaign technologies.

Just after the passage of the FECA, the NCs and CCCs tried to work together to meet their financial obligations to their constituents through legal means. The Republicans had a cordial relationship among their organizations; the Democrats' relationship was more distant. Former NRCC executive director Nancy Sinnott Dwight explained that the RNC and the NRCC had a good relationship in the late 1970s because many of the staff members had worked together when there was a shortage of Republican campaign professionals (understandable in the post-Watergate era) and the talent pool was small. Also, RNC chair Bill Brock (also a former NRSC chair) and NRCC chair Guy Vander Jagt had a good personal relationship. The RNC showed an interest in both House and Senate elections, an interest enhanced by the fact that the Republicans were the "party out" (i.e., did not control the White House).[42] The Democrats suffered from being the "party in." The DNC was filled with President Jimmy Carter's patronage appointees who cared little about the plight of specific congressional Democrats. All CCCs assumed that the national committees would continue to provide some money and that the CCCs would then direct these resources to their constituencies.[43] When it became apparent that the national committees would no longer supply funds,[44] one of the CCCs, the NRSC, challenged the new campaign finance law and permanently changed the service role of the CCCs.

In 1978 the newly solvent NRSC creatively interpreted the law on coordinated expenditures. They entered into what they called "agency agreements" with a number of state parties, which allowed the NRSC to raise and disburse the coordinated expenditure (see table 5.1) the state party could make in a U.S. Senate race on its behalf. The NRSC would act as a designated agent for the state party, freeing the state organization's resources for other political efforts and candidates. The NRSC was expanding the interpretation of section 441a(d) of the 1971 FECA. However, its Democratic counterpart, the DSCC, challenged this action. The FEC supported the legitimacy of agency agreements, but the Court of Appeals reversed their decision. The case was then taken to the Supreme Court as *Federal Election Commission v. Democratic Senatorial Campaign Committee et al.*

Table 5.1
Coordinated Expenditure Limits for Campaigns
for the House of Representatives, Adjusted for
Consumer Price Index Increases

Election Cycle	Expenditure Limit (for state party or national committee)	Expenditure Limit Doubled (amount CCC can spend if both agency agreements obtained)
1974	$ 10,000	$ 20,000
1976	$ 10,910	$ 21,820
1978	$ 12,290	$ 24,580
1980	$ 14,720	$ 29,440
1982	$ 18,440	$ 36,880
1984	$ 20,200	$ 40,400
1986	$ 21,810	$ 43,620
1988	$ 23,050	$ 46,100
1990	$ 25,140	$ 50,280
1992	$ 27,620	$ 55,240
1994	$ 29,300	$ 58,600
1996	$ 30,910	$ 61,820

Source: *FEC Record*, March 1976; March 1978; March 1980; June 1982; March 1984; April 1986; March 1988; March 1990; March 1992; March 1994; March 1996.

In a unanimous opinion, handed down on November 10, 1981, Justice Byron White held that "while 441a(d) (3) does not authorize the NRSC to make expenditures in its own right, it does not follow that it may not act as agent of a committee that is expressly authorized to make expenditures. Nothing in the statute suggests that a state committee may not designate another committee to be its alter ego and to act on its behalf."[45]

This decision shaped the future of the CCCs, the role of the NCs in congressional elections, and the expectations of both incumbent and challenger congressional candidates. In finding these agency agreements to be legal, the Court led the way for the CCCs to increase their financial involvement in congressional campaigning.

Now the CCCs could not only arrange to make coordinated expenditures for the states on behalf of candidates, they could also effectively double their value by entering into a similar arrangement with the national committee. Since the law designated both NCs and state parties to make coordinated expenditures, a CCC could double the expressed limit of $10,000 in each House race (or the state-by-state limits determined by VAP in a Senate race). It was a relatively simple matter to get both the national and state committees to agree to enter into these agency agreements; they simply did not have the time, desire, or money to pursue coordinated expenditures themselves. Since the CCCs had the best information on the races under their purview and were designed to look out for the best interests of their constituencies (incumbents and challengers), it was only logical that they should want to spend money on behalf of their candidates. To preserve their mission of pursuing majorities in Congress, the CCCs looked for ways to raise and distribute money to candidates instead of cleansing already raised funds.

After the 1982 election cycle coordinated expenditures from the NCs in House and Senate races virtually disappear. In the 1982 cycle this loss of the NCs' coordinated expenditures was offset by a surge in NC contributions, but this was only temporary, and NC contributions continued to drop in congressional races throughout the 1980s and into the early 1990s. Tables A.6, A.7, A.12, and A.13 show the contribution and expenditure patterns of the two national committees. Meanwhile, the contributions and expenditures of the CCCs continued to rise. The two Republican CCCs and the DSCC have contributed to a fairly steady number of candidates, either meeting or approaching the number of a full slate of general election candidates, while the DCCC has been able to achieve this only recently (see tables A.8, A.10, A.14, and A.16).

The legal limits on contributions make this issue relatively simple: the CCCs can generally afford to give the maximum allowable direct contribution ($5,000 per election[46] to House candidates, $17,500 per election cycle to Senate candidates) to *all* their candidates, incumbents as well as challengers, although they do not generally do this.[47] The major variation comes in the expenditures. For the senatorial CCCs, the number of races in which expenditures are made remains roughly the same as the number contributed to; the difference is the amount. For example, in table A.15 we see that the DSCC went from an expenditure of $589,316 in 19 races in 1980 to $6,207,437 in 38 races in 1988; table A.9 shows that the NRSC doubled its expenditures, from $5,025,802 in 34 races in 1980 to $10,250,538 in 34 races in 1988. The amount each CCC may spend in a coordinated expenditure effort on behalf of its candidates is tied to a formula in the 1974 law which allows each committee (national and state) to spend $10,000 times a COLA in House races and $0.02 $\times$ VAP $\times$ COLA for Senate races. The amounts are recalculated for each election cycle (see table 5.1).[48]

For the House committees, both the frequency and amounts of expenditures differ from contributions. Tables A.10 and A.11 show that the NRCC was making expenditures in only about half the number of the races to which it contributed. These expenditures were generally four to five times the amount of contributions. Of course, these are aggregate figures, so the number of races that the NRCC actually makes a maximum expenditure in is quite a bit smaller than the total number contributed to. The DCCC, by contrast, has increased both numbers of races contributed to and numbers of races on which expenditures were made. Tables A.16 and A.17 show that from 1984 to 1989 numbers of contributions and expenditures reached near-parity, though both have risen in the 1990s.

The newfound power of coordinated expenditures solved some problems and caused others. It solved the problem of how the CCCs would best help incumbents cope with contribution limits and the financial demands of new technology; it also created the problem of setting funding priorities between incumbents and challengers. Before the proliferation of agency agreements, the committees could do little for candidates financially other than give the legally limited direct contribution. Now the CCCs could contribute up to $46,000 directly or indirectly (in the 1982 cycle) to campaigns. Suddenly, more candidates wanted their share.

The 1980 Elections

While the agency agreements were being tested by the NRSC, the 1980 elections took place and had a dramatic impact on all four committees. The economy was moving from bad to worse, and President Carter's approval ratings were slipping. Republicans capitalized on the Democrats' misfortunes and won both the White House and the Senate. Because of the Democrats' unpopularity, Republicans in all three campaign organizations were optimistic about the 1980 elections. Indeed, both the NRCC and NRSC believed they had a good chance of achieving majorities in their chambers. To take advantage of the political opportunities in 1980, the NRCC, the RNC, and the NRSC joined forces to stage a high-profile media campaign with the theme "Vote Republican—For a Change." Together the three committees spent $9 million on this effort. Though Republicans gained only thirty-four seats in the House, they won control of the Senate and many believed the party-orchestrated media blitz gave Reagan's fortunes a boost.[49] Sen. John Heinz (R-PA) chaired the NRSC for the 1980 cycle. The NRSC gained substantial legitimacy following the 1980 elections because of its proven fund-raising capabilities and new targeting strategies. The NRSC spent more than $5 million in the 1980 cycle, compared with just under $3 million in the 1978 cycle (see table A.9). The average expenditure in incumbent senators' races dropped from $178,363 in 1978 to $50,169 in 1980, while open seat expenditures rose from an average of $48,922 to $254,564.

The DSCC was stunned and temporarily immobilized after 1980. Sen. Wendell Ford (D-KY) headed the committee from 1977 to 1982. Despite the dramatic losses in 1980, Ford was retained as DSCC head.[50] Many Democratic insiders contend that the senatorial party was in shock over their new minority status and was unable to reorganize. After the 1982 cycle the DSCC adopted a divided yet effective leadership arrangement with Sen. Lloyd Bentsen (D-TX) as chair and Sen. Alan Cranston (D-CA) raising funds for the DSCC through the Leadership Circle, a separate but affiliated committee targeting primarily large donors.[51] In the 1984 cycle the DSCC doubled its funds and helped gain two seats. The DSCC was also encouraged by the renewed activities at the DCCC.

Rep. James Corman (D-CA) had been head of the DCCC since Wayne Hays's resignation in 1976. However, he lost his own bid for reelection in 1980, an embarrassment for congressional Democrats. They reluctantly turned the DCCC over to a young, brash representative from California, Tony Coelho. Coelho, first elected in 1978 but a Hill staff veteran, decided to stop using the traditional Democratic tactic of bemoaning the Republicans' war chest and started building one himself. Coelho proved tremendously successful but drew criticism from his colleagues over his nontraditional sources, mainly big business.[52] The NRCC had great success in fund-raising and staff development after the 1980 elections. It was able to offer money and services not thought possible in the post-Watergate era.

Paul Herrnson published the most comprehensive accounting of services offered by the CCCs in the 1980s. He argues that the activities of the six party committees (the four CCCs and the two NCs) from the late 1970s to the mid-1980s reveal a new role for political parties: national party as intermediary between candidates and campaign resources, instead of the nineteenth-century model of party as political machine or the 1960s–1970s model of party as peripheral organization. Herrnson shows that in the 1980s party receipts grew tremendously, the six committees moved to permanent nongovernmental headquarters, the staff became permanent and full time, and each organization became functionally diversified with five or six distinct divisions each.[53] These divisions, which still exist, are executive/administrative; finance/fund-raising; political/campaign; research; and communications/media center/press. Ironically, these divisions correspond to those found for the CCCs in the 1950s. Several things did change after the early 1980s. First, the CCC staffs became larger and were more likely to be permanent. Second, as Herrnson describes, campaign finance reform allowed the CCCs to become major brokers with the PAC community and devote staff and resources exclusively to the purpose of matching PACs with appropriate candidates for their donations. Though such a channeling function had obviously been a CCC technique for decades, its high-profile professionalization is a significant development. Indeed, Herrnson writes, "national party services in campaign management, communications, fundraising, and in some traditional local party activities now enhance, supplement, and even replace campaign services that candidates previously had to purchase from professional campaign consultants."[54] While I do not entirely agree with Herrnson's interpretation of new party activity in the 1980s, his argument is certainly compelling. Herrnson takes the position that the national parties (which includes all six party committees, although he is careful to notice their distinct compositions and tasks) were peripheral to congressional elections from the time of the decline of the political machine until the party resurgence of the 1980s. I contend that Herrnson's argument overstates the case on both ends: the CCCs were not entirely peripheral over the last century, nor are they central to the outcomes of congressional elections today. Herrnson's study also refers primarily to the relationship of the CCCs to the NCs and their common relationship to congressional candidates. No link to the parties in government is established.

Though it is unclear whether CCCs can substitute for professional campaign consultants in the modern era (at least for candidates with the potential to win races),[55] it is clear that CCCs have adopted many of the highly sophisticated campaign technologies. What changed in the 1980s was the nature of incumbent demands for CCC services and funds. While CCCs had always been formed by and for incumbents, the new campaign finance law and new campaign technology meant that members had to rely on outside help to achieve reelection. At the same time, they were spending more time in Washington, D.C. Thus during the 1980s, while CCCs were mastering direct mail and high-dollar fund-raising techniques, incumbents came to expect that the CCCs would relieve them of a certain number of campaign duties. Though in an earlier era there was little problem with this position, in the 1980s it meant that a CCC could spend less time focusing on its original mission to win majorities. Tensions developed between CCC chairs and the members of the congressional party when the CCCs and the leadership wanted to focus on majorities rather than incumbent requests (especially from those who had no genuine need for assistance). The next transition for the CCCs came when they began to favor challenger candidates rather than incumbents in the provision of modern campaign and fund-raising services.[56]

Incumbents and Challengers: The Dilemma of Success

After 1980 it was clear that what had once been sufficient to protect incumbents was no longer enough: only 90.7 percent of incumbent House members were reelected, down from 93.7 percent in 1978. All lawmakers needed to take public opinion polls and use mass media to get their reelection messages across. If they did not have a precise perception of their electorate, it was possible that a challenger would, thereby overcoming the advantages of incumbency. All the CCCs took similar stances: (1) they had to bring their incumbents into the technology age, and (2) they had to pay attention to attractive challengers in races where the other party's incumbents were weak. Correspondingly, the activities of the CCCs in their role as Washington-oriented service organizations needed modification. The incumbents, who had depended on the CCCs to tend to many of their mundane campaigning tasks, would have to learn to lead themselves into the new electoral age. Before, they had taken care of their own campaigning at home and looked to the CCCs for Washington-based resources; now they no longer felt confident on their own turf. For those CCCs not protecting majorities, recruiting promising candidates became a more pressing interest. Indeed, all four CCCs became more involved in candidate recruitment for open seat and challenger races. However, none of the CCCs would violate their policy of not giving preprimary endorsements. So, although the CCCs sent field representatives to recruit candidates, they could make no concrete promises until after the race was defined.[57]

Beyond recruitment, there is the matter of setting priorities for funding incumbents and challengers. This problem is fundamentally different by chamber, reflecting the distinct concerns of the House and Senate parties. The senatorial committees have fewer races, so the decision is easier: they deal with all of them. Both Senate committees have the staff and resources to become involved in all thirty-three or thirty-four Senate races in a given cycle. Incumbents are still their highest priority, but every challenger receives serious consideration for funding.

The House committees have a different predicament. Despite their larger staffs, they cannot focus on all 435 races simultaneously, nor do they have the money to provide each with adequate support.[58] Marginality (the chance of losing or winning a seat) became their common litmus test. The House CCCs have had to sacrifice some attention to safe incumbents for the sake of supporting challengers with a good chance of winning. This was especially true for the NRCC in 1994 and to a lesser extent the DCCC in 1996 (see chap. 7). Likewise, some incumbents are in desperate trouble while others may have only token opposition. At the DCCC, for example, Tony Coelho wanted to alleviate Democratic nervousness by recouping some of their losses in the House after the 1980 elections by helping good challengers win elections. This would show senior incumbents the importance of learning contemporary campaign techniques.

Still, Coelho's main task was to protect incumbents. If there were no incumbent losses, then the Democrats retained control. The tactics adopted by the two House CCCs were understandably different.

The NRCC quickly learned that success can breed contempt. In the wake of the triumphant 441a(d) decision, the NRCC found itself in a bind. Once the agency agreements were declared legal, the incumbents lined up for their share. They figured that since the NRCC could now raise and spend close to $50,000 for each of their races, it ought to save the incumbents the trouble of having to raise that much themselves[59] and allocate it to their campaign. The NRCC could not afford to expend the maximum contribution on all of the candidates asking for money. It especially could not fund all the incumbents and expect to have any money left over for challenger races. The Incumbent Review Panel was born.

As of the 1980 election (and indeed until 1985), it was the NRCC's policy to give the maximum allowable contribution to each incumbent: $5,000 in the primary and $5,000 in the general election. Beyond this initial contribution, the committee staff thought that incumbents could raise their own money and did not need the extra money the NRCC could legally spend in coordinated expenditures. In 1982 the committee had more money in the bank than before, and the Court decision allowed them to spend money through agency agreements. The incumbents, who despite election successes felt electorally insecure, wanted the available cash. The committee staff was not in a position to say no to their "board of directors." The chair did not want to make such tough allocation decisions himself. Therefore Vander Jagt and NRCC's executive director, Nancy Sinnott Dwight, came up with the idea of creating a peer review mechanism. The Incumbent Review Panel (IRP), a subset of the NRCC's executive committee, consisted of three incumbent congressmen,[60] the chair, and the executive director of the NRCC in a nonvoting capacity. The panel heard the pleas of the incumbents who requested full coordinated expenditures. If the panel felt that the incumbent was in trouble, then the request would be granted. If the request was frivolous, or demonstrated that the incumbent had not come into the technology age or realized his full fund-raising potential, it was usually denied.[61] Such peer review was helpful not only to the committee but also to the incumbents who had not been using the new technology. One had to think carefully about asking colleagues for this money. Review panels remain an important part of CCC operations.

The DCCC did not have a formal structure such as the Incumbent Review Panel but informally considered the merits of incumbents' requests. Coelho was under attack from Democratic incumbents during the 1982 cycle for doing much the same thing the Incumbent Review Panel had done for the Republicans: denying incumbent requests. Coelho was determined to make financial assistance need based, but the incumbents were used to getting spoils from the committee.[62]

The Republicans' electoral success and organizational superiority would not last, however, in part because the Democrats finally took notice of the NRCC's methods and began to emulate them. When Coelho became chair of the DCCC in 1981 he set out to breathe life into the nearly moribund operation by using the same solutions the NRCC had discovered. At a press conference with NRCC chair Vander Jagt in 1982, Coelho had this to say:

> I do have great admiration for Guy and the job that he has done. I think he's done an absolutely fantastic job for the Republican Committee and has done something that I'm really interested in doing, in making the party a factor again in politics. It is so critical that we do that. That's my goal for House Democrats, and, if I can just do half the job that he has done, in half the time, we'll get there, and we'll do it quick! I intend to do it quick! I intend to do it a lot faster than that, Guy! But, he has been a great example to follow.[63]

During Coelho's tenure the DCCC grew rapidly. Coelho worked closely with the business PAC community, reminding them that House Democrats controlled important decision-making positions in Congress and that the business community's attention to Republicans was misplaced. Coelho's efforts gave the DCCC a needed boost, and its viability was secured. As a result of his DCCC efforts, Coelho became the House Democratic whip in 1986.

Although both the NRCC and the DCCC moved to wean incumbents from the gravy train, this did not diminish their commitment to reelecting incumbents. The House committees were eager to try their new expertise on open seat races and promising challenger races and wished to use resources normally committed to incumbents for this purpose. Never, however, would they knowingly sacrifice an incumbent.

New Campaign Activities

By the end of the 1980s the CCCs had mastered fund-raising on their own. They developed mailing lists targeted at small donors, cultivated a circle of high-dollar ($1,000 or more) donors who could legally donate twenty times more to the party than to any individual candidate, and experimented with ways to circumvent the legal spending limits. Each party had different problems. The Republicans had the greatest fund-raising successes overall with the cultivation of small donors rather than large donors, probably because their rank-and-file supporters are wealthier than those of the Democrats. They also needed to find ways to channel more money to the closest races once the CCC already made the maximum contribution. The Democrats had better success extracting funds from wealthy individuals and the PAC community by touting their majority status. Eventually, they could solicit more from these sources than they could legally collect, so they learned to maximize the use of these funds by designating them "soft money." Coelho and the DCCC maximized this method.

In the early 1980s Coelho had begun to experiment with the use of soft money at the DCCC. Soft money consists of funds that cannot legally be used as direct contributions in federal elections. Normally, this means that the donor has already exceeded his maximum contribution limit to the party organization or is prohibited from making any contributions in Federal elections. Coelho took advantage of the opportunity to get these donors, mostly individuals, labor unions, and corporations, to give more money to the DCCC for use in "nonfederal" party activities. The most common use was for "building funds,"where soft money could be used to pay for updating party facilities and other overhead expenses. The Democrats built their state-of-the-art Harriman Communications Center this way.[64] Soft money allowed the Democrats to conduct their operation more like a business, according to Coelho, and allowed them to compete with the Republicans' hard money fund-raising advantage.[65]

The Republicans faced different issues. When the NRSC first raised more money than it could legally spend in 1990, it sought creative solutions. Under its chair, Don Nickles (R-OK), the NRSC engaged in three significant activities: bundling, transfers to state parties, and creation of a new "agent" for itself. The first, bundling, involves linking donors and candidates directly with NRSC assistance. The NRSC does not spend more than the legal amount but provides a critical link for funneling additional funds to candidates by encouraging these NRSC donors to give money to targeted senatorial candidates. Second, the FECA allows national party committees to give (or in the legal sense, transfer) money to state party organizations to spend on efforts that help the party slate generally, though it is often clear what candidate the money will benefit. Last, the NRSC created the Republican Senatorial Inner Circle as a joint fund-raising committee. This entity previously raised funds from high-dollar donors solely for the NRSC. But when the NRSC raised more than it could spend, it redesigned the Inner Circle to maximize candidates' resources.[66]

In the 1990s the CCCs became expert at maximizing the money they had to give to candidates. In 1991 the FEC required full disclosure of soft money expenditures as well as set limits as to how much soft money could be used for party expenses. According to Diana Dwyre, the use of soft money can actually result in a greater net of hard money by allowing many overhead expenses to be absorbed by soft money, leaving more hard money available for direct spending on candidates. Also, the NRCC gave soft money to state parties who in turn made legitimate "hard" contributions to candidates running for the U.S. House.[67]

Now that the committees were working with roughly the same materials and intent, they spent the next few cycles working on making better incumbents. The DSCC expanded its staff under Lloyd Bentsen (D-TX) in 1984 and George Mitchell (D-ME) in 1986. Sen. Alan Cranston (D-CA) helped Bentsen raise funds in 1984 because of his interest in running in the presidential race. The year 1984 was the beginning of a positive turnaround in DSCC fund-raising. When Mitchell took over in 1985 he made a significant effort to develop a professional staff and create a collegial attitude. His efforts and the new majority in 1986 improved the environment at the DSCC and brought more fund-raising success. Mitchell's leadership of the DSCC in the 1986 cycle contributed to his elevation to Senate majority leader in 1988. Sen. John Kerry's (D-MA) leadership of the DSCC improved fund-raising levels even more. In 1989 the DSCC had fifty-five employees and ten interns in four divisions: fund-raising, political, administration, and communications among all Democratic senators.[68]

The NRSC became a formidable fund-raising force under Senators Bob Packwood (second term), Richard Lugar (R-IN), and John Heinz (second term), with a combination of direct mail successes and high-dollar donors. Coelho's behavior at the DCCC became legitimized when the Democratic leadership (at Coelho's insistence) made the DCCC chair position part of its official leadership circle.[69] The NRCC became more specialized, splitting its staff between incumbent and challenger races because, according to former executive director Joseph Gaylord, they were as different as "battleships and sailboats."[70] In addition, all the CCCs, but especially the House committees, offer extensive orientation services for newly elected members to guide them through their critical first reelection. For example, the NRCC's freshman orientation includes seminars on campaigning, advice on hiring staff, and introductions to the PAC community.[71]

Several distinct changes in CCC operations came about because of the FECA. The generation and distribution of funds, as described above, is one. The tailoring of services around stipulations in the law is another. Indeed, the CCCs believed that these new services—campaign finance law information, connections to PACs, schooling in advanced technology such as computers, media, and polling, and connections to consultants—had a profound impact on their candidates. Candidates, however, seem to like money more than services.[72]

Although there is no question that the CCCs became successful at raising money and could contribute substantial sums to certain congressional candidates, these amounts must be taken in the context of the overall increase in the cost of campaigns. For example, the average Republican candididate for an open Senate seat in 1992 spent $2,831,067. The average combined disbursement (both contribution and coordinated expenditures) by the NRSC in open Senate races that year was $505,197. Only direct contributions would count in the Senate candidates' receipts, so each candidate in this instance received an average of $11,759 from the NRSC. The remaining $493,618 was spent by the NRSC on behalf of the candidate. This means that in an average race in which $3,324,685 was spent, the candidate had to raise $2,819,308 apart from the NRSC, or 85 percent of all monies spent on his behalf (see tables A.8, A.9, and A.19). An example from the House Democrats is more striking. Democratic candidates for an open House seat in 1992 spent an average of $478,930, and the DCCC made contributions to such races of $2,453 on average and coordinated expenditures of $13,536. In this case, when $492,466 is spent by the candidate and the DCCC combined, the candidate had to raise $476,477, or 97 percent apart from the DCCC (see tables A.16, A.17, and A.18). This does not include the assistance candidates may get from the CCCs in locating potential funding sources such as PACs, and it does not speak to the concentration of funds in particular races that the CCC considers to be very close (where CCC monetary contributions would then make up a significantly higher percentage of receipts or amounts spent in the race than these averages reveal), but it is easy to see why candidates do not consider the CCC to be decisive in their electoral outcomes, although they remain happy to cash whatever checks are sent.

The FECA also caused an explosion in the campaign industry. Today's consultants, who are now independent players in the election process, frequently were yesterday's CCC service providers. As described above, the CCCs began to offer technically sophisticated services in the early 1980s. Interestingly, as the 1980s progressed, many CCC employees joined specialized consulting firms or started their own organizations. This movement led the NRCC in the 1994 cycle to stop offering a full range of in-house services in favor of subcontracting these services from consultants, many of whom they had a hand in training.

Conclusion: The Invincible Incumbent?

Campaign finance reform permanently changed the activities of the CCCs. Candidates now considered CCCs important sources of money, instead of simple money conduits. However, CCCs also trained a new army of campaign technology providers. The CCCs' strengths remain true to their initial mission: they are creating stronger candidates, both incumbents and challengers, in pursuit of majority status. The task started with incumbents. Throughout the 1980s, the CCCs, especially the NRCC and the DCCC, educated their incumbents on how to stay in office in the face of well-qualified challengers and sophisticated technology. These campaign committees taught themselves how to handle modern-day campaigning and in their mission as protectors of incumbents, forced their constituencies to pay attention. According to Martin Franks (former executive director of the DCCC), DCCC chair Coelho would say to Democratic incumbents, "I love you, but your seat means more to me than you do," as a way to shock them into modernizing their campaign techniques and strategies.[73] CCCs came to occupy a different position in the congressional constellation. When the CCCs were less money oriented they would not have been able to confront the Republican and Democratic incumbents in such an abrupt manner. Instead, as campaigning changed, and continues to change so quickly, incumbents learned that it is in their best interests to be led by the CCCs' technological expertise. Given campaign finance reform, CCCs must service incumbents in a new way, but continue to service them nonetheless. They have found that incumbents who in the past would not have requested much CCC assistance now expect a considerable amount. This leads to an inefficient use of CCC resources, as demonstrated by Gary Jacobson's analysis of CCC spending in the mid-1980s.[74] This has put the minority party CCCs in the position of choosing between pursuing majorities and supporting incumbents.

Large amounts of money were raised and spent by the CCCs in the 1980s and early 1990s, but very few electoral gains or losses were directly attributed to CCC activities. Despite the increasingly larger amounts of money the CCCs can provide, it is still only a fraction of what it costs to run a competitive campaign and tends to come very late in the election cycle. However, the CCCs are considered more important than in the past. This is due to internal congressional party concerns about the need for constant campaigning and fund-raising, which explains more about the CCCs' continued existence and mission than wins and losses after each election cycle. The CCCs adapted to the radically changed congressional campaign environment because the leadership of the four congressional parties wanted them to and not necessarily because their monetary resources were believed to address the new fund-raising demands on candidates due to the FECA. Rather the CCCs were expected to help candidates perform these functions more efficiently for themselves. This also made the CCCs more valuable commodities for congressional leadership ambition. The next chapter considers CCC chairs' careers in detail.

CHAPTER 6

LEADERSHIP AND THE ORGANIZATION OF THE CONGRESSIONAL PARTY
WHERE DOES THE CONGRESSIONAL CAMPAIGN COMMITTEE CHAIR FIT IN?

ALTHOUGH CCCs PERFORM IMPORTANT FUNCTIONS for the congressional party, most lie outside of our traditional conceptions of congressional party leadership activity. Therefore, CCCs have not been discussed much in the literature on Congress. Activities of the congressional party in government, and hence its leadership, are usually described in terms of what is required to get specific laws through the legislative process, and congressional leadership strength is usually seen in the success of legislation with the clear backing of party leaders (i.e., when the congressional party expresses preference homogeneity).[1] The issue of party majority status is taken as a given in these discussions.[2] This means that traditional leadership studies are predominantly "postelectoral," and make only passing mention of the relationship between electoral concerns and leadership actions. Majority status is a fundamental precondition for these analyses.[3]

Such lack of attention to the ongoing project of majority acquisition is not surprising because of the nebulous nature of party campaigning in congressional elections. Working toward majority status is not as linear a process as passing the budget.[4] Though there is an end date for the acquisition of majority status (namely, the day of the general election), there is no one uniform starting date for each congressional district (except to say that one can begin preparing for an election the day after the previous general election—a two-year time frame) and, most problematically, no expectation for a clear return on increments of campaign resource investment. In other words, when working on legislative outcomes, party leaders are in a better position to calculate the concessions that must be made to build a majority vote coalition. Because of the large number of uncontrollable factors related to attaining majority status, party leaders are uncertain about the outcomes associated with the allocation of resources to elections.[5] It is therefore more attractive for leaders to allocate time and resources to dealing with the immediate legislative questions at hand, regardless of whether the party is in the majority or the minority. Hence the role of leadership in legislative activity preoccupies both lawmakers and scholars.

Nevertheless, party leaders and all those who aspire to these positions appreciate the need for a constant pursuit of majority status. Indeed, two things party leaders must do almost simultaneously are argue for the validity of their legislative agenda and campaign for majority status. These roles must occur both inside and outside Washington, D.C., and may at times appear indistinguishable. Leaders, however, do not view them as exactly the same, for policy items may only be won by making points with their colleagues, the president, organized groups, and on occasion with the public, while majority status is in the hands of voters scattered among a handful of marginal congressional districts (with a few surprises on election day) and normally depends on factors determined locally rather than nationally. Party leaders want to head the majority party (and rank-and-file members want to belong to it) for the obvious reason that they wield more power in Washington, D.C., that way. Also, leaders recognize that almost every move they make can influence the public's perception of the majority or its candidates. But party leaders are also interested in securing their positions within their party and realize that they must give members an incentive to continue to support them. Though the literature has thoroughly covered the implications of pork barrel politics, it has been less clear about the leadership's command of campaign resources. To both maintain or attain majority status and secure one's position in the party, leaders must campaign for other members. So campaigning is critical to achieving a governing position both individually and collectively.

The same logic that applies to the creation and maintenance of the CCCs applies to the goals of party leaders: CCCs provide an efficient and centralized vehicle for the coordination of campaign activity. For party leaders, CCCs identify priority races at which their appearance is helpful and assist in fund-raising for the collective use of the congressional party. Thus party leaders have historically had an important role in the operation of the CCCs, usually selecting CCC chairs and often CCC staff. The CCC chair, then, is generally someone known to the party leader but who has volunteered (or been recruited) to take on the task of campaigning over governing as a way to satisfy their ambitions.

This constant interest in majority status is why the congressional parties have always maintained their CCCs, although they have at times been small organizations with little material effect on election outcomes. Still, all four congressional parties want control of the internal structures of Congress, even when their prospects for majority status seem dim. The immediate goal of the CCCs is to maintain incumbents in office. In the case of the majority party, protecting incumbents amounts to pursuing majority status, though as Gary Jacobson points out, majority parties do not believe in the minimum winning coalition concept and therefore will seek to increase their numbers to some degree even though it may be a pointless project.[6] In the minority party, the maintenance of incumbents is crucial to the party's survival; the pursuit of majority status, through the cultivation of challenger or open seat candidates, is an immediate secondary goal. Maintaining incumbents in office is a universal goal of all members of Congress, which is facilitated by each chamber's internal organization in the course of legislative business.[7] Lawmakers want as much access as possible to universal benefits that will improve their reelection prospects, and they

The Connection of CCC Chairs to Party Leadership

The connection between CCCs and leadership is multifaceted. First, the CCCs began in the 1860s, *before* leadership structures were developed and during the time that congressional committees were emerging as powerful individual fiefdoms. Since the late nineteenth century the CCC chair was fairly prominent, since there were few other positions to compete with it. As congressional leadership matured, the CCC position remained but was eclipsed by newly created internal positions. Thus the place of the CCC chair in the four parties' leadership structures is quite sensitive to other changes in the congressional party, reflecting an elision of campaigning needs by increasingly complex legislative needs.

Second, given this environment of leadership expansion and development, we must examine who becomes a CCC chair and what may follow from holding that position. Here we are looking for patterns in the careers of CCC chairs, asking if the CCC chair position attracts a certain type of member, and assessing how the later careers of chairs may have changed because of their CCC experience. Given the histories previously presented, we can hypothesize that CCC chairs believe that their CCC service will lead to a position of higher party leadership. We will look at the extent to which these expectations have been realized.

Third, as the CCCs became full-time, fully professionalized institutions, competition for chair positions became more visible. Brief case studies of CCC contests and leadership contests involving CCC chairs are provided here for all four congressional parties. These case studies highlight what remains the fundamental tension of the CCCs: How aggressively is majority status to be pursued? This is where the tension between pursuit (or expansion) of a majority can conflict with incumbent protection. In the end, the biases of congressional leaders, which lean toward incumbent protection, tend to prevail.

Fourth, the control of CCC chairs by other leaders is considered. Leaders do care about controlling majorities *and* the promises to be made or kept in the course of pursuing majority status. We return then to a discussion of legislative strategy and the CCCs.

The Structure of Leadership in Congress

Members of Congress can lead from a variety of positions. The most prominent are Speaker (in the House), floor leader, and whip. The congressional campaign committee chair is one of several lower-level leadership positions. All of these less prominent positions are widely coveted for the promise they hold for advancement. All warrant research concerning their utility as leadership positions and as training grounds for future leaders. Below I attempt to situate the CCC chair in the congressional party leadership structure.

LEADERSHIP IN THE HOUSE

Leadership positions in the House are more clearly defined than in the Senate because of the greater power individual senators have. In both House parties the leadership structure is extensive and hierarchical. Because of the clear flow of power to the top of the structure, most leadership positions are held by different individuals (this is not the case for the Senate Democrats). The phenomenon of recognizable leadership succession in the House is predominantly a post–World War II development. Clear patterns of succession gradually emerged: first from floor leader to Speaker, then from whip to floor leader.[8] When leadership succession began to occur we see the relationship between the CCC chair and leadership recruitment, as more CCC chairs emerged as potential candidates for an increasing number of leadership contests. (See fig. 1.)

House Democrats

Though the two House parties' leadership structures have more in common with each other than their respective Senate co-

FIG. 1. LEADERSHIP IN THE HOUSE

Speaker (1789)

House Democrats

Floor Leader (mid-nineteenth century)
Congressional Campaign Committee Chair (1868)
Caucus Chair (1910)
Whip (1899, elected 1986)
Zone Whips (1923)
Deputy Whip (1955)
Second Deputy Whip (1970)
Chief Deputy Whip (1973)
Caucus Vice Chair (1986; transformed from Caucus Secretary 1960–86)
Multiple Chief Deputy Whips (1991)
Leadership Advisory Group (1995)
Vice Chairs, Steering and Policy Committee (1995)

House Republicans

Floor Leader (mid-nineteenth century)
Congressional Campaign Committee Chair (1866)
Whip (1897)
Assistant Whips (1931)
Conference Vice Chair (1955)
Conference Secretary (1955)
Policy Committee Chair (1959)
Research Committee Chair (1965)
Chief Deputy Whip (1981)
Second Deputy Whip (1989)
Expanded Whips (1995)

partisans, there are differences in their development and current configuration. In the late nineteenth century House Democrats had a floor leader, but that individual was part of the committee system (usually chair of the Ways and Means Committee) and served at the pleasure of the Speaker (when in the majority). It was not until the overthrow of Speaker Joseph Cannon (R-IL) and the Democrats' return to majority status in 1910 that the Democratic party developed the structure we see today. At that time, the Democrats invested their caucus with the power to elect the floor leader, although the Democratic whip was appointed by the Speaker or floor leader from about 1900 until 1987, when the position became elective by the entire Democratic caucus.[9] The greatest expansion of the House Democratic whip system happened after 1933, with the designation of several assistant whips and a multiplicity of "zone" whips selected by state delegations.[10] The whip system has been the location of the most leadership expansion in the House Democratic party, especially since the reforms of the 1970s, due to myriad institutional and personal factors in rapid succession.[11] Since that time the whip system has been used to satisfy the demands of various factions.

Because the Democrats held a majority in the House from 1955 to 1995, most members wanted access to standing committee assignments so they could take credit for legislative accomplishments. During the reforms of the 1970s the Steering Committee (originally formed in 1933 to take over committee assignments from the Ways and Means Committee), merged with the Policy Committee, a political committee authorized by the Congress to formulate party positions on issues, to create the contemporary Steering and Policy Committee. In 1974 the committee appointment function was shifted entirely to the Steering and Policy Committee, where it had earlier been under the Speaker's authority, transforming both the nature of that institution and the role of leadership in the committee assignment process.[12] The transformation of the Steering and Policy Committee stemmed from the reforms within the House Democratic party to curtail the power of the seniority and committee systems. One consequence was to strengthen the power of formal party leaders. Elected party leaders were (and many argue are) considered more responsive to the rank-and-file who elected them than the more insulated committee chairs who had previously controlled the flow of policy.[13] Today's House Democratic leadership structure has an extensive whip system, consisting of eighty-five House members. Many positions in the whip system have been added recently. In 1995 the leadership again expanded its ranks to help assist the party in regaining majority status.

House Republicans

The floor leader for the House Republicans became an independent position, separate from the chair of the Ways and Means Committee, in 1919. Beginning in 1923 the floor leader has been elected in a meeting of the Republican conference.[14] The first known whip was appointed in 1897, and Republican Speakers or floor leaders continued to appoint whips until 1919. From 1919 to 1965 the Committee on Committees, which also made assignments to the standing committees, selected the whip, subject to conference approval. Since 1965 the whip has been selected by the entire Republican conference. As with the Democrats, the appointment of deputy whips is the prerogative of the whip. Unlike the Democrats, the Republicans had not seen much need to create an extensive whip system until 1995 when they became the majority party. The chief deputy whip position was not established until 1981, following a change in the upper rungs of the leadership ladder.

Randall Ripley believes that House Republicans deliberately sought to give their party a hierarchical chain of command, especially during the mid-1960s. He argues that the leaders (the minority leader, the conference chair, the whip, the chair of the Policy Committee, and the chair of the Research and Planning Committee) thought the minority party should be putting forth alternatives to majority proposals.[15] Since they had not had control for such a long time, they created more policy development positions rather than foster an extensive whip system to keep track of legislative events over which they had limited control. For most of the post–New Deal period, the House Republicans tended to have a more hierarchical leadership structure and more collegiality due to their inability to control the committee structure, marking a significant party culture difference between House Republicans and House Democrats.

LEADERSHIP IN THE SENATE

Although congressional scholars argue that the Senate was institutionalized by the turn of the century, the leadership posts were not well defined until the direct election of senators. Floor leaders had been present since the late nineteenth century, but party whips did not exist as formal positions until 1913 for the Democrats and 1915 for the Republicans.[16] It was not until much later (almost twenty years) that patterns of succession to leadership positions formed, unlike the House, which established patterns of succession from floor leader to Speaker soon after 1910. This reflects the still informal nature of Senate transactions as compared to those in the House. The Senate did have strong leadership, but this smaller body of powerful politicians each with similar experience in public office and more individual power, required less structured leadership than the larger, less professional House. Figure 2 depicts the leadership structures of the two Senate parties. The more intimate and individualistic nature of the Senate has fostered a bipartisan working atmosphere, interfering with the development of strong party leadership.

Senate Democrats

The leadership of the Senate Democrats has been the least hierarchical of all four congressional parties. This is due to the extensive monopoly of power granted to their floor leader. The floor leader of the Senate Democrats chairs the Senate Democratic Conference and the Senate Democratic Policy Committee. Until the 101st Congress (and the change of floor leader from Robert Byrd [D-WV] to George Mitchell [D-ME]), the floor leader also

FIG. 2. LEADERSHIP IN THE SENATE

Senate Democrats

Floor Leader (late nineteenth century)
Whip (1913)
Democratic Senatorial Campaign Committee Chair (1920)
Conference Chair (held by Floor Leader)
Policy Committee Chair (held by Floor Leader)
Steering Committee Chair (separate individual since 1989)
Conference Secretary (1949)
Chief Deputy Whip (1977)
Policy Committee Co-Chair (1989)
Technology and Communications Committee Chair (1995)
Assistant Floor Leader (1995)

Senate Republicans

Floor Leader (late nineteenth century)
Whip (1915)
National Republican Senatorial Committee Chair (1920)
Conference Chair (1949)
Conference Secretary (1949)
Policy Committee Chair (1949)
Committee on Committees Chair (1953)

served as chairman of the Steering Committee, which makes committee assignments.

The structure of the Senate Democratic party invites relatively strong leadership,[17] but this may be because of the abundance of opportunities to lead in the committee system when the Democrats are in the majority. Senate Democrats expanded their ranks to include more members, specifically, chief deputy whip in

1977 and co-chair of the Democratic Policy Committee in 1989. The addition of the Policy Committee co-chair accompanied the separation of the Steering Committee from the majority leader's portfolio. Both changes were made when George Mitchell became majority leader in 1989. When the Senate Democrats again became a minority in 1995, they created two new leadership positions to compensate for the prominence some Senators lost when Republicans gained control of the committee system. Traditionally, Senate Democrats have been able to realize their ambitions just as easily through prime committee positions as through leadership positions, which are relatively scarce in their party.

Senate Republicans

The Republicans followed the Democrats' lead in the creation of a whip and selected their first in 1915.[18] However, they have used this position less consistently than their Democratic counterparts. Because of their small number from 1935 to 1944, the Republicans did not select a whip; instead, various senators performed whip-like functions on an ad hoc basis.[19] After 1944 the whip position quickly developed into an heir apparent's slot for floor leader of the party. The whip position was even renamed assistant floor leader. Since 1949 Senate Republicans have selected different individuals to be conference chair, conference secretary, Policy Committee chair, and NRSC chair. As of 1953 the Committee on Committees was also chaired by someone other than the floor leader. Until the mid-1970s the Senate Republican leader had appointive powers for the Committee on Committees, the Policy Committee, and the NRSC.[20] Today, all these positions are elected by the conference.

The CCC Chair

DEVELOPMENT

The CCCs arose during the development of the strong Speakership and before the first floor leaders were established in the

House. Although the House CCCs have been re-created continuously since 1866, their institutionalization has been a twentieth-century development. The CCCs are officially composed of partisan members of the respective chambers of Congress. The original formula for both House committees specified that there would be one member from each state that had representation from that party in the chamber, though this requirement has not always been strictly adhered to (in fact, the NRCC did away with it entirely in 1993). The membership of the Senate committees depends on a combination of self-selection and leadership appointment. Over time, additional appointees have been added to each of the four committees by their congressional party's leadership.

The chairs of each of the CCCs normally belong to the committee as their state delegation's representative. From the 1860s to the 1940s the chairs were selected four to six months before the regular biennial election. The Senate committees had an informal tradition (now a rule for the Senate Republican Committee) that no senator would chair the committee during the cycle in which he was personally up for reelection. Senate Democrats have sometimes disregarded this concern. This policy accounts for the higher turnover in the chairmanship of the Senate committees relative to the House committees. In the House, some individual chairs held on to the CCC position for a decade or more. Recently, however, both House parties have frowned on long tenures at CCCs and are now championing a two-term limit on CCC chairs.

In the post–World War II congresses, the Democrats of both chambers have considered the CCC chair an appointed position, which the congressional party leadership selects and asks the full committee to ratify. The Senate Democrats have on occasion had elections for the DSCC chair within the full caucus, although the Democratic floor leader has the power to appoint DSCC chairs and tends to do so when no contestants emerge voluntarily. The DCCC chair remains largely a gift of the party leader, who selects the nominee subject to full caucus approval. The

Republicans, however, held some form of vote until 1994, when the Republican Conference decided to adopt the Democrats' tradition and allow the party's leader to appoint a chair,[21] a move intended to bring the position under more direct control of the party leadership.

ATTRACTION

Some say that the CCCs have had little effect on election outcomes (at either the individual or the aggregate level). However, the major intent of the campaign committees from the congressional standpoint is not to win particular elections but to support incumbents and keep peace in the family.[22] Some would say that this statement goes too far, that the CCCs now put a great deal of time and resources into winning additional seats, especially open ones. While the increased activities of CCCs is not disputed, the question of whether they aggressively seek to influence the outcomes of particular races (i.e., pick the candidates themselves or endorse a candidate before the primary election) must be answered in the negative. Indeed, marginality (especially regarding incumbents) is the only truly distinguishing factor in CCC allocation decisions, a revealing fact. There is a strong desire to keep members in the chamber, even though specific individuals' votes may make no material difference in the fate of party-sponsored legislation (i.e., there is nothing to keep them from voting against the party leadership's wishes). In fact, enactment of legislation is not a fundamental consideration in evaluating partisan needs; it is instead the imperatives of congressional organization in the form of majority control of the chamber. The party that has a majority controls the legislative schedule and committee composition. Substantive legislative decisions are structured by these critical organizational variables.

The previous chapters have documented what the CCCs have done to pursue majority control. If the CCCs do not seek ideological purity (either because of potential alienation or because no such thing exists) in determining which candidates to support for reelection, and they are only expected to provide universal perquisites to all party candidates, what is their connection to the congressional party leadership? The duties of CCC chairs allow them to contribute to the sensitive and personal goal of reelection for each member of their party. Learning the constituency concerns of various members gives the chair a rich perspective on the complexity of the congressional party and promotes a personal understanding of individual members' constraints.[23] For these reasons, the CCC chair position serves as a leadership training ground.[24] In the House this position is especially attractive to relatively junior members with the ambition to move on to higher leadership positions but without the legislative experience to move up through the whip system. In the Senate the CCC chair provides other opportunities in the standing committee structure or in exposure to fund-raising opportunities needed for potential presidential primary bids.

CAREER ANALYSIS

Two forms of analyses follow: an examination of the CCC chair position through the tenures of CCC chairs over time and an investigation of the careers of CCC chairs *after* their CCC service. A word about the data collection is in order. To date, ninety-six individuals have been identified as chairs of the CCCs. Unfortunately, there is no one authoritative source on CCC chairs during certain periods. Even contemporary sources contain errors. Consequently, the lists of the chairs were garnered from various archival sources,[25] including records of individual CCC chairs, files of the secretary of the Senate (when available), reports to the clerk of the House of Representatives filed under the Federal Corrupt Practices Act (currently housed at the National Archives), and various sources on the NCs or congressional leadership that occasionally describe particular chairs. The latter sources were not systematic; finding secondary works was a happy accident. The data presented here should be viewed with caution.

I gathered biographical profiles on each of the ninety-six individuals, including their activities leading up to their election to Congress and subsequent appointment as CCC chairs and their careers after serving as CCC chairs. The analysis of how members are recruited to be a CCC chair is important to understanding the congressional party, but it is not the main focus here. This analysis focuses on the fate of CCC chairs after their CCC service.

Tables A.2 through A.5 show the tenure of each CCC chair. The information includes how many cycles each served at the CCC, how long each served in the House or Senate before becoming chair,[26] the number of years each served in the chamber after CCC service, age at becoming chair, the total number of years in the chamber, and the individual's next formal career after CCC service.

As Congress matured and individuals launched full-time congressional careers, leadership positions should have become more coveted, as ambitious politicians were drawn to Congress to satisfy their career aspirations.[27] Here, David T. Canon's interpretation of the institutionalization of leadership is applied to my investigation of the development of the CCC chair position.[28] Canon's analysis uses the whip's position in all four congressional parties to assess the degree of party institutionalization (a term he adopts from Nelson W. Polsby).[29] For Canon, institutionalization of leadership institutions is assessed by examining institutional durability, institutional boundaries (nonpermeable career structures), internal complexity, and universalistic practices. Though Canon's theory is meant to explain the development of a leadership career ladder, he recognizes that individual leaders have significant impacts on their positions and thus the shape of the entire party leadership structure. Canon states, "This link between durability, internal complexity, and the boundedness of leadership can be presented as a hypothesis: leaders are promoted if they maintain and develop their current positions. If a leader is ineffective in using the current office, it is not likely to become a springboard for higher office."[30] Using Canon's analysis as a guide, the integration of the CCC chair into the leadership structure is examined.

In assessing the boundedness of the CCC chair position, I am particularly interested in whether the time spent in the chamber before CCC tenure increased or decreased, whether the chairs were younger or older than their predecessors, and how the length of their careers compared. Table 6.1 provides summary statistics from the detailed information in tables A.2 through A.5. The averages are collapsed into the time periods corresponding to the chapters describing CCC activities. During the first period, 1866–1920, formal leadership positions were not well developed. Here, members serve relatively few terms as CCC chair and do so after serving about three terms in the House. The second period, 1920–72, includes the beginning of the development of leadership positions. In both House CCCs the number of cycles chairs serve increases (in the case of the DCCC, one outlier, Michael Kirwan, skews all the averages), as does the number of years served in the chamber before becoming a CCC chair and the total length of the congressional career. This indicates a general trend in the professionalization of Congress. The average age of the NRCC chair becomes younger while the DCCC chair gets older. Those who become NRCC chairs serve in the House for fewer years than do Democrats, which also follows from their shorter overall careers until the 1990s. The Democrats' long-standing majority status, electoral stability in many regions, and strong reliance on seniority for advancement accounts for the differences with their Republican counterparts. The post-reform period, 1974–96, finds younger chairs who have had careers of a length comparable to their predecessors, reflecting the growing tendency to view Congress as a primary career goal.

The Senate CCC figures are startling for their stability. In both parties and both time periods senatorial CCC chairs serve relatively few cycles early in their careers. That there is so little change in senatorial CCC service compared to House CCC service shows both that Senate leadership is very fluid and that CCC positions may be coveted because of their scarcity. On average, Senators serve over half their first six-year term before

Table 6.1
Average Careers for CCC Chairs

	Average Cycles Served[a]	Average Years before CCC	Average Years after CCC	Average Age	Average Career (years)
NRCC	**2.5**	**6.9**	**4.3**	**51.5**	**16.0**
1866–1920	2.0	5.3	2.3	54.3	11.2
1920–72	2.9	8.4	6.9	49.8	21.1
1974–96	3.3	8.3	4.8	47.3	18.8[b]
DCCC	**3.1**	**11.6**	**2.9**	**50.9**	**19.8**
1870–1920	1.9	8.0	4.4	47.0	16.0
1920–72	6.0	15.5	2.7	56.3	27.0
1974–96	2.2	13.2	1.0	51.3	18.2[b]
NRSC	**1.3**	**5.8**	**6.3**	**52.3**	**15.2**
1920–72	1.4	4.7	6.5	54.4	14.5
1974–96	1.3	7.2	6.1	49.3	16.2[b]
DSCC	**1.4**	**4.7**	**10.8**	**52.9**	**18.8**
1920–72	1.4	5.5	12.5	54.4	19.5[b]
1974–96	1.4	3.2	7.3	50.1	13.9[b]

[a] Average cycle can mean as much as 2 years service or, as in 1868, only 6 months.
[b] Many members still serving. Calculated through 1996.

chairing a CCC. Many scholars of the Senate contend that the informal nature of the Senate retards well-bounded leadership structures. Although a few members left the chamber immediately after CCC service, the remainder either pursued leadership opportunities or returned to regular member responsibilities. Canon calls these groups "ladder climbers" and "dabblers," respectively.[31] Generally, the CCC chair position has not been particularly well bounded in either chamber, though especially not in the Senate. It is still not unusual for relatively junior members to assume this position, although in recent decades it is likely that CCC service will lead to some perceptible reward. So although the qualifications to become CCC chair remain unspecified, appreciation by the leadership for a CCC chair's job well done is rather well established.

As previously stated, the congressional party leadership desires majority status. However, leaders cannot personally commit daily resources to this pursuit since the administration of the legislative agenda demands much of their time. So the leadership wants the CCC chair to be one who has the necessary skills to campaign for a wide variety of members, both present and potential. This usually means that the CCC chair is not known as a particularly ideological member, although there have been exceptions.[32] Also, unlike other key leadership positions, the CCC chair does not demand a high level of legislative skill but rather a high level of political skill, something that can be acquired without long congressional experience. Key leaders can monitor or control the actions of the CCCs since the leaders themselves are the principal political capital for the CCCs (in terms of fund-raising and appearances). So if CCC chair activity is deemed inappropriate or ineffective, the leadership may withhold their support of the CCC and pursue majority election goals independently, circumvent CCC chairs, or replace them entirely. This has seldom been necessary as CCC chairs are chosen with considerable care. Certainly the performance of the CCC chair (or the perceived performance) in political skill and fund-raising has formed the basis of judgment for leadership advancement from the CCC position in both chambers. These skills, not electoral gains or losses, are what matter.

It is difficult to ascertain why certain members advance their careers while others do not. Burdett Loomis explains that "as with most steps up the political ladder, advancing into the legislative leadership includes elements of self-starting from below as well as being tapped from above."[33] The current leaders generally want to be succeeded by members like themselves, and they will therefore seek lieutenants from whom they expect loyalty. Since the primary allegiance of members of Congress is to their constituents and not to their congressional party, the party's formal leaders in Congress typically lack disciplined party followers. Still, leadership is necessary for the congressional parties to maintain identities separate from the presidential parties and is especially important if their party does not control the White House.

Attempting to predict which of the many members of Congress will become formal leaders of their parties is very difficult because of the multiple factors at work. Robert Peabody has characterized the variables that explain leadership succession and leadership contests, but this schema applies only after the contestants have emerged.[34] Those who have studied leadership recruitment have also focused on voting behavior, the so-called middleman hypothesis. According to David Truman, only members who demonstrate moderate opinions in voting within their party win leadership positions. More recent studies have challenged this claim. William Sullivan suggests that party-supporting voting behavior *before* leadership ascension is not a consideration for selecting leaders. Once leadership is assumed, a more moderate stance in voting is usually adopted.[35] Roll call voting alone is obviously not a reliable indicator of leadership ascension. If we acknowledge that campaigning is a critical facet of governing, then potential leaders must demonstrate a commitment to the electoral concerns of fellow members, an ability to articulate the party's governing agenda, and a willingness and talent to mobilize scarce electoral resources. Below, the fates of the CCC chairs are categorized by their next position. The results do show that the CCC is a proving ground for potential leaders rather than a secure, well-bounded leadership position.

CAREER MOVES

The CCC chair position often produces high-ranking formal party leaders, though such career promotion is hardly automatic. Most CCC chairs do not become members of the formal leadership. The argument is that the CCC post serves as either a screening tool for potential leadership talent or a reward for service to the leadership or one's colleagues. Its value as a screening tool is that it is one position (among others) from which prospects can be observed. There are a variety of reasons why CCC chairs may not move up, some of which reinforce the utility of the CCC post as a training ground. It may be better to know the stamina and limits of potential leaders before they take on more responsibility for the congressional party's fate. Winning leadership positions in the U.S. Congress is not like winning public office; one must demonstrate the ability to manage an unwieldy congressional party.

What happened to the ninety-six chairs after they headed a CCC? Five members died in office, and sixteen were not reelected (this includes both primary and general election defeats). As leadership studies explain, a safe district is a highly desirable requirement for formal leadership. Therefore, individuals must demonstrate their ability to continue in office by consistently winning reelection with comfortable electoral margins. Obviously, losing reelection excludes one from continuous leadership service, so CCC chairs who lost reelection were eliminated as leadership prospects. Senators in this category lost their elections at the next regular election after their CCC tenure rather than while they were chair, since the policy has been to exclude from the CCC chair senators who were up for reelection. Many of the losing CCC chairs went down in years that were costly for the party generally: Republican defeats in 1932, 1934, 1936, and 1974 and Democratic defeats in 1980 were common because of other structural factors in the American political context. The leadership may not have erred in choosing these individuals, since such catastrophic political events cannot easily be prevented, only mitigated at best.

Of course, others may not have moved up the career ladder after CCC leadership for personal reasons. One may leave Congress voluntarily. Twelve CCC chairs retired or sought higher office after their service. These individuals chose not to wait for an opportunity to progress into the leadership of their chambers. Instead, they sought other legislative positions (i.e., the U.S. Senate) or positions with the presidential administration, or chose to leave Congress. Most of the chairs in this category left Congress before 1920. Only one, Wayne Hays, left after the FECA, and that was because personal scandal forced him to resign.

Five CCC chairs became chair of their party's NC as a consequence of their CCC experience. This shows how the potential fluidity of party organization can encourage the national committees to look to successful CCC operations for cues and potential personnel. However, the relatively small number of cases does not permit extrapolation. Some additional cases deserve further attention. Rep. Joseph Martin chaired the RNC while serving as House minority leader in 1940 (after his successful service as CCC chair in 1938), and Sen. Thruston Morton was chair of the RNC (while a sitting senator) before he chaired the NRSC in 1964 and 1966. (After leaving Congress, Tony Coelho became a major adviser and fund-raiser for the DNC because of his DCCC successes.)

What of those who did succeed to higher leadership positions, or those who believed they could? Tables 6.2 and 6.3 demonstrate the CCCs' relationship to leadership. We may conclude that it is more than coincidence that twenty-four former CCC chairs became congressional leaders. Several of the CCC chairs in table 6.2, such as Martin, Halleck, Dirksen, Mitchell, and Coelho—were quite direct about their ambitions. Others, such as Clements, Ford, and Fazio, already had other leadership duties and their CCC position demonstrated a service obligation to the party.

It is also interesting to consider those CCC chairs who attempted other leadership posts and were unsuccessful. Five individuals named in table 6.3 made their unsuccessful attempt for a leadership position immediately after their tenure at a CCC, and all of them made their attempts since 1968.[36] The perception that service at a CCC warranted a leadership bid is a significant finding in the matter of leadership recruitment. It means that CCC chairs expect that their activities will be rewarded by the congressional parties at large. These twenty-nine individuals, both successful and unsuccessful leadership aspirants, clearly saw themselves as leadership "ladder climbers." There are some remaining individuals who cannot be as easily categorized. Of course, the four individuals who are currently serving as chairs have yet to see what CCC service may do for their careers.

The remaining twenty-six individuals did not achieve (or attempt) formal leadership positions immediately after their tenure at a CCC. They also did not depart Congress soon after their CCC tenure. At this point we must consider some special options for senators. Because of the lack of leadership options and the relatively powerful position of each senator without regard to leadership status, we may look for other motivations for Senate CCC chairs. One possibility is that a senator may have presidential aspirations and wish to use the CCC chair to explore fund-raising opportunities in other parts of the country. Four senators are known to have used the CCC to explore the viability of their own potential presidential candidacy: Republicans Barry Goldwater and Phil Gramm and Democrats Charles Robb and Robert Kerrey (who is also cited as a current chair as of this writing). Another option is to use service at the CCC as leverage for desirable committee assignments. In recent years both the Finance and the Appropriations committees were cited as desirable enough to persuade senators to head the CCC in return for future assignment to them. Two senators, Democrats John Breaux

Table 6.2
CCC Chairs Who Rose in Leadership Ranks

Committee	Cycles at CCC	Leadership Position	State	Name
DCCC	1869–70	Speaker	Pennsylvania	Rep. Samuel Randall
	1898–1902	Minority leader	Tennessee	Rep. James Richardson
	1902–08	Ways and Means	Georgia	Rep. James M. Griggs
	1924–26	Minority whip	Arkansas	Rep. William Oldfield
	1928–34	Majority leader	Tennessee	Rep. J. W. Byrns, Sr.
	1970–72	Majority whip	Massachusetts	Rep. Thomas P. O'Neill
	1982–86	Majority whip	California	Rep. Tony Coelho
	1992–94	Caucus chair	California	Rep. Vic Fazio
NRCC	1938	Minority leader	Massachusetts	Rep. Joseph Martin
	1944–46	Majority leader	Indiana	Rep. Charlie Halleck
	1974	Minority whip	Illinois	Rep. Bob Michel
	1994–96	Chair, Speaker's Advisory Group	New York	Rep. Bill Paxon
DSCC	1934	Minority whip	Illinois	Sen. James H. Lewis
	1946–48	Minority whip	Illinois	Sen. Scott Lucas
	1952–54	Democratic whip	Kentucky	Sen. Earle Clements

Table 6.2 (continued)
CCC Chairs Who Rose in Leadership Ranks

Committee	Cycles at CCC	Leadership Position	State	Name
	1955–60	Secretary, Democratic Conference	Florida	Sen. George Smathers
	1978–82	Majority whip	Kentucky	Sen. Wendell Ford
	1986	Majority leader	Maine	Sen. George Mitchell
	1990	Chief deputy whip	Louisiana	Sen. John Breaux
NRSC	1951–55	Minority whip	Illinois	Sen. Everett Dirksen
	1970	Chair, Policy Committee	Texas	Sen. John Tower
	1976	Republican whip	Alaska	Sen. Ted Stevens
	1978, 1982	Chair, Republican Conference	Oregon	Sen. Bob Packwood
	1990	Chair, Policy Committee	Oklahoma	Sen. Don Nickles

Table 6.3
CCC Chairs Who Were Unsuccessful Leadership Contestants

Committee	Cycles at CCC	Position Attempted	State	Name
DCCC	1987–90	Majority whip June 1989	Arkansas	Rep. Beryl Anthony
NRCC	1975–92	Minority leader December 1980	Michigan	Rep. Guy Vander Jagt
DSCC	1967–68	Majority whip (aborted)	Maine	Sen. Edmund Muskie
NRSC	1983–84	Majority leader 1984	Indiana	Sen. Richard Lugar
	1979–81 1985–86	Conference chair 1980	Pennsylvania	Sen. John Heinz

and Bob Graham, may have negotiated this trade (Breaux also became chief deputy whip). This connection should be viewed with some caution as seniority is a strong norm in the Senate when committee assignments are considered, and the CCC connection could be entirely spurious.

The remaining twenty-two chairs returned to regular roles and may have been leadership "dabblers," or informal leaders.[37] Interestingly, eighteen of these CCC chairs served in the Senate and only four in the House. Thirteen of the eighteen senators are Democrats, confirming that the options for leadership are extremely limited for Senate Democrats.[38] It is also entirely possible that some of these members failed to impress the party leaders during their CCC tenures and had no choice but to return to so-called ordinary status in the chamber. That many of these individuals rose to prominent committee leadership or became informal leaders perhaps shows only that they lacked effective campaigning skills.

What Chairs Expect

Since we are considering the CCCs to be leadership positions with potential for career advancement in the leadership structure, we can assume that members want to be CCC chairs for the power, influence, and exposure that the position carries with it. The way in which these benefits manifest themselves may differ by chamber (internal leadership for the House, presidential potential for senators). Because CCCs provide other members with scarce Washington resources, many may be grateful for CCC assistance. The counterposition is not likely. That is, candidates who believe CCCs helped them too little, or accuse them of inadequate service, tend not to be election winners. Although members may see CCC help as insignificant, they rarely see it as harmful. At worst, it is irrelevant. Also, if the election is a success, the CCC chair can claim some credit. At the same time, if there is a loss, it is easy for the CCC chair to avoid blame. This is because electoral loss is usually considered a collective or individual (candidate) problem: either the party's fortunes nationally were dim or the individual candidate failed in some way. CCCs are rarely considered to bear primary responsibility for a loss, although leaders have chastised them for not paying more attention to surprise winners. The CCC chair is also an easier position for relatively junior members to attain.[39] It requires no parliamentary finesse, only raw political skill and loyalty to the existing leadership. Lack of either of these qualities can lead to quick replacement.

The case studies below demonstrate the utility of the CCC chair as a leadership training ground and explore the leadership value of the CCC position in its own right. It is clear that a leadership connection exists between the CCC chair and the congressional leadership and that this connection has been more overt in recent years because of the attention the FECA drew to the fund-raising power of the CCCs. Since campaigning is now recognized as a constant need, CCC chairs have a more solid claim to centrality in the life of the congressional party. When CCC chairs were picked just a few months before an election, even they knew their work was less central to the party than that of legislative managers. Now that the FECA and modern campaign technologies mandate a perpetual campaign apparatus, CCC chairs are chosen simultaneously with other leadership positions immediately after biennial elections. As the case studies below show, some CCC chairs have convinced the congressional party that their campaign experience qualifies them to move into legislative leadership positions.

Case Studies

The NRCC: 1975–Present

Guy Vander Jagt became NRCC chair when a vacancy occurred in 1975 after Bob Michel, chair for the 1974 cycle, was named minority whip. A contest developed among three candidates: Vander Jagt (R-MI), Pierre "Pete" du Pont (R-DE), and John Rousselot (R-CA). Vander Jagt won on a second ballot vote because he was perceived to be the most moderate of the three candidates.⁴⁰ There were clear ideological delineations. Rousselot was a member of the John Birch Society, and DuPont was considered to be the liberal candidate. Vander Jagt says that he was drafted to run precisely because there was so much ideological room, and many Republicans preferred a moderate in the post. He held this position from 1975 to 1992, when he lost his own primary, an unusually long tenure for any of the four CCC posts. Vander Jagt oversaw a financial revitalization of the post–FECA NRCC and was able to provide significant financial assistance to candidates in the 1978 and 1980 elections.

Vander Jagt's success at the NRCC prompted him to challenge Michel for the vacant minority leader position following the 1980 elections. Minority leader John Rhodes (R-AZ) announced his plans to retire from Congress and not seek reelection in 1980. This meant there would be new leadership of the House Republicans after the 1980 elections and potentially many new faces among their ranks. Michel had been House minority whip since Vander Jagt had been NRCC chair and had developed a reputation as a good parliamentarian who could engineer compromises on the House floor. Vander Jagt, by contrast, was more of an outsider. His public speaking tours and appeals nationwide on behalf of the Republican party were applauded but at the same time were thought to have precluded opportunities for him to develop legislative skills.⁴¹ The candidates appealed to different segments of the House Republican party. Michel, a member since 1956, courted and received the support of the more senior Republicans who appreciated his skills at bipartisan negotiation and were less likely to value the campaign assistance Vander Jagt provided. Vander Jagt, first elected ten years later, looked for support from those who benefited from his leadership at the NRCC since the mid-1970s. Most of these junior members *did* support Vander Jagt, but their numbers were not enough.⁴²

Michel's victory surprised few; that he won by a modest margin, 103 to 87, did come as a surprise. Vander Jagt returned to the NRCC, where he remained chair without contest until 1990. After surviving that challenge, he served through his own election defeat in the 1992 primary. After Vander Jagt's challenge to Michel, the two men had an uneasy relationship. Without the challenge, the two might have complimented each other, as Michel enjoyed legislative strategy and Vander Jagt thrived on campaign politics.[43]

Until 1990, NRCC chairmanship contests, bitter as they were, took place only when the position was vacant.[44] In the 1990 contest a sitting chairman faced a challenge. Given Vander Jagt's overall success as NRCC chair, we must wonder why he was challenged by four-term Rep. Don Sundquist (R-TN). Two events proved critical: Minority whip Newt Gingrich's position in opposition to President Bush's 1990 budget compromise package, and NRCC co-chair Ed Rollins's advice to Republican congressional candidates on how to react to it.

Ed Rollins's role is critical. He had a long career as a political consultant, having worked as adviser to President Reagan and as a top manager in the Reagan-Bush reelection effort in 1984. After the 1988 elections Vander Jagt brought Rollins to the NRCC because he thought it needed some reorganization. The size of Rollins's salary and his high visibility became controversial. Vander Jagt thought this a small price to pay for Rollins's professionalism.

Meanwhile, battle lines were being drawn in the House over the budget. In June 1990 President Bush indicated that he might abandon his "no new taxes" pledge, featured prominently in the 1988 elections, to obtain a favorable budget deal with the Democratic leadership. Many rank-and-file Republicans felt that they had been ignored in the decision-making process and that even worse, they had been left echoing the president's "no new taxes" pledge in the face of an election year when Bush was ready to abandon it with little consequence. As a result, minority whip Newt Gingrich led a crusade against the president's plan.

The budget issue began to have an effect in the electoral arena. Louisiana's fourth district was the critical election. Louisiana has an unusual electoral system: the candidates of all parties for any given office run in the fall of an election year (in 1990, it was on

October 6). The candidate who wins an absolute majority of the votes wins the seat and does not need to compete in the general election in November. If no candidate receives a majority, the two candidates with the highest numbers of votes run against each other in the general election. Therefore, it was prudent for the NRCC to try to achieve Republican victories in these primary races. Rep. Jim McCreary (R-LA) was a freshman who won his seat by just 1,376 votes in 1988. McCreary and the NRCC were understandably nervous about this campaign.

On October 4, two days before the Louisiana primary and the morning of the vote on the president's budget, McCreary had still not decided which way to go. Rollins at the NRCC suggested that McCreary vote against the president's budget plan and reiterate his support for no new taxes, even if the president himself had reneged. The NRCC worked with the campaign to create ads that highlighted McCreary's opposition to President Bush.[45] McCreary won the race with a comfortable 55 percent of the vote. His success was exciting for the NRCC, and they decided to recommend the same strategy to other candidates in close races. This way, they could remain true to previous campaign promises and capitalize on the current anti-Washington sentiment. Rollins decided to write a memo to this effect and to circulate it among Republican House candidates whose victories were the central concern of the NRCC. President Bush responded by publicly demanding the resignation of Ed Rollins.[46]

There was only one problem: Bush was not Rollins's employer. Bush thought he could count on Vander Jagt's support, believing that Vander Jagt would realize that the Republican party should not be moving in two directions at once. But Vander Jagt had worked hard to get Rollins on board, and he had an obligation to win elections for House Republicans. Consequently, when Bush and Vander Jagt met shortly after the Rollins memo was made public, the result was not what the president would have wished. According to the *Washington Post*, "The president did not directly demand Rollins's resignation, but did tell Rep. Guy Vander Jagt (Mich.), chairman of the NRCC, that it would be impossible to work with the committee as long as Rollins was dispensing such advice. Vander Jagt reported that he was 'black and blue' from the meeting."[47]

Since Bush could not sway Vander Jagt, the Washington press corps speculated that the White House's strategy was to find someone else who would fire Rollins. To do that, someone who would vow to fire Rollins would have to mount a leadership challenge to Vander Jagt. Don Sundquist of Tennessee, a longtime Bush supporter, decided to challenge Vander Jagt. The timing, just a week before the 1990 elections, brought the beginning of what would be five weeks of exaggerated allegations. The perception that Sundquist was Bush's foot soldier hurt him greatly. Newt Gingrich's role in the contest also proved decisive. Since Gingrich led the forces against the Bush budget, which in turn brought about the Rollins memo, it was logical that Gingrich would support Vander Jagt. As it turned out, Gingrich not only supported Vander Jagt, he was considered one of his campaign managers.

The leadership votes took place on December 3, 1990. Vander Jagt had the support of the minority leader, Bob Michel, as well as Gingrich. The unofficial report of the vote was 98 to 66, indicating that Vander Jagt did have the firm support he claimed. Nevertheless, the 66 votes that Sundquist received indicated substantial displeasure.

In a personal interview conducted after the leadership vote, Vander Jagt listed five variables that he believed made him especially vulnerable to a challenge in 1990: (1) the NRCC's decision to eliminate automatic contributions to members; (2) a general mood in the country that it was time for a change; (3) the fact that Republicans had not gained seats in the last several elections; (4) the multifaceted Rollins factor; and (5) opposition to Gingrich.[48] The first variable is quite interesting, as no mention had been made of it in press reports. Both Vander Jagt and Sundquist confirmed that automatic contributions to incumbents were at an all-time low. That the size of automatic contributions to incumbents dwindled steadily during the 1980s probably caused many congressmen to wonder what, if any, utility the NRCC could have if it did not aid their reelection efforts. This suggests a preference for incumbent protection over majority pursuit. Vander Jagt's second and third variables are hardly unique to this particular race, but the last two are. As Vander Jagt described it, the Rollins factor cut two ways: those who were irritated by his attack against the president and those who were irritated by his attack against them. The circumstances for the first attitude have been described. The second stems from a lead quote by Rollins in a feature article in the *Washington Post*: "I hate this place. I hate my job. I hate congressmen. I hate candidates."[49] It appears that the NRCC's co-chair had managed to alienate a wide variety of congressmen within the congressional party. Last, Vander Jagt named the Gingrich factor, saying that some members believed that Gingrich's fervent support of Vander Jagt suggested an attempt by Gingrich to control all of the leadership positions. Perhaps this sentiment was not misguided. Gingrich had always been involved with NRCC affairs since his own election in 1978 and had a good working relationship with Vander Jagt.

After Vander Jagt's defeat in 1992, Bill Paxon won the NRCC post without contest. Since Paxon became chair, the NRCC has changed its by-laws to make the chair an appointee of the Speaker. Perhaps this was to avoid battles like that in 1990. For now, NRCC chairs are appointed for terms lasting two election cycles. Paxon was reappointed by Gingrich in 1996, and John Linder of Georgia now leads the NRCC for the 1998 cycle (and presumably for 2000 as well).

The DCCC: 1980–Present

The circumstances of Tony Coelho's assumption of the DCCC chairmanship are reminiscent of those of Vander Jagt's. Coelho's predecessor, Jim Corman (D-CA), had been a low-profile chair and was in jeopardy of losing his own seat in the 1980 elections. When Corman did lose, the DCCC was in a demoralized state. Though the party leadership had overseen its operations since the FECA,⁵⁰ the DCCC had not raised tremendous sums of money. But neither the DCCC's sluggishness compared to the NRCC nor Corman's defeat worried House Democrats as much as the overall results of the 1980 elections. When Ronald Reagan won the White House, he was joined by thirty-five new Republicans in the House and a Republican majority in the Senate. Although these numbers were not sufficient to rob the Democrats of actual control of the House of Representatives, the Democratic leadership felt that they had lost philosophical and political control of the House agenda and they feared that the 1982 elections might bring further erosion of liberal Democrats' power.⁵¹

The Democratic leadership, specifically Speaker Tip O'Neill and the majority leader, Jim Wright, interviewed several members for the vacant DCCC slot. Coelho said that he would raise $5 million, double what the DCCC raised in 1980 if made DCCC chair.⁵² Despite his youth and relative inexperience as a second-term member, the leadership was willing to take a chance on Coelho. He headed the DCCC for the 1982, 1984, and 1986 cycles.

When asked why he wished to be DCCC chair, Coelho responded that it was the best way for him to get power for his constituency quickly. Coelho was elected in 1978, replacing B. F. Sisk (for whom Coelho had worked as chief of staff), who was a member of the powerful Rules Committee. Coelho believed that going from a powerful Rules member to a freshmen member would be a big loss in prestige for his district. So he figured that devoting his efforts to fund-raising on behalf of other Democrats would give him better access to important players. Coelho raised funds aggressively for President Carter's reelection effort, as well as for DCCC chair Corman's own House race and for Jim Wright. As a result, Corman suggested Coelho as his replacement at the DCCC after the 1980 elections.⁵³

When Coelho obtained this position, which he received much earlier in his career than he would have any other legislative leadership position, he ran the DCCC as a real competitor to

Vander Jagt's NRCC. In a dramatic shift from previous practices, Coelho ran the DCCC like a business. Fund-raising became a central priority for the DCCC, and substantial efforts were made to approach high-dollar donors, to cultivate direct mail small-money donors, and to press the PAC community for support. Coelho made significant inroads with the PAC community, especially with business interests, for both hard and soft money donations. Coelho was able to do this by reminding these PACs that Democrats controlled all the important committees in the House and assuring them access in return for their support. Coelho even set up weekly meetings with important lobbyists and key committee chairs.[54] This meant that the DCCC was in a position to shore up incumbents in the 1982 cycle, a year in which the Republicans met with significant losses. As a result of that victory, Coelho got attention from his fellow partisans and the news media. This put him in a stronger political position, which he used to insist that the DCCC be made into an official leadership position in the Democratic leadership circle. The DCCC chair officially became the fifth position on the leadership ladder and held a slot on the Steering and Policy Committee, which among other duties makes committee assignments. This leadership designation remains in effect today. Coelho also makes no secret of the fact that rumors of Tip O'Neill's impending retirement after the 1986 elections piqued his interest in running for higher leadership positions. Though he briefly toyed with the idea of running for majority leader (against the majority whip, Thomas Foley), he ultimately decided to pursue the whip position and joined the movement to change it from an appointed to an elected position, since he believed himself more likely to become whip if it was chosen by rank-and-file members rather than by party leaders.[55] Coelho easily won over two other candidates after the 1986 election. According to Lynne Brown and Robert Peabody, Coelho's win over Charles Rangel and Bill Hefner was in large part due to his DCCC service.[56] In addition to his successful fund-raising efforts and campaign advice, Coelho was credited with great understanding of the political problems of individual members. This was considered a good skill for a successful whip, although some thought such knowledge came more from DCCC staff efforts than Coelho himself. Though there were charges that Coelho lacked parliamentary skills because of his emphasis on campaign work (a similar charge made against Vander Jagt in 1981), Coelho overcame this hesitation in his resounding victory, reminding us that campaigning skills are viewed as a dimension of legislative skills.

Coelho's successor at the DCCC was Beryl Anthony (D-AR). Anthony, a successful fund-raiser, was anxious for the position. He was chosen by Speaker-elect Jim Wright over two others: Dennis Eckart of Ohio and Vic Fazio of California (Fazio would later chair the DCCC for the 1992 and 1994 cycles).[57] Although Anthony had a reputation as an excellent fund-raiser, no campaign talent could have compensated for the double catastrophe of having the Speaker of the House (Wright) and the majority whip (Coelho) resign their seats at the same time.[58] As a result of those resignations, several leadership positions opened up, including the whip position which Anthony made a run for. Anthony was upset at his dismal showing in the 1989 Democratic whip's race in which he believed he was due the same consideration Coelho had enjoyed and announced his intention to resign shortly thereafter.

By February 1990 the word was out that the new Speaker, Tom Foley (D-WA), was interviewing candidates for Anthony's replacement. Many complained that the demands associated with chairing the CCC were not worth the potential benefits, thinking they would have to sacrifice attention to legislative duties (as Coelho did) to maximize DCCC opportunities.[59] Such a gamble was not attractive to many Democrats who became socialized to the House's emphasis on legislative work. Though Vic Fazio was ultimately named DCCC chair for the 1992 and 1994 election cycles, he was a reluctant convert who had lost his earlier zeal for the position. However, Speaker Foley was set on Fazio and in an unusual move, agreed to allow Fazio to serve as vice chair of the Democratic Caucus while he was chairing the

DCCC.⁶⁰ Although Fazio chaired the DCCC during one of the worst election cycles ever (the Democrats lost fifty-two seats and control of the House of Representatives in 1994), he was promoted subsequently to chair of the Democratic Caucus. Rep. Martin Frost (D-TX) was named as his replacement for the 1996 cycle and continues for the 1998 cycle.

The NRSC: 1978–Present

Sen. Robert Packwood (R-OR) twice served as chair of the NRSC. The first time was for the 1978 election cycle, when he was credited with making the NRSC a meaningful money-raising vehicle. In 1979 Packwood was elected chair of the Republican Conference, a position he relinquished to run for the NRSC chair in 1981 for the 1982 cycle. Sen. Robert Dole (R-KS) campaigned against Packwood for the NRSC position then but dropped out of the race at the last minute.⁶¹ Packwood's victory left a vacancy for the conference chair position, and a contest developed between Sen. James McClure (R-ID) and the outgoing NRSC chair, Sen. John Heinz (R-PA). McClure soundly beat Heinz 33 to 20. Despite Heinz's fund-raising successes at the NRSC, he was thought to be aloof, and his personal wealth was seen as a potential political problem.⁶²

So Packwood again chaired the NRSC for the 1982 election cycle. The circumstances this time were very different. In 1978 the Senate Republicans had been in the minority for more than two decades. In 1982 they had been in the majority for two years. Understandably, senators were interested in what their campaign chairman might do (this is especially so since Senator Heinz, who chaired the NRSC in 1980, was credited with raising enough funds to enable the NRSC to provide some useful services and contributions). They were also understandably interested in the tensions that developed between Packwood and (then-popular) President Ronald Reagan.

The tensions started when Packwood said that Reagan had an "idealized concept of America" that was making it impossible for the Republican party to reach out to women, blacks,

Hispanics, and Jews in the midterm elections.[63] Though Packwood later apologized for the remark, he made it clear that he still believed it to be true and planned campaign strategies for Republican senatorial candidates that excluded Reagan or references to him. As a result the White House insisted that a fund-raising letter bearing Reagan's signature not be mailed, a move that cost the NRSC a considerable amount of potential income as well as expenses for production costs.[64] Also, the White House approached the Senate majority leader, Howard Baker, with the idea that Packwood ought to be ousted from the NRSC. This strategy was articulated publicly by former Reagan aide Lyn Nofziger: "If the Republican majority in the U.S. Senate want to keep their majority they ought to get themselves a new chairman."[65] Despite this pressure, Baker would not make any moves to eliminate Packwood. The Republican party in the Senate at that time was less concerned about Reagan's feelings than about retaining a majority. Packwood's poll data were clear: Reagan's America was perceived as insensitive, especially as the recession progressed. Knowing that midterm losses were common, the Republican senators chose not to capitulate to the pressure. Ultimately, Baker and the White House chief of staff, James Baker, worked out a truce: Packwood would stop criticizing the president (while continuing to vote his conscience in the Senate) and Reagan would sign a new fund-raising letter for the NRSC.[66]

Though the campaign continued without further public rifts, this episode was not forgotten. The Republicans held on to their majority after the 1982 elections. Still, rather than retain Packwood as NRSC chair, Sen. Richard Lugar (R-IN) ran for the post with White House encouragement. He won the contest against Packwood and chaired the NRSC for the 1984 campaign. Whether Lugar would have sought this post regardless of Reagan's feelings is unknown. The vote was close, 29 to 25, and probably reflects a more conservative shift in the Senate rather than an explicit rejection of Packwood.[67] However, Lugar's NRSC service did entice him to run for majority leader after the 1984 elections to replace Baker, who was retiring, so perhaps Lugar's own career ambitions fueled his desire for the NRSC. Lugar was among five contestants in a race in which Bob Dole was the eventual winner.[68] Lugar instead became chair of the Foreign Relations Committee, leaving the NRSC chairmanship vacant once again. John Heinz ran for the post again against Sen. Malcolm Wallop (R-WY). Heinz prevailed, but by only one vote.

Rudy Boschwitz (R-MN) became chair for the 1988 cycle. He had expressed earlier interest in leadership, having run for conference secretary in 1984, but lost his own bid for reelection in 1990. Don Nickles (R-OK) was chair for the 1990 cycle, defeating John McCain of Arizona. Nickles was the NRSC chair who figured out how the committee could spend more than its legal limits through bundling, as explained in chapter 5. After the 1990 election, Nickles was elected chair of the Policy Committee. In June 1996 he became majority whip. Nickles represented the new center of the Republican party better than Heinz did, and had a more engaging personal manner compared to Heinz's aloofness.

Sen. Phil Gramm (R-TX), chair for 1992 and 1994, was fairly blatant in his use of the NRSC as an exploratory tool for his probable 1996 bid for the presidency. His use of the NRSC for his own political purposes brought a challenge from Mitch McConnell (R-KY) for the NRSC chairmanship for the 1994 cycle. Gramm did prevail, though he continued to house staff at the NRSC to coordinate his presidential campaign and NRSC schedules. Though some senators were concerned about the blatant overlap of Gramm's interests, none of them thought he sacrificed the goal of a Senate majority (achieved in 1994) for his personal agenda.[69] Alfonse D'Amato (R-NY) chaired the committee for the 1996 cycle. McConnell chairs it for the 1998 cycle.

The DSCC: 1978–Present

Wendell Ford (D-KY), DSCC chair for the 1978, 1980, and 1982 cycles, became the minority whip in late 1982 despite the losses that occurred in the Senate during his tenure (including the loss of Democratic control in 1980). When Lloyd Bentsen again chaired the DSCC in 1984 (after his previous 1974 stint), he considerably broadened the financial base of the committee. Though Bentsen was a powerful senator, he did not enter the leadership ranks but chose to make his senatorial career at the powerful Finance Committee.

George Mitchell of Maine became DSCC chair for the 1986 cycle, while the Democrats were still in the minority. During that cycle, Mitchell was a very active chair, making room in his schedule for fund-raising and coordinating appearances for members. When the 1986 elections were over and the Democrats regained their majority, Mitchell expressed his interest in the majority leader position. Robert Byrd of West Virginia was still leader, however, and Mitchell was named assistant leader as a placeholder title for that slot. After the 1988 elections Byrd stepped aside and Mitchell became the majority leader. However, his interest in the DSCC continued. Mitchell still exercised great control over DSCC events, making campaign appearances on behalf of other candidates and overseeing DSCC Washington operations despite his new responsibilities.[70] Since Mitchell appointed the DSCC leaders, there was no resistance to his involvement in DSCC affairs.

Byrd named Massachusetts senator John Kerry to head the DSCC in the 1988 cycle. Byrd was thought to have offered the position to Kerry in an effort to prevent him from supporting J. Bennett Johnston in a potential leadership challenge to Byrd.[71] At the time there were fears that Kerry's opposition to accepting PAC money would ruin the DSCC's fund-raising chances. However, the DSCC had great fund-raising success under Kerry. Sen. John Breaux of Louisiana headed the DSCC for the 1990 cycle. Breaux was known as a good one-on-one campaigner who expanded professional staff operations at the DSCC. He became chief deputy whip immediately after his DSCC chairmanship.

Sen. Charles Robb (D-VA) became chair of the DSCC for the 1992 cycle in part so that he could explore fund-raising opportunities for a potential presidential bid. Then Robb developed his own personal and political problems in his home state, which put an end to any further ambitions for him in 1992. For the 1994 cycle Bob Graham (D-FL) reluctantly agreed to lead the DSCC, which turned out to be a bad year for Democrats. Though Graham harbored no leadership or presidential aspirations at that time, some believe he was interested in a position on the Senate Finance Committee, an assignment he received immediately after his DSCC tenure.[72]

Sen. Bob Kerrey of Nebraska headed the DSCC for the 1996 and 1998 cycles. Like Coelho before him, Kerrey is forging strong ties to the business community. Kerrey ran unsuccessfully for the 1992 Democratic presidential nomination and has clearly not ruled out another future run. Some believe he agreed to stay on at the DSCC to help his own fund-raising for a 2000 presidential primary campaign.

Moving from CCCs to Party Leadership

The above discussion shows that leadership ambitions are clearly present in CCC chairs. In addition, the incentives for becoming and staying CCC chair are greater in the House parties, where opportunities for career advancement are more plentiful, than in the Senate parties. In the Senate it is clear that Democrats have a harder time inducing members to chair the CCC than they do in the House. The primary reason for this is that chairing a CCC requires a great deal of work outside Washington, D.C., and there are very few rewards awaiting those who undertake CCC service. Senatorial Republicans have been better rewarded overall.

When legislation is being forged in Congress, compromise is essential. Later, members of Congress are left to defend their positions to their individual constituencies. More often, then, coalitions form across parties to achieve common goals for a particular region, industry, or social group. This norm of legislative cooperation extends into much of Congress's business.

The organization of the chamber itself and control of the structure of congressional business (i.e., majority or minority status) is not, however, a negotiated aspect of our governmental system. The difference between majority and minority status is a finite number of seats: one-half of the body plus one. Thus the electoral connection is the heart of a congressional party's organizational identity. For the maintenance or attainment of majority status, a continuing support agency is justified. Fear or hope of a change in numerical status is very real in both chambers. The members seek reassurance that numerical status will not be reduced at the very least and that it will be increased at best.[73] A CCC chair must do whatever is possible for every other member who might be in the majority party. This is not always an easy task, because both parties are quite ideologically diverse and some members do not deserve to be defended in an election. However, part of the attraction of the CCC position is to allow the CCC chair to be evaluated by his peers for leadership potential. The evidence shows that members can have a reasonable expectation that CCC service will lead to promotion, though the simple fact of CCC service is not a guarantee.

Unfortunately, we find little information about early CCC chairs and the institutional development of the CCCs. It is difficult to explore the leadership connection in this early period, because the CCCs developed before the formal floor leader and whip positions. Therefore, much caution should be used in strict definitions of formal leadership. The information on the tenures of the ninety-six House and Senate chairs shows that the CCCs have endured over time, and are becoming more coveted. Though we know that the service of CCC chairs is valued by congressional leaders, we also know from this analysis that appreciation does not automatically bring rewards. The CCC chair has no clear place in the leadership promotion practices of any of the four congressional parties. Nevertheless, it allows members to demonstrate campaign talents, which have always been an important part of leadership responsibilities.

CHAPTER 7

THE CONTRACT WITH AMERICA AND THE NATIONAL REPUBLICAN CONGRESSIONAL COMMITTEE

INNOVATION OR ADAPTATION?

THE CONTRACT WITH AMERICA drew significant, unprecedented attention to CCCs. The Contract, a common party agenda championed by Republican House incumbents and challenger candidates, marked a departure in the type of campaign activities associated with the CCCs since the late 1970s. Specifically, the NRCC abandoned its provision of highly skilled in-house services in favor of concentrating money donations to nonincumbent candidates. The way in which it channeled this money, using incumbents as sources or conduits, was not new, but it was an approach that had largely been ignored since FECA. In essence, the NRCC adopted a philosophy that held that spreading services thinly to incumbents was unlikely to bring a forty-year-old minority party into the majority. Taking the mandate for achieving a majority seriously, the NRCC saw that the only form of CCC assistance that clearly mattered to candidates' electoral success was money, and they came up with ways to get as much money as possible to as many promising races as it could. The NRCC also recognized the value of having a broad campaign message and increased media exposure, which led them to develop the Contract. This marks a decision by the NRCC to put the pursuit of majority status ahead of incumbent protection. After the NRCC realized a majority in 1994, the Democrats began a less ambitious change in their own thinking for the 1996 election cycle.

The Contract with America was devised as a campaign tool for the use of Republican candidates to the House of Representatives in the 1994 midterm congressional elections. What makes the Contract fundamentally different from other campaign tools is that Republican leaders in the House presented it as the governing document that the party would follow if the electorate made Republicans a majority party. The Contract was constructed and articulated in precisely the way many believe that political parties should go about their business. Congressional Republicans met collectively to determine what their public policy positions would be and how to articulate them. Then they pledged to work systematically to enact them. This is significantly different from the traditional approach to issues by congressional parties. Since their inception, the CCCs compiled issue books with facts, figures, and partisan positions on the issues of the day. Candidates used these as reference books for issues with which they were unfamiliar. But in this case the NRCC was using an entirely different strategy: they were orchestrating a national plan of action involving all candidates, versus the more traditional view that all politics is local. In the past this led to an exclusively race-by-race approach to congressional elections.

The Contract was created by a subgroup of House Republicans who were quite committed to the idea of obtaining a majority and engaging in responsible party governance. Though they declared the Contract to be a governing document, it was hastily assembled to attract attention in the fall campaign. In the 104th Congress, when Republicans in both chambers had their majorities, the House Republicans were unable to see many of their proposals become law because of opposition from their fellow Republicans in the Senate.[1] This is because the Contract was a creation of the House Republicans alone. The Senate Republicans never endorsed the document or embraced the idea of a common electoral strategy. This speaks to the institutional party interest the CCCs are designed to protect.

The House Republicans before the Contract with America

The idea for an integrated, national congressional campaign did not emerge in a few weeks over the summer of 1994. It was the product of a long evolution of House Republicans' view of their own minority status. Until the election of Ronald Reagan in 1980, the Republican party generally was perceived as economically conservative and socially moderate. After Reagan's nomination, it became clear that the party had taken a more conservative turn on social issues. The ideological changes in the House Republican Conference in the 1980s led to perceptible changes in its outlook and behavior. Instead of being conciliatory participants in the policy-making process, many House Republicans began to focus on ideology. Eventually, some of the members who preferred confrontation to conciliation began to command more attention.[2] The most important subgroup, the Conservative Opportunity Society (COS), founded by Newt Gingrich, exposed an evolving schism in the House Republican Conference. The COS championed a partisan, confrontational approach to campaigns as well and worked closely with the NRCC to develop national campaign themes. The NRCC, however, chose not to stick strictly to the COS plan and stayed focused on the local dimensions of congressional campaigns.[3]

Starting after the 1990 elections, there was much speculation over the retirement plans of the House minority leader, Bob Michel. The presumption was that the minority whip, Newt Gingrich, would become the new party leader on Michel's departure. Anticipating Michel's retirement, Gingrich became heavily involved in the 1992 and 1994 elections with the hope that these years would witness a significant increase in the number of Republican members who might in turn support his leadership and deter any potential challengers for the top Republican job. Gingrich's substantial efforts formed the basis of his consideration for the position of floor leader and for his ultimate acclamation as Speaker at the beginning of the 104th Congress.

The House Republicans believed the 1992 election cycle afforded significant possibilities: sixty-six House members, many of them Democrats, announced their retirement. This near-record number was precipitated by the grandfather clause for members' retention of excess campaign funds for personal use, new redistricting plans, and political scandals (especially the House Bank scandal). In the wake of these retirements, the House Republicans often chanted the mantra "100 open seats," which indicated the number of open seats they expected to be available given retirements and the rearrangement and creation of congressional districts through redistricting. These opportunities provided great motivation for NRCC chair Guy Vander Jagt who had just survived a leadership challenge amid allegations of sloppy management, improper strategic decision making, and disagreements with the White House. Vander Jagt felt extra pressure to mount a major effort in the 1992 cycle.[4] Despite the considerable anticipation, the election was a near-bust for Republicans, gaining them only ten seats. There were signs of growing GOP strength in the House, however. The 1992 election was the first time since 1882 that a president's party gained seats in the House while the president himself lost reelection.[5]

Vander Jagt was defeated in his own primary election in the summer of 1992, which many believe was due to the amount of time he spent in Washington, D.C., on NRCC affairs. This created a vacancy at the NRCC and led to the emergence of Rep. Bill Paxon (R-NY) as the NRCC's new chair. When Paxon, who was considered to be a Gingrich protégé, took over the organization he was confronted with a large debt left from the 1992 election cycle. He also had a different approach to the role the NRCC should play in congressional elections. In the recent past, members relied on the NRCC for a steady stream of cash and other resources for their own reelection campaigns, which earned it a reputation as an "incumbent protection committee."[6] Paxon and Gingrich had a more aggressive view of the NRCC. First, Paxon sought and received assistance from the RNC to alleviate the NRCC's debt. Second, Paxon's NRCC looked to maximize cash assistance to candidates in a variety of ways. One important start was limiting the NRCC's overhead, which meant cutting services and reducing staff. The litmus test for keeping services included two key assessments. First, the NRCC should only offer services that could not be obtained outside the organization. The major division retained under this criterion was research, which engages in opposition research, issue research, and incumbent members' legislative voting records. Second, the NRCC should not engage in activities that were considered poor returns on investment to individual campaigns. This meant eliminating the radio actualities service, which is the daily message of the party made ready for broadcast by members to their hometowns, and the survey research division as well as scaling down the field division. The NRCC had no field representatives until July 1994, and even then they hired only three contact persons, all to be located in Washington, D.C. All the field contact work was done by telephone. The NRCC also worked closely with the RNC to avoid duplication of effort. In fact, the new RNC chair, Haley Barbour, not only assisted the NRCC with loans in early 1993 but also fully funded coordinated expenditures to congressional races in consultation with the NRCC in 1994. The RNC and NRCC divided up the country for coordinated expenditures, ensuring there would be no violation of agency agreements.[7] This relationship with the RNC was a new one, and was largely due to the RNC's lack of an immediate constituent (that is an incumbent president) and the NRCC's real needs. This funding relationship was not continued in the 1996 cycle.

One of the most notable efforts at the NRCC was the insistence by Paxon (together with Gingrich) that incumbent members contribute money out of their own campaign funds to the NRCC for use by challenger and open seat candidates. The argument, of course, was that the collective goal of majority status was more valuable to these incumbents than the extra few thousand dollars would be. This became the basis for the 1994 electoral strategy and prompted the evolution of the Contract.[8]

Inventing the Contract with America

Bill Paxon was not the only new leader in the Republican party after the 1992 elections. Haley Barbour was elected chair of the RNC at about the same time Paxon became chair of the NRCC. After a contentious vote for the RNC chairmanship, Barbour inherited an organization weakened by President Bush's defeat. Barbour sought a working relationship with Republicans in Congress since he did not have the immediate concern of a presidential race. There was resistance from the NRCC because the RNC had more of a reputation for ignoring congressional Republicans than for helping them. But with a regime change at both the NRCC and the RNC, communications became easier. Barbour formed good working relationships with Gingrich as well. Together with Paxon, these three constructed an integrated strategy for achieving majority status in the House in 1994.

Barbour created the Office of Congressional Affairs at the RNC to ease this relationship. Barbour intended this office to parallel the work of the Republican Governors' Association, which, he explained, "has strengthened our relationship with our GOP state chief executives." He hoped that the Office of Congressional Affairs would "coordinate strategy and message with Republicans in Congress."[9] The office was staffed with two principals: a House liaison and a Senate liaison. This illustrated Barbour's commitment to work directly with the congressional Republicans. Indeed, Barbour stated in his 1993 report, "There is nothing we can do to help elect a Republican president in 1996 that is nearly as important as winning a big Republican victory in 1994."[10] The RNC's commitment to the midterm congressional elections was also evident in the amounts of money raised and spent. The RNC lent the NRCC funds early in 1993 when debts threatened the NRCC with bankruptcy and directly spent more than $5.1 million on House elections.[11] An additional $400,000 was spent on disseminating the Contract message alone.¹² Several members of the RNC staff were involved in the development of the Contract from the time it was formally initiated in the spring of 1994 through its debut in September 1994.¹³ The RNC also paid for the production of the paperback book version of the Contract with America.¹⁴

Part of the strategy Gingrich, Paxon, and Barbour wanted to pursue for the 1994 elections was a common, public agenda for challenger candidates. Using an idea Gingrich had long espoused, the House Republican Conference agreed to develop task forces to flesh out legislative ideas for a potential Republican majority. Gingrich believed that House Republicans could enact a historic program, similar to Roosevelt's New Deal agenda, in one hundred days. During the 103d Congress, House Republican leaders surveyed their freshmen, challenger, and open seat candidates about what issues they would like to see in a Republican majority's one hundred-day agenda. The results were tabulated, and the most common answers became the foundation for the specific items in the Contract with America. Accordingly, eleven task forces of House Republicans were formed to hammer out the specific legislative proposals for the first one hundred days of the 104th Congress under Republican control.¹⁵

In July and August 1994 the task forces went to work. They were aided by information gleaned from focus group studies conducted by the RNC and the NRCC concerning the phrasing that should be used in various Contract items. Some items were fairly simple to compose, being based on bills previously introduced by Republican members. Other ideas, such as the proposal for welfare reform, were considerably more contentious. The members were under severe time constraints to complete their work, and many particulars were glossed over. One of the more creative aspects of the Contract was the clause in which members and candidates would promise to bring these proposals to the floor of the House and hold a vote on all of them, but it deliberately did not promise a vote in the affirmative on all the items in the agenda.

Use of the Contract in the 1994 Elections

After the Contract was completed, the NRCC and the RNC arranged an elaborate unveiling. On September 27, 1994, they assembled all the Republican candidates who agreed to sign the Contract on the steps of the Capitol.[16] Though the assembly made for an impressive media event, most observers and many participants did not fully accept the possibility of achieving majority status or enacting the Contract. News of its existence quickly died out in the national media, and the remainder of the general election continued to be reported on the basis of race-by-race dynamics, not in terms of a national Republican agenda.

Candidates used the Contract in their own election campaigns according to their individual needs. Most senior Republican House members made little use of the Contract or ignored it entirely. Though incumbents all desired the collective party outcome of majority status, they all held two beliefs: that it was unlikely that a Republican majority would be an outcome of the 1994 elections; and that they knew how to campaign successfully for their own reelections and needed no additional help from the Contract. Previous research on congressional elections suggests that nonincumbents generally run more issue-oriented campaigns than incumbents, who tend to emphasize their record of service activities.[17] Still, the general feeling by incumbent and challenger candidates alike was that the Republican party would see gains in the 1994 elections, but that belief stemmed more from the historic trend of a president's party losing seats in midterm elections rather than from the power of the Contract itself.

The utility of the Contract for nonincumbent candidates was another matter. Without the benefit of previous electoral success in the House of Representatives (or, in many cases, any electoral experience whatsoever),[18] challenger and open seat candidates were more receptive to using the Contract as a campaign tool. The NRCC conceded that few nonincumbents used the notion of a party agenda for a potential majority party in their campaigns. Rather, the NRCC found challengers using specific elements in the Contract to "localize national issues."[19] Most of the Contract's proposals were chosen because of members' belief that they had saliency with the public. Therefore, challenger candidates had the benefit of concrete proposals at their fingertips. Challengers used the Contract as a resource for campaign issue themes, choosing from the balanced budget amendment, welfare reform, legal reform, and so on, as it suited their needs. Many of the new freshmen members of the 104th Congress believe their campaigns benefited from the existence of the Contract and its collective party agenda.[20] There were other aggressive moves by the NRCC besides the Contract. In addition to the solicitation of funds from members for the NRCC, members with safe seats did not receive any NRCC contributions. Also, the NRCC aggressively pursued PACs to get them to give to their candidates.[21] Together, these efforts indicated a stark reversal of the previous cycle's incumbent protection mode.

The 1994 Elections and Their Aftermath

The 1994 elections brought the first Republican majority in both the House and the Senate in forty years. The 104th Congress had 236 Republicans, 198 Democrats, and 1 Independent (because of a special election and five party switchers; the original election results were 230 Republicans, 204 Democrats, and 1 Independent). All Republican incumbents won reelection, and 34 Democratic incumbents were defeated. Of the 52 open seats, Republicans won 39 and Democrats won 13. Moreover, of the 31 previously Democratic open seats, 22 were won by Republicans; of the 21 Republican open seats, 17 were won by Republicans.

Virtually all Republican members, with the possible exception of Gingrich and his closest followers, were shocked.[22] The much-hyped majority had been achieved, despite the general ignorance of the Contract by the voting public at large. Polls showed that only 28 percent of the electorate had heard of the Contract before the election.[23] Several other factors help to explain the Republican victory. In many areas of the South a significant realignment appears to be under way. Money also played an important role, with nonincumbent Republicans being significantly better funded than they had been in the past. Also, Republicans accounted for eighteen of the richest twenty-five challenger candidates in terms of cash received.[24] On a national level, many believe that the election contained a significant element of white male backlash. Gary Jacobson argues that an unusually large portion of the electorate voted locally as they had been voting nationally; that is, Republicans gained House seats in areas where they had traditionally led in presidential races but where Democrats still held on in congressional and state-level elections. Overall, Gary Jacobson reports that Republican electoral opportunities improved in all types of races (incumbent reelection, open seats previously held by both parties, and challengers defeating Democratic incumbents), with improved candidate quality an important factor.[25] There is no single explanation for the Republicans' success. The Contract itself was not decisive, but it is proof of precisely the kind of help the CCCs can best provide: collective goods for pursuing majorities.

The real impact of the Contract was not felt until the immediate postelection period. Having ignored it during the election campaign, the media scrambled to cover the Contract. Republican members who had not taken the idea of a Republican majority or the Contract agenda seriously were also scrambling to find direction. Consider their extraordinary situation: their previous leader had retired, they had few members and almost no staff who had served in a Republican majority, and they had promised to act on a legislative agenda that included very few details. Out of both convenience and necessity, the new Republican majority grasped the Contract to give them a starting point. Suddenly, Speaker-elect Gingrich and many from the Republican majority were talking about the "mandate" that the voters had just given them. Undaunted, the new Republican majority, including those members who had not expected to be part of a majority and campaigned under that expectation, acted as though they believed they had been given a clear mandate from the people.²⁶ The connection between campaigning and governing was largely realized by the House Republicans in 1994.

The Contract's Role in 1996

The NRCC actively prepared their members for a dramatically different task in the 1996 elections: how to defend a governing position instead of attacking one. The NRCC did not create a new Contract for 1996. Paxon and Gingrich said that the issues in the Contract were not fully addressed and should therefore continue to be considered by the electorate. They also had many more vulnerable freshmen incumbents to protect than promising challengers to support. For this reason, the NRCC stepped up its incumbent protection efforts, which were more formally institutionalized for the 1994 election cycle in the form of the Incumbent Support Fund and the Incumbent Review Panel.

The Incumbent Support Fund is a separate account held by the NRCC as an "insurance fund" for incumbent members. Each incumbent was asked to contribute to this fund on the basis of seniority or status in the chamber. The assessment for the 1996 cycle was $2,500 for freshman, $5,000 for "regular" members, $6,500 for subcommittee chairs, and $7,500 for leaders and full committee chairs. The NRCC raised $1.1 million in 1994 through this fund, with contributions from 135 out of 178 members running for reelection. In 1996 they raised $1.7 million. The idea behind the fund is that all members contribute (in a progressive fashion roughly commensurate with the level of influence one gains by being in the majority) and only those who need extra funds for their reelection efforts will receive money from it (hence the life insurance analogy: you pay premiums hoping you never need a payoff, but the payoff is there when needed).²⁷

The mechanism used to decide who may receive funds from the Incumbent Support Fund is the IRP. This is the same panel that had its origins in the 1980s, but in the 1990s it has a larger role. Originally, members would go before the board if they needed money to plead their case, then a vote was held on whether to provide the funds. In 1994 the process was sped up so that members in need could get money early. The panel established clear criteria for evaluating need, using information from primaries and FEC reports. The IRP developed into a support group for these vulnerable members. For 1996 the IRP had even more demands placed on it, with 73 freshman incumbents and 110 total incumbents elected within the last three years. Thirteen members sat on the panel, and each had between one and five members assigned to them. The IRP members talked with new members individually on a monthly basis and met monthly to review districts they might have problems with. Freshmen had special assistance in securing speakers to go to their districts, and the NRCC also provided assistance with fund-raisers, especially in Washington. The NRCC also helped these members to find staff and set up full-time campaign operations in their districts.

Not all of these services were new. What was distinctive about the NRCC's efforts in 1994 was the emphasis on nonincumbent candidates. Incumbents were told they did not need the automatic services the NRCC normally provided and were forced to plead the merits of their case to receive maximum assistance, rather than receive such assistance as an entitlement of their incumbency. However, this focus necessarily changed when the Republicans became the majority party because now majority pursuit *was* incumbent protection, as it had been for their Democratic counterparts for the previous four decades. Still, the situation was not quite the same because of the size of the Republican freshman class (typically the most vulnerable type of incumbent) and the relatively small size of the majority. The idea of denying support to secure incumbents was still in place in 1996, but the proportion of secure to insecure incumbents dwindled.

In response to the Contract and NRCC efforts in 1996, the DCCC changed its tactics, though not nearly as significantly as the NRCC had. The Democrats introduced their own congressional legislative agenda, Families First. This 21-point agenda was dubbed "modest, moderate, and achievable" by Democratic congressional leaders who said, "We do not want to replace the extremism of one party with the extremism of another."[28] The agenda included many ideas already championed by Republican moderates (such as welfare reform and balanced budget proposals) since polling data gathered by Democratic leaders indicated that the public reacted badly to the rhetoric of the Contract, though not to the substance of its more moderate proposals. Families First did not contain the binding provisions for congressional candidates that the Contract with America did. Whereas the Contract was literally a "contract" to bring certain pieces of legislation up for a vote and was signed by more than three hundred Republican candidates, Families First did not ask Democratic members and candidates for such promises. The party leaders wanted to focus on saying something positive about what a Democratic Congress would do.

The Democrats did not stick to the proposal as their major campaign theme, choosing instead to capitalize on the Republican Speaker's unpopularity and the Democratic president's popularity. According to *Roll Call*, in the days following the introduction of Families First, the paper received hundreds of press releases from Democratic congressional candidates attacking Speaker Gingrich and Republican activities, but only one candidate sent a press release supporting the Democratic agenda.[29] At the time of the announcement neither the DCCC nor prominent Democratic campaign consultants had any intention of promoting the agenda intensely, choosing instead to highlight specific issues (as Republican candidates did with the Contract in 1994) or to attack Speaker Gingrich. Though President Bill Clinton endorsed Families First, it was not developed in coordination with the DNC the way the Contract was developed with the RNC.

Since 1996 was a presidential election year, the DCCC had only modest cooperation with the DNC (the same holds true for RNC-NRCC cooperation). The DCCC did adopt another strategy from Republicans—that of using wealthy incumbents as funding sources. The president invited congressional candidates to join him during campaign appearances. Still, the DCCC had a sense that the president was ambivalent about a Democratic Congress and worried more about his own reelection. That the DNC money decisions were made by the president's deputy chief of staff, Harold Ickes, and not DNC officers is evidence of this.[30]

This discussion of the Contract and Families First shows that the CCCs can reorient their priorities. Although the CCCs have always been dedicated to winning majorities, the traditional expectation was that incumbent needs would come first. Nonincumbent candidates would be considered secondarily. In 1994 the NRCC, with the blessing of the party leadership, changed this tradition and told most incumbents not to expect significant CCC assistance. Instead, they were called on to assist the NRCC in any way possible, especially in procuring money for potentially close races. The benefits of majority status were stressed as inducements for compliance. The NRCC was responsible for channeling a great deal of money to many of the 1994 House races. In some cases it was able to give the maximum legal contribution itself. In other cases it arranged for the RNC to give the contribution and coordinated expenditures (in essence dissolving the agency agreements discussed in chapter 5). In addition, the NRCC got the cooperation of many senior Republicans in donating funds to campaigns directly. As a result, all members benefited from the effort, since the result was majority status. This example also demonstrates the fluid relationship the NRCC has with the RNC. The level of cooperation in place for 1994 was remarkable and was not duplicated for 1996. The presidential race made the retention of a House majority a lesser concern for the RNC. After the 1996 race the NRCC and the RNC again selected new chairs (now that the NRCC has changed their rules in this regard) and the entire relationship is open for renegotiation for the 1998 cycle. Bill Paxon, whose two-cycle term ended with the 1996 election, was made chair of the Speaker's Advisory Group and therefore a member of the leadership.

Conclusion

Today's congressional campaign committees are active, professional, full-time organizations. They offer more services and raise and distribute more money than at any point in their history. But does this mean that the CCCs have become part of an invigorated national party organizational effort, or rather, as this book suggests, that the CCCs have achieved a successful adaptation to the current campaign needs of incumbent members of Congress?

The histories of the CCCs show their continuous existence since the 1860s. The CCCs are not traditionally described as modern incarnations of long-standing institutions but rather as contemporary constructs activated as a result of party revitalization. Looking at the CCCs from their inception gives us a better perspective on their role in the congressional party, a linkage that has been largely missing from treatments of the CCCs. The importance of the distinction between congressional and presidential arms of the political parties cannot be overstated. If the institution of political parties could not result in a joint campaign agency at the beginning, it is difficult to believe that their further retrenchment today leads to unity of purpose.

Since their inception, the CCCs offered nationally based campaign services to candidates for Congress, with the intention of attaining majority status. Majority status is a collective good that brings individual rewards. Because any member of the majority has more access to power and influence than virtually any member of the minority, majority status is coveted. Members of Congress, rationally, believe the pursuit of majority status begins by assisting incumbents and then by assisting challenger candidates. Therefore, the location of the CCCs in Washington, D.C., was a logical move since incumbents do most of their work there. Throughout the CCCs' history, these services have been orchestrated through a Washington office, making it impossible to serve candidates who have not yet been nominated. This has made the job of pursuing majorities somewhat difficult and has given the CCCs a reputation for being incumbent protection agencies. As campaign methods changed, however, members made different or additional demands on these congressional party organizations designed to meet their common electoral needs. As campaigning becomes more time-consuming because of mass media techniques and the need for constant fund-raising, the pressure from incumbents to make campaigning easier for them while they are in Washington increases and explains why the CCCs have augmented their services over the course of their histories.

Because campaigning for reelection is fundamentally an individual pursuit, these electoral services are normally quite limited and fairly generic. While members agree that they want access to Washington resources in a noncompetitive, mutually beneficial manner with their fellow members, they are not usually willing to devote the resources to such a project that would make CCCs actually able to attain majorities. However, 1994 proved an exception for House Republicans. Consequently, CCCs are not set up to work toward the actual winning of elections. Instead, they exist to help the congressional parties retain their membership, preferably in the form of a majority, which fosters organization of the chamber and the movement of congressional business.

Also, CCCs have never really had the power to win majority status. They are far too limited to be able to direct congressional elections in the same way European parties can. They lack both the authority and the inclination to determine who will run for congressional seats by staying out of primary races. Because of this, they often become involved too late in the game to make any material difference in the outcome. The literature on congressional elections indicates that the results are determined by the local contexts of the candidates and their personal political abilities. Nothing this book reveals refutes that conclusion.

Nevertheless, some have interpreted the post-FECA services of the CCCs as evidence of their institutionalization.[31] That is not necessarily the case. In every cycle it seems a new chair has to recover from a burdensome debt left by his predecessor. We in academia and journalism are too easily convinced that the cycle that follows indicates a transition to something different. A new chair such as Coelho or Paxon comes along, creates a dramatic new fund-raising plan, hires new people, offers some new services, and we are quick to call this party revitalization. Why should this pattern be so extraordinary? Why would a CCC want a surplus of funds coming out of an election cycle? Why would they want to retain a full complement of staff? We must remember that for the first seventy-five years of the CCCs' existence, they were not activated until six months prior to the election. We must therefore consider what it takes for CCCs to function full time in the modern campaign context. If they are going to help campaigns in the final critical days, they are going to have to deliver the maximum in resources they can muster.

Likewise, CCCs are hardly designed to be the primary innovators in the campaign arena. Though they serve an important centralizing purpose, few candidates rely on them as their primary campaign adviser, choosing instead to rely on their privately hired campaign consultants or local party organizations. Thus the CCCs are only one of a number of campaign organizations candidates use for assistance.

The relationship between the CCCs and the NCs is also significant. We cannot feel comfortable referring to "party activity" without specifying which level, or arm, of the party we mean. The evidence here shows that CCCs and the NCs have distinct though related lives. Interestingly, there is no one clear pattern to CCC-NC cooperation or lack thereof. The information is too sketchy. Also, no one factor (type of election, in/out party status of the NCs, personalities of the chairs) seems dominant over time. The only clear constant is inconsistency. This lends credence to the assertion that CCCs reinvent their electoral strategies after each election cycle. CCCs are more likely to get NCs to cooperate with them during off-year elections, but as the NCs have their own agenda, constituency, and political constraints, the relationship between them is highly fluid. For the 1998 election cycle, with two new NC chairs and three new CCC chairs, creative innovation in the CCC-NC relationship may again take place.

Members desire to chair the CCCs for reasons unrelated to party electoral goals. That is, they wish to deliver funds and services in a way that will enhance their own personal goals. CCC chairs usually seek higher leadership positions within their chambers. Historically, the CCC chair has been a position from which party leaders can observe members' performance, specifically with regard to the more public aspects of governing. In more recent years, especially in the Senate, we find that CCC chairs may be interested in fostering presidential ambitions and are using their time at the CCC to enhance their fund-raising connections, or they may be using the experience to argue for improved leverage for themselves in the chamber, in more prestigious committee assignments or in increased legislative influence. Interestingly, to realize rewards for CCC service, it is not necessary to have achieved electoral success. The *perception* of great effort is what counts. One need only look at years such as 1974 and 1994. Bob Michel, NRCC chair in 1974 when House Republicans lost forty-eight seats, was immediately elevated to minority whip. Vic Fazio, DCCC chair in 1994 when House Democrats lost fifty-two seats and control of the chamber, became Democratic Caucus chair immediately thereafter. This leadership connection is critical because it points to the explicitly *congressional* nature of the CCCs. It also explains why CCCs have not been eliminated for failing to provide clear electoral benefits. Unlike the NCs, the CCCs are ruled by the officeholders whose elections they hope to secure. Therefore, the motivations of CCC chairs and their programs while chair are directly related to their ambitions in the chamber (or in the case of the Senate, beyond the chamber). This is why we need to know something about Congress and its leadership to properly understand the CCCs.

The need for constant campaigning is an integral part of the lawmaking process. The campaign committees arose to ensure that this need would always be met by creating institutions staffed by those who stood to gain the most from their existence. Early in the development of the national committee organizations, congressional leaders recognized that their interests would not mesh easily or consistently with the interests of the presidential party organizations. Therefore, although it made sense to be part of a party family, especially when voters and contributors liked the party in general, it did not make sense to give that family a single head who dictated positions from above to subordinate children. Instead, a more "cousin-like" approach evolved, allowing the various parts of the party family (presidential, senatorial, congressional) to work together when convenient and to work separately or even at odds with each other when other circumstances warranted.

Where does this take us? Perhaps, as other scholars have suggested, we need to reexamine our traditional conception of the political party as a tripartite structure. Instead of looking at party in government, party as organization, and party in the electorate, we should acknowledge that the party as organization is really not separate from the party in government. In fact, this study shows that the idea that party organizations are separate from the party in government is really a legal distinction arising out of the last major reform of campaign activity. The party as organization has no independent life of its own. This is in contrast to the national committees when there is no president controlling the White House. As Philip A. Klinkner shows, the out-party organization must reinvent itself in the years between a presidential election loss and the next presidential nominating season.[32] The congressional parties are never in this position, because they always have a core constituency whether they are in the minority or the majority. The CCCs operate at the behest of the party in government, and the party leaders are integral parts of this structure. They have a tremendous influence over who will head the CCC, and can supervise the party's activities. You can not have a "Speaker's Club" for high-dollar fund-raisers (like the DCCC did) without the cooperation of the Speaker.

So we should look at the CCCs not just for the broad array of services they provide but for their contribution to the operations of party in government. Given the results of the 1994 elections, party leaders are less likely to believe that their majority or minority status will continue for the long term. Will party leaders make decisions about congressional initiatives based on their potential impact on the next set of elections? Will the leadership only encourage CCC chairs who exhibit loyalty to the party as it is currently constituted? This study comes to the conclusion, without regret or joy, that separation of powers in a presidential system prevents meaningful, overarching political parties. CCC activities prove that the separation of interests and strategies often happens without fanfare or great publicity, but the underlying separation is omnipresent. Perhaps we can look to studies of politics with the institutional basis originally intended, instead of hoping that the harmful effects of the system can somehow be offset by political parties.

APPENDIX

TABLES A.1–A.20

Table A.1
Election Results, 1866–1996

Year	House				Senate				President	
	Democrats	Republicans	Other	Total	Democrats	Republicans	Other	Total	Name	Party
1866	49	143		192	11	42		53	Johnson	R
1868	73	170		243	11	61		72	Grant	R
1870	104	139		243	17	57		74	Grant	R
1872	88	203		291	19	54		73	Grant	R
1874	181	107	3	291	29	46		75	Grant	R
1876	156	137		293	36	39	1	76	Hayes	R
1878	150	128	14	292	43	33		76	Hayes	R
1880	130	152	11	293	37	37	2	76	Garfield	R
1882	200	119	6	325	36	40		76	Arthur	R
1884	182	140	4	326	34	41		75	Cleveland	D
1886	170	151	4	325	37	39		76	Cleveland	D
1888	156	173	1	330	37	47		84	Harrison	R
1890	231	88	14	333	39	47		86	Harrison	R
1892	220	126	8	354	44	38	3	85	Cleveland	D
1894	104	246	7	357	30	44		74	Cleveland	D
1896	134	206	16	356	34	46	10	90	McKinley	R
1898	163	185	9	357	26	53	11	90	McKinley	R
1900	153	198	5	356	29	56	3	88	McKinley	R
1902	178	207		385	32	58		90	T. Roosevelt	R

Table A.1 (continued)
Election Results, 1866–1996

Year	House				Senate				President	
	Democrats	Republicans	Other	Total	Democrats	Republicans	Other	Total	Name	Party
1904	136	250		386	32	58		90	T. Roosevelt	R
1906	164	222		386	29	61		90	T. Roosevelt	R
1908	172	219		391	32	59		91	Taft	R
1910	228	162	1	391	42	49		91	Taft	R
1912	290	127	18	435	51	44	1	96	Wilson	D
1914	231	193	8	432	56	39	1	96	Wilson	D
1916	210	216	9	435	53	42	1	96	Wilson	D
1918	191	237	7	435	47	48	1	96	Wilson	D
1920	132	300	1	433	37	59		96	Harding	R
1922	207	225	3	435	43	51	2	96	Coolidge	R
1924	183	247	5	435	40	54	1	95	Coolidge	R
1926	195	237	3	435	47	48	1	96	Coolidge	R
1928	163	267	1	431	39	56	1	96	Hoover	R
1930	216	218	1	435	47	48	1	96	Hoover	R
1932	313	117	5	435	59	36	1	96	FDR	D
1934	322	103	10	435	69	25	2	96	FDR	D
1936	333	89	13	435	75	17	4	96	FDR	D
1938	262	169	4	435	69	23	4	96	FDR	D
1940	267	162	6	435	66	28	2	96	FDR	D

Table A.1 (continued)
Election Results, 1866–1996

Year	House				Senate				President	
	Democrats	Republicans	Other	Total	Democrats	Republicans	Other	Total	Name	Party
1942	222	209	4	435	57	38	1	96	FDR	D
1944	243	190	2	435	57	38	1	96	FDR	D
1946	188	246	1	435	45	51		96	Truman	D
1948	263	171	1	435	54	42		96	Truman	D
1950	234	199	2	435	48	47	1	96	Truman	D
1952	213	221	1	435	47	48	1	96	Eisenhower	R
1954	232	203		435	48	47	1	96	Eisenhower	R
1956	234	201		435	49	47		96	Eisenhower	R
1958	283	154		437	64	34		98	Eisenhower	R
1960	263	174		437	65	35		100	Kennedy	D
1962	258	177		435	67	33		100	Kennedy	D
1964	295	140		435	68	32		100	Johnson	D
1966	247	187	1	435	64	36		100	Johnson	D
1968	243	192		435	57	43		100	Nixon	R
1970	254	180	1	435	54	44	2	100	Nixon	R
1972	239	192	4	435	56	42	2	100	Nixon	R
1974	291	144		435	60	37	3	100	Ford	R
1976	292	143		435	61	38	1	100	Carter	D
1978	276	157	2	435	58	41	1	100	Carter	D

Table A.1 (continued)
Election Results, 1866–1996

Year	House				Senate				President	
	Democrats	Republicans	Other	Total	Democrats	Republicans	Other	Total	Name	Party
1980	243	192		435	46	53	1	100	Reagan	R
1982	269	165	1	435	46	54		100	Reagan	R
1984	252	182	1	435	47	53		100	Reagan	R
1986	258	177		435	55	45		100	Reagan	R
1988	260	175		435	55	45		100	Bush	R
1990	267	167	1	435	56	44		100	Bush	R
1992	258	176	1	435	57	43		100	Clinton	D
1994	204	230	1	435	47	53		100	Clinton	D
1996	207	227	1	435	45	55		100	Clinton	D

Table A.2
Democratic Congressional Campaign Committee Chairs

Chair	No. Cycles at CCC	Election Years	No. Years before CCC	No. Years after CCC	Age at CCC	Total Years in Chamber	Next Position after CCC Chair
Samuel Randall	2	1870–72	6	18	41	28	Speaker
Sen. William Wallace	1	1880	4	0	52	6	Lost reelection
Sen. Charles J. Faulkner	1	1894	6	4	47	12	Unknown
James Richardson	2	1898–1900	12	4	55	20	Minority leader
James M. Griggs	3	1902–6	4	3	36	13	Ways and Means
James T. Lloyd	3	1908–12	10	4	50	20	Retired
Frank Doremus	2	1914–16	2	4	48	10	None
Scott Ferris	2	1918, 1922	10	2	40	14	Ran for Senate
Henry D. Flood	1	1920	18	1	54	21	Died in office
William Oldfield	3	1924–28	14	0	49	20	Minority whip
Joseph W. Byrns	3	1930–34	20	2	60	28	Majority leader
Patrick Drewry	6	1936–46	15	0	60	27	Died in office
Michael Kirwan	21	1948–68	10	0	60	33	Died in office
Thomas O'Neill	2	1970–72	16	14	57	34	Majority whip
Ed Edmondson	1	1972	18	0	52	20	Ran for Senate
Wayne Hays	1.5	1974	24	0	62	27	Resigned
James Corman	2.5	1976–80	15	0	56	20	Lost reelection
Tony Coelho	3	1982–86	2	2	39	10	Majority whip
Beryl Anthony	2	1988–90	8	2	49	14	Lost Race for whip
Vic Fazio	2	1992–94	12	3+	49	19+[a]	Caucus chair
Martin Frost	2	1996–98	18	0	53	21+[a]	Currently serving

[a] Currently serving in the chamber

Table A.3
National Republican Congressional Committee Chairs

Chair	No. Cycles at CCC	Election Years	No. Years before CCC	No. Years after CCC	Age at CCC	Total Years in Chamber	Next Position after CCC Chair
Robert C. Schenck	1	1866	2	4	56	8	Lost reelection
Sen. Edwin Morgan	1	1868	4	2	56	6	Chair, RNC
Sen. Zachariah Chandler	2	1870–72	12	2	58	16	Chair, RNC
Sen. John Logan	1	1874	2	2	47	6	None
Sen. Simon Cameron	1	1876	8	0	76	10	Retired
Jay Hubbell	3	1878–82	4	0	48	10	Retired
J. J. Belden	1	1890	2	6	64	10[a]	Retired
Joseph Babcock	6	1894–1904	0	2	43	14[a]	Retired
James Sherman	2	1906–8	16	0	50	20	Vice president
William McKinley	2	1910–12	4	6	53	14[a]	Lost reelection
Frank Woods	2.5	1914–16	4	1	44	10	Lost reelection
Simeon Fess	1.5	1918–20	5	2	56	10	Ran for Senate
Will Wood	6	1922–32	6	0	60	18	Lost reelection
Chester Bolton	2	1934–36	4	0	51	8	Lost reelection
Joseph Martin	1	1938	12	28	51	42	Minority leader
William Ditter	2	1940–42	6	0	53	10	Died in office
Charles Halleck	2	1944–46	8	22	43	34	Majority leader
Leonard Hall	3	1948–52	8	0	47	14	Chair, RNC
Richard Simpson	3	1954–58	16	0	53	22	Died in office
William Miller	1	1960	8	4	45	14	Chair, RNC
Robert Wilson	6	1962–72	8	8	45	28	None
Robert Michel	1	1974	16	18	50	36	Minority whip
Guy Vander Jagt	9	1976–92	9	0	45	27	Lost reelection
Bill Paxon	2	1994–96	4	1	39	9+[b]	SAG chair
John Linder	1	1998	4	0	55	5+[b]	Current chair

[a] Nonconsecutive service
[b] Currently serving in the chamber

Table A.4
Democratic Senatorial Campaign Committee Chairs

Chair	No. Cycles at CCC	Election Years	No. Years before CCC	No. Years after CCC	Age at CCC	Total Years in Chamber	Next Position after CCC Chair
David Walsh	1	1922	2	23	49	27[a]	None
Millard Tydings	1	1930	2	20	39	24	None
Claude Swanson	1	1932	21	0	69	23	Secretary of the navy
James H. Lewis	1	1934	8	4	70	14[a]	Majority whip
Joseph Guffey	2	1936,42	0	4	65	12	None
Prentiss Brown	1	1938	0	4	48	6	Lost reelection
Theodore F. Green	1	1940	2	20	72	24	None
Joseph O'Mahoney	1	1944	9	14	59	25[a]	None
Scott Lucas	2	1946–48	6	2	53	12	Minority whip
Clinton Anderson	1	1950	0	22	54	24	None
Earle Clements	2	1952–54	1	2	55	7	Minority whip
George Smathers	3	1956–60	4	8	42	18	Conference secretary
Vance Hartke	1	1962	2	14	42	18	None
Warren Magnuson	2	1964–66	18	14	58	36	None
Edmund Muskie	1	1968	8	11	53	21	Lost whip's race
Daniel Inouye	1	1970	6	27+[b]	47	35+[b]	None
Ernest Hollings	1	1972	5	25+[b]	49	32+[b]	None
Lloyd Bentsen	2	1974, 1984	2	8	52	22	None
J. Bennett Johnston	1	1976	2	20	43	24	None
Wendell Ford	3	1978–82	2	13+[b]	53	25+[b]	Majority whip
George Mitchell	1	1986	5	8	52	15	Majority leader
John Kerry	1	1988	2	9+[b]	43	13+[b]	None
John Breaux	1	1990	2	7+[b]	45	11+[b]	Chief deputy whip
Chuck Robb	1	1992	2	5+[b]	52	9+[b]	Presidential aspirant
Bob Graham	1	1994	6	3+[b]	58	11+[b]	Finance Committee
Bob Kerrey	2	1996–98	6	0	53	9+[b]	Presidential aspirant

[a] Nonconsecutive service
[b] Currently serving in the chamber

Table A.5
National Republican Senatorial Committee Chairs

Chair	No. Cycles at CCC	Election Years	No. Years before CCC	No. Years after CCC	Age at CCC	Total Years in Chamber	Next Position after CCC Chair
Charles McNary	1	1920	2	23	45	27	Unknown
Medill McCormick	1	1922	2	2	44	6	Lost reelection
George Moses	2	1924, 1930	4	2	54	14	Lost reelection
Lawrence Phipps	1	1926	6	4	53	12	None
Henry Hatfield	1	1932	2	2	56	6	Lost reelection
John Townsend	1	1938	8	2	64	12	None
Owen Brewster	1	1950	8	2	61	12	Lost reelection
Everett Dirksen	2	1952-54	0	14	55	18	Minority whip
Barry Goldwater	3	1956, 1960-62	2	18	46	30[a]	Presidential nominee
Andrew Schoeppel	1	1958	8	2	63	12	None
Thruston Morton	2	1964-66	6	2	56	12	Retired
George Murphy	1	1968	2	2	65	6	Lost reelection
John Tower	1	1970	8	14	44	24	Chair, Policy Comm.
Peter Dominick	1	1972	8	2	56	12	Lost reelection
William Brock	1	1974	2	2	43	6	Lost/RNC chair
Ted Stevens	1	1976	6	21+[b]	52	27+[b]	Minority whip
Robert Packwood	2	1978, 1982	8	12	45	26	Chair, Conference
John Heinz	2	1980, 1986	2	4	41	14	Lost conference chair
Richard Lugar	1	1984	6	13+[b]	51	21+[b]	Lost majority leader
Rudy Boschwitz	1	1988	8	2	57	12	Lost reelection
Don Nickles	1	1990	8	7+[b]	41	17+[b]	Chair, Policy Comm.
Phil Gramm	2	1992-94	6	3+[b]	49	13+[b]	Presidential aspirant
Alfonse D'Amato	1	1996	14	2+[b]	59	17+[b]	None
Mitch McConnell	1	1998	12	0+[b]	55	13+[b]	Currently serving

[a] Nonconsecutive service
[b] Currently serving in the chamber

Table A.6
RNC Contributions

Cycle	Presidential Candidates			Senate Incumbents			Senate Challengers			Senate Open Seats		
	#	Total $	Avg. $	#	Total $	Avg. $	#	Total $	Avg. $	#	Total $	Avg. $
1977–78	0	–	–	13	61,886	4,760	3	18,056	6,019	1	736	736
1979–80	5	8,280	1,656	0	–	–	6	69,813	11,636	0	–	–
1981–82	0	–	–	0	–	–	1	4,500	4,500	0	–	–
1983–84	0	–	–	0	–	–	0	–	–	0	–	–
1985–86	0	–	–	0	–	–	1	397	397	0	–	–
1987–88	0	–	–	0	–	–	0	–	–	0	–	–
1989–90	0	–	–	0	–	–	0	–	–	0	–	–
1991–92	0	–	–	0	–	–	1	5,000	5,000	0	–	–
1993–94	0	–	–	0	–	–	1	5,000	5,000	1	84	84

Source: Federal Election Commission, *FEC Reports On Financial Activity: Final Report, Party and Non-Party Political Committees*, vol. 1, Summary Tables, for Cycles 1977–78 through 1993–94. Table E in all reports.

Table A.7
RNC Expenditures

Cycle	Presidential Candidates			Senate Incumbents			Senate Challengers			Senate Open Seats		
	#	Total $	Avg. $	#	Total $	Avg. $	#	Total $	Avg. $	#	Total $	Avg. $
1977–78	0	–	–	3	3,719	1,240	4	9,573	2,393	5	9,614	1,923
1979–80	1	4,504,176	4,504,176	2	2,666	1,333	6	307,037	51,173	0	–	–
1981–82	0	–	–	0	–	–	0	–	–	0	–	–
1983–84	1	6,811,061	6,811,061	0	–	–	0	–	–	0	–	–
1985–86	0	–	–	0	–	–	0	–	–	0	–	–
1987–88	1	8,289,173	8,289,173	0	–	–	0	–	–	0	–	–
1989–90	0	–	–	0	–	–	0	–	–	0	–	–
1991–92	1	10,417,766	10,417,766	0	–	–	0	–	–	0	–	
1993–94	0	–	–	0	–	–	1	5,000	5,000	1	84	84

Source: Federal Election Commission, *FEC Reports On Financial Activity: Final Report, Party and Non-Party Political Committees*, vol. 1, Summary Tables, for Cycles 1977–7. through 1993–94. Table K in all reports.

House Incumbents			House Challengers			House Open Seats			Totals		
#	Total $	Avg. $	#	Total $	Avg. $	#	Total $	Avg. $	#	Total $	Avg. $
42	182,916	4,355	81	360,166	4,446	56	281,484	5,026	196	905,244	4,619
15	41,845	2,790	90	513,549	5,706	37	210,968	5,702	153	844,455	5,519
81	577,916	7,135	98	658,778	6,722	54	458,984	8,500	234	1,700,178	7,266
23	144,995	6,304	67	525,969	7,850	25	177,830	7,113	115	848,794	7,381
22	122,700	5,577	22	92,221	4,192	25	135,109	5,404	70	350,427	5,006
21	62,730	2,987	27	130,250	4,824	17	133,500	7,853	65	326,480	5,023
9	28,185	3,132	22	90,043	4,093	18	137,350	7,631	49	255,578	5,216
43	222,257	5,169	86	333,746	3,881	51	224,000	4,392	181	785,003	4,337
2	336	168	69	344,381	4,991	39	194,352	4,983	112	544,153	4,859

House Incumbents			House Challengers			House Open Seats			Totals		
#	Total $	Avg. $	#	Total $	Avg. $	#	Total $	Avg. $	#	Total $	Avg. $
2	8,085	4,042	40	224,327	5,608	17	81,663	4,804	71	336,981	4,746
5	26,641	5,328	49	341,982	6,979	19	169,767	8,935	82	5,352,269	65,272
4	19,549	4,887	10	89,031	8,903	10	124,384	12,438	24	232,964	9,707
0	–	–	2	3,954	1,977	2	2,795	1,398	5	6,817,810	1,363,562
0	–	–	0	–	–	1	2,100	2,100	1	2,100	2,100
0	–	–	0	–	–	0	–	–	1	8,289,173	8,289,173
0	–	–	1	25,000	25,000	1	21,344	21,344	2	46,344	23,172
21	392,564	18,694	16	200,272	12,517	17	239,511	14,089	55	11,250,113	204,548
2	336	168	69	344,381	4,991	39	194,352	4,983	112	544,153	4,859

Table A.8
NRSC Contributions

Cycle	Presidential Candidates			Senate Incumbents			Senate Challengers			Senate Open Seats		
	#	Total $	Avg. $	#	Total $	Avg. $	#	Total $	Avg. $	#	Total $	Avg. $
1977–78	0	–	–	13	131,524	10,117	16	196,830	12,302	10	127,731	12,773
1979–80	0	–	–	8	110,727	13,841	20	229,041	11,452	5	75,125	15,025
1981–82	0	–	–	51	213,260	4,182	21	295,044	14,050	4	50,023	12,506
1983–84	1	422	422	38	300,054	7,896	12	163,925	13,660	9	98,650	10,961
1985–86	0	–	–	26	300,160	11,545	20	163,908	8,195	7	124,404	17,772
1987–88	0	–	–	15	192,178	12,812	17	245,915	14,466	6	99,496	16,583
1989–90	0	–	–	22	248,505	11,296	35	232,703	6,649	4	41,801	10,450
1991–92	0	–	–	13	211,000	16,231	19	280,639	14,770	9	140,556	15,617
1993–94	0	–	–	9	157,454	17,495	14	200,222	14,302	12	141,103	11,759

Source: Federal Election Commission, *FEC Reports On Financial Activity: Final Report, Party and Non-Party Political Committees*, vol. 1, Summary Tables, for Cycles 1977–78 through 1993–94. Table E in all reports.

Table A.9
NRSC Expenditures

Cycle	Presidential Candidates			Senate Incumbents			Senate Challengers			Senate Open Seats		
	#	Total $	Avg. $	#	Total $	Avg. $	#	Total $	Avg. $	#	Total $	Avg. $
1977–78	0	–	–	7	1,248,544	178,363	11	861,525	78,320	10	489,221	48,922
1979–80	0	–	–	9	451,522	50,169	20	3,301,459	165,073	5	1,272,821	254,564
1981–82	0	–	–	11	2,027,394	184,309	18	4,672,832	259,602	3	2,007,311	669,104
1983–84	0	–	–	20	3,029,330	151,466	12	1,827,737	152,311	5	1,875,084	375,017
1985–86	0	–	–	26	4,884,035	187,848	21	3,411,948	162,474	7	1,663,347	237,621
1987–88	0	–	–	13	3,575,941	275,072	15	4,574,392	304,959	6	2,100,205	350,034
1989–90	0	–	–	18	3,693,360	205,187	23	3,558,049	154,698	3	432,745	144,248
1991–92	0	–	–	14	7,340,121	524,294	13	5,433,060	417,928	8	3,704,206	463,026
1993–94	0	–	–	8	1,847,781	230,973	10	4,121,542	412,154	10	4,936,177	493,618

Source: Federal Election Commission, *FEC Reports On Financial Activity: Final Report, Party and Non-Party Political Committees*, vol. 1, Summary Tables, for Cycles 1977–7 through 1993–94. Table K in all reports.

APPENDIX 229

House Incumbents		House Challengers			House Open Seats			Totals		
#	Total $	Avg. $	#	Total $	Avg. $	#	Total $	Avg. $	#	Total $	Avg. $
0	–	–	1	25	25	0	–	–	40	456,110	11,403
0	–	–	0	–	–	0	–	–	33	414,893	12,573
0	–	–	0	–	–	0	–	–	76	558,327	7,346
0	–	–	0	–	–	0	–	–	60	563,051	9,384
0	–	–	2	15,000	7,500	3	26,000	8,667	58	629,472	10,853
5	25,000	5,000	14	90,000	6,429	10	105,000	10,500	67	757,589	11,307
4	25,000	6,250	6	35,000	5,833	14	113,000	8,071	85	696,009	8,188
4	20,000	5,000	6	25,000	4,167	3	15,000	5,000	54	692,195	12,818
4	20,000	5,000	11	67,500	6,136	6	35,000	5,833	56	621,279	11,094

House Incumbents		House Challengers			House Open Seats			Totals		
#	Total $	Avg. $	#	Total $	Avg. $	#	Total $	Avg. $	#	Total $	Avg. $
0	–	–	0	–	–	0	–	–	28	2,599,290	92,832
0	–	–	0	–	–	0	–	–	34	5,025,802	147,818
0	–	–	0	–	–	0	–	–	32	8,707,537	272,111
0	–	–	0	–	–	0	–	–	37	6,732,151	181,950
0	–	–	0	–	–	0	–	–	54	9,959,330	184,432
0	–	–	0	–	–	0	–	–	34	10,250,538	301,486
0	–	–	0	–	–	0	–	–	44	7,684,154	174,640
0	–	–	0	–	–	0	–	–	35	16,477,387	470,782
0	–	–	0	–	–	0	–	–	28	10,905,500	389,482

Table A.10
NRCC Contributions

Cycle	Presidential Candidates			Senate Incumbents			Senate Challengers			Senate Open Seats		
	#	Total $	Avg. $	#	Total $	Avg. $	#	Total $	Avg. $	#	Total $	Avg. $
1977–78	0	–	–	0	–	–	0	–	–	0	–	–
1979–80	0	–	–	0	–	–	5	3,013	603	0	–	–
1981–82	0	–	–	0	–	–	2	2,185	1,092	0	–	–
1983–84	0	–	–	0	–	–	2	95	48	1	658	658
1985–86	0	–	–	2	10,000	5,000	2	10,000	5,000	2	875	438
1987–88	0	–	–	0	–	–	7	44,943	6,420	4	15,733	3,933
1989–90	0	–	–	2	10,000	5,000	10	78,579	7,858	3	16,824	5,608
1991–92	0	–	–	2	10,000	5,000	3	15,000	5,000	2	10,000	5,000
1993–94	0	–	–	2	10,000	5,000	8	37,104	4,638	8	35,496	4,437

Source: Federal Election Commission, *FEC Reports On Financial Activity: Final Report Party and Non-Party Political Committees*, vol. 1, Summary Tables, for Cycles 1977–78 through 1993–94. Table E in all reports.

Table A.11
NRCC Expenditures

Cycle	Presidential Candidates			Senate Incumbents			Senate Challengers			Senate Open Seats		
	#	Total $	Avg. $	#	Total $	Avg. $	#	Total $	Avg. $	#	Total $	Avg. $
1977–78	0	–	–	0	–	–	0	–	–	0	–	–
1979–80	0	–	–	0	–	–	0	–	–	0	–	–
1981–82	0	–	–	0	–	–	0	–	–	0	–	–
1983–84	0	–	–	0	–	–	0	–	–	0	–	–
1985–86	0	–	–	0	–	–	1	697	697	0	–	–
1987–88	0	–	–	0	–	–	0	–	–	0	–	–
1989–90	0	–	–	0	–	–	0	–	–	0	–	–
1991–92	0	–	–	0	–	–	0	–	–	0	–	–
1993–94	0	–	–	0	–	–	0	–	–	0	–	–

Source: Federal Election Commission, *FEC Reports On Financial Activity: Final Report Party and Non-Party Political Committees*, vol. 1, Summary Tables, for Cycles 1977–78 through 1993–94. Table K in all reports.

APPENDIX

House Incumbents			House Challengers			House Open Seats			Totals		
#	Total $	Avg. $	#	Total $	Avg. $	#	Total $	Avg. $	#	Total $	Avg. $
133	973,888	7,322	104	512,018	4,923	53	331,518	6,255	290	1,817,424	6,267
152	1,091,150	7,179	169	618,484	3,660	45	293,016	6,511	371	2,005,663	5,406
193	1,444,419	7,484	134	626,192	4,673	70	482,128	6,888	399	2,554,924	6,403
165	1,261,165	7,643	179	1,052,037	5,877	33	267,624	8,110	380	2,581,579	6,794
182	823,619	4,525	91	447,255	4,915	55	363,501	6,609	334	1,655,250	4,956
174	700,130	4,024	127	525,879	4,141	33	284,422	8,619	345	1,571,107	4,554
161	275,778	1,713	61	277,808	4,554	33	287,678	8,718	270	946,667	3,506
143	326,482	2,283	152	248,735	1,636	60	118,227	1,970	362	728,444	2,012
172	135,079	785	197	346,378	1,758	53	223,884	4,224	440	787,941	1,791

House Incumbents			House Challengers			House Open Seats			Totals		
#	Total $	Avg. $	#	Total $	Avg. $	#	Total $	Avg. $	#	Total $	Avg. $
16	98,869	6,179	45	354,249	7,872	40	386,303	9,658	101	839,421	8,311
23	218,778	9,512	55	667,527	12,137	32	342,805	10,713	110	1,229,110	11,174
69	1,874,024	27,160	60	1,722,673	28,711	47	1,346,552	28,650	176	4,943,249	28,087
52	1,529,608	29,416	113	3,745,526	33,146	28	988,928	35,319	193	6,264,062	32,456
53	1,464,138	27,625	67	1,222,479	18,246	35	1,411,075	40,316	156	4,098,389	26,272
41	1,247,532	30,428	51	1,760,854	34,527	25	1,100,966	44,039	117	4,109,352	35,123
24	729,473	30,395	30	863,646	28,788	29	1,237,366	42,668	83	2,830,485	34,102
39	1,059,192	27,159	112	2,616,652	23,363	53	1,513,896	28,564	204	5,189,740	25,440
41	1,195,355	29,155	65	1,670,457	25,699	23	1,064,502	46,283	129	3,930,314	30,468

Table A.12
DNC Contributions

Cycle	Presidential Candidates			Senate Incumbents			Senate Challengers			Senate Open Seats		
	#	Total $	Avg. $	#	Total $	Avg. $	#	Total $	Avg. $	#	Total $	Avg. $
1977–78	1	8,246	8,246	2	350	175	1	150	150	0	–	–
1979–80	2	15,000	7,500	0	–	–	0	–	–	0	–	–
1981–82	1	41,376	41,376	0	–	–	0	–	–	0	–	–
1983–84	1	820,922	820,922	0	–	–	0	–	–	0	–	–
1985–86	7	20,000	2,857	0	–	–	0	–	–	1	500	500
1987–88	0	–	–	0	–	–	0	–	–	0	–	–
1989–90	0	–	–	0	–	–	0	–	–	0	–	–
1991–92	2	3,101	1,550	0	–	–	0	–	–	0	–	–
1993–94	2	10,000	5,000	0	–	–	2	17,534	8,767	0	–	–

Source: Federal Election Commission, *FEC Reports On Financial Activity: Final Report, Party and Non-Party Political Committees*, vol. 1, Summary Tables, for Cycles 1977–78 through 1993–94. Table E in all reports.

Table A.13
DNC Expenditures

Cycle	Presidential Candidates			Senate Incumbents			Senate Challengers			Senate Open Seats		
	#	Total $	Avg. $	#	Total $	Avg. $	#	Total $	Avg. $	#	Total $	Avg. $
1977–78	0	–	–	4	17,978	4,494	8	27,554	3,444	2	6,061	3,031
1979–80	1	3,386,793	3,386,793	17	216,554	12,738	16	227,175	14,198	3	63,530	21,177
1981–82	1	106,157	106,157	0	–	–	2	23,507	11,754	1	14,500	14,500
1983–84	2	2,659,678	1,329,839	0	–	–	1	506	506	0	–	–
1985–86	2	343,348	171,674	0	–	–	0	–	–	0	–	–
1987–88	2	8,077,044	4,038,522	0	–	–	0	–	–	0	–	–
1989–90	2	112,652	56,326	0	–	–	1	1,393	1,393	0	–	–
1991–92	2	10,160,172	5,080,086	1	107,039	107,039	6	63,779	10,630	3	24,533	8,178
1993–94	0	–	–	1	106,058	106,058	1	38,545	38,545	1	15,507	15,507

Source: Federal Election Commission, *FEC Reports On Financial Activity: Final Report, Party and Non-Party Political Committees*, vol. 1, Summary Tables, for Cycles 1977–7 through 1993–94. Table K in all reports.

APPENDIX

House Incumbents			House Challengers			House Open Seats			Totals		
#	Total $	Avg. $	#	Total $	Avg. $	#	Total $	Avg. $	#	Total $	Avg. $
25	25,300	1,012	3	2,207	736	16	28,054	1,753	48	64,307	1,340
4	6,551	1,638	4	11,500	2,875	5	8,000	1,600	15	41,051	2,737
16	6,650	416	47	36,498	777	33	40,050	1,214	97	124,574	1,284
10	14,500	1,450	18	46,750	2,597	14	43,500	3,107	43	925,672	21,527
0	–	–	0	–	–	0	–	–	8	20,500	2,563
9	45,000	5,000	10	50,000	5,000	7	42,998	6,143	26	137,998	5,308
0	–	–	2	6,150	3,075	8	40,000	5,000	10	46,150	4,615
0	–	–	0	–	–	0	–	–	2	3,101	1,551
6	23,693	3,949	2	10,000	5,000	5	25,000	5,000	17	86,227	5,072

House Incumbents			House Challengers			House Open Seats			Totals		
#	Total $	Avg. $	#	Total $	Avg. $	#	Total $	Avg. $	#	Total $	Avg. $
21	3,747	178	22	5,522	251	20	7,960	398	77	68,822	894
13	18,397	1,415	18	26,643	1,480	4	3,434	858	72	3,942,526	54,757
0	–	–	0	–	–	1	578	578	5	144,742	28,948
0	–	–	0	–	–	1	5,000	5,000	4	2,665,184	666,296
0	–	–	0	–	–	0	–	–	2	343,348	171,674
0	–	–	1	15,000	15,000	2	15,000	7,500	5	8,107,044	1,621,409
1	1,301	1,301	0	–	–	0	–	–	4	115,346	28,837
89	706,446	7,938	18	114,414	6,356	10	93,075	9,308	129	11,269,458	87,360
1	7,302	7,302	0	–	–	2	11,453	5,726	6	178,865	29,811

Table A.14
DSCC Contributions

Cycle	Presidential Candidates			Senate Incumbents			Senate Challengers			Senate Open Seats		
	#	Total $	Avg. $	#	Total $	Avg. $	#	Total $	Avg. $	#	Total $	Avg. $
1977–78	0	–	–	13	173,500	13,346	12	160,000	13,333	7	93,500	13,357
1979–80	0	–	–	17	295,000	17,353	9	124,000	13,778	5	62,500	12,500
1981–82	0	–	–	18	297,500	16,528	11	180,000	16,364	3	52,500	17,500
1983–84	0	–	–	7	115,000	16,429	20	222,985	11,149	6	82,050	13,675
1985–86	1	100	100	11	139,658	12,696	18	288,234	16,013	7	138,917	19,845
1987–88	0	–	–	14	145,582	10,399	15	188,891	12,593	11	89,035	8,094
1989–90	0	–	–	15	221,793	14,786	10	142,600	14,260	3	52,500	17,500
1991–92	0	–	–	21	216,000	10,286	13	227,500	17,500	8	140,000	17,500
1993–94	0	–	–	14	227,500	16,250	8	140,000	17,500	9	157,500	17,500

Source: Federal Election Commission, *FEC Reports On Financial Activity: Final Report, Party and Non-Party Political Committees*, vol. 1, Summary Tables, for Cycles 1977–78 through 1993–94. Table K in all reports.

Table A.15
DSCC Expenditures

Cycle	Presidential Candidates			Senate Incumbents			Senate Challengers			Senate Open Seats		
	#	Total $	Avg. $	#	Total $	Avg. $	#	Total $	Avg. $	#	Total $	Avg. $
1977–78	0	–	–	0	–	–	0	–	–	0	–	–
1979–80	0	–	–	11	367,169	33,379	6	176,792	29,465	2	45,355	22,678
1981–82	0	–	–	17	1,008,230	59,308	11	677,099	61,554	3	191,916	63,972
1983–84	0	–	–	13	684,049	52,619	18	1,757,731	97,652	5	1,506,870	301,374
1985–86	0	–	–	3	1,681,800	560,600	14	2,959,881	211,420	7	1,423,691	203,38
1987–88	0	–	–	13	2,014,496	154,961	15	2,911,101	194,073	9	1,280,540	142,28
1989–90	0	–	–	13	2,723,173	209,475	12	1,519,138	126,595	3	282,611	94,20
1991–92	0	–	–	16	3,212,071	200,754	21	5,377,448	256,069	9	2,643,593	293,73
1993–94	0	–	–	12	6,198,205	516,517	11	1,270,756	115,523	10	4,826,941	482,69

Source: Federal Election Commission, *FEC Reports On Financial Activity: Final Repor Party and Non-Party Political Committees*, vol. 1, Summary Tables, for Cycles 1977–7 through 1993–94. Table K in all reports.

APPENDIX

House Incumbents		House Challengers			House Open Seats			Totals		
#	Total $	Avg. $	#	Total $	Avg. $	#	Total $	Avg. $	#	Total $	Avg. $
0	–	–	0	–	–	0	–	–	32	427,000	13,344
0	–	–	0	–	–	0	–	–	31	481,500	15,532
0	–	–	0	–	–	0	–	–	32	530,000	16,562
1	150	150	0	–	–	0	–	–	34	420,185	12,358
8	16,396	2,050	0	–	–	0	–	–	45	583,305	12,962
4	6,174	1,544	0	–	–	0	–	–	44	429,682	9,766
0	–	–	0	–	–	3	15,000	5,000	31	431,893	13,932
0	–	–	1	5,000	5,000	1	5,000	5,000	44	593,500	13,489
0	–	–	1	5,000	5,000	1	5,000	5,000	33	535,000	16,212

House Incumbents			House Challengers			House Open Seats			Totals		
#	Total $	Avg. $	#	Total $	Avg. $	#	Total $	Avg. $	#	Total $	Avg. $
0	–	–	0	–	–	0	–	–	0	–	–
0	–	–	0	–	–	0	–	–	19	589,316	31,017
0	–	–	0	–	–	0	–	–	31	1,877,245	60,556
0	–	–	0	–	–	0	–	–	36	3,948,650	109,685
0	–	–	0	–	–	1	1,000	1,000	25	6,066,372	242,655
1	1,300	1,300	0	–	–	0	–	–	38	6,207,437	163,354
0	–	–	0	–	–	0	–	–	28	4,524,922	161,604
1	2,600	2,600	0	–	–	0	–	–	47	11,235,712	239,058
0	–	–	0	–	–	0	–	–	33	12,295,902	372,603

Table A.16
DCCC Contributions

Cycle	Presidential Candidates			Senate Incumbents			Senate Challengers			Senate Open Seats		
	#	Total $	Avg. $	#	Total $	Avg. $	#	Total $	Avg. $	#	Total $	Avg. $
1977–78	0	–	–	0	–	–	0	–	–	0	–	–
1979–80	0	–	–	0	–	–	0	–	–	0	–	–
1981–82	0	–	–	0	–	–	1	25	25	0	–	–
1983–84	0	–	–	0	–	–	0	–	–	1	1,695	1,695
1985–86	0	–	–	1	2,687	2,687	2	3,800	1,900	1	6,000	6,000
1987–88	1	2,102	2,102	0	–	–	0	–	–	0	–	–
1989–90	0	–	–	3	399	133	1	100	100	0	–	–
1991–92	0	–	–	3	10,300	3,433	3	950	317	4	7,432	1,858
1993–94	0	–	–	1	5,000	5,000	0	–	–	5	11,750	2,350

Source: Federal Election Commission, *FEC Reports On Financial Activity: Final Report, Party and Non-Party Political Committees*, vol. 1, Summary Tables, for Cycles 1977–78 through 1993–94. Table K in all reports.

Table A.17
DCCC Expenditures

Cycle	Presidential Candidates			Senate Incumbents			Senate Challengers			Senate Open Seats		
	#	Total $	Avg. $	#	Total $	Avg. $	#	Total $	Avg. $	#	Total $	Avg. $
1977–78	0	–	–	0	–	–	0	–	–	0	–	–
1979–80	0	–	–	0	–	–	0	–	–	0	–	–
1981–82	0	–	–	0	–	–	0	–	–	0	–	–
1983–84	0	–	–	0	–	–	0	–	–	0	–	–
1985–86	0	–	–	0	–	–	0	–	–	0	–	–
1987–88	0	–	–	0	–	–	0	–	–	0	–	–
1989–90	0	–	–	0	–	–	0	–	–	0	–	–
1991–92	0	–	–	0	–	–	0	–	–	0	–	–
1993–94	0	–	–	0	–	–	0	–	–	0	–	–

Source: Federal Election Commission, *FEC Reports On Financial Activity: Final Repor Party and Non-Party Political Committees*, vol. 1, Summary Tables, for Cycles 1977–7 through 1993–94. Table K in all reports.

APPENDIX

	House Incumbents			House Challengers			House Open Seats			Totals	
#	Total $	Avg. $	#	Total $	Avg. $	#	Total $	Avg. $	#	Total $	Avg. $
65	236,500	3,638	31	95,000	3,065	46	205,938	4,477	142	537,438	3,785
82	335,303	4,089	38	131,033	3,448	37	147,761	3,994	157	614,097	3,911
71	262,072	3,691	111	193,336	1,742	37	107,672	2,910	220	563,105	2,560
95	429,327	4,519	97	188,226	1,940	36	143,519	3,987	229	762,767	3,331
108	175,844	1,628	72	237,634	3,300	51	184,875	3,625	235	610,840	2,599
124	225,574	1,819	109	227,301	2,085	51	214,777	4,211	285	669,754	2,350
125	169,804	1,358	56	105,266	1,880	37	172,163	4,653	222	447,732	2,017
221	337,578	1,528	117	231,364	1,977	102	250,204	2,453	450	837,828	1,862
206	521,066	2,529	111	195,311	1,760	105	257,862	2,456	428	990,989	2,315

	House Incumbents			House Challengers			House Open Seats			Totals	
#	Total $	Avg. $	#	Total $	Avg. $	#	Total $	Avg. $	#	Total $	Avg. $
0	–	–	0	–	–	0	–	–	0	–	–
3	5,800	1,933	2	19,020	9,510	1	9,866	9,866	6	34,686	5,781
22	38,789	1,763	53	66,458	1,254	15	92,689	6,179	90	197,936	2,199
35	536,984	3,978	124	391,056	3,154	22	196,007	8,909	281	1,124,047	4,000
59	483,203	8,190	117	222,479	1,902	35	388,900	11,111	211	1,094,582	5,188
76	1,169,074	15,383	89	828,937	9,314	26	427,592	16,446	191	2,425,603	12,699
92	1,082,416	11,765	88	1,157,288	13,151	31	637,579	20,567	211	2,877,283	13,636
91	1,510,545	7,909	115	1,745,450	15,178	65	879,866	13,536	371	4,135,861	11,148
52	3,373,421	22,194	110	2,132,578	19,387	51	2,224,816	43,624	313	7,730,815	24,699

Table A.18
Average Campaign Disbursements, Democrats

Cycle	Senate Incumbents Avg. $	Senate Challengers Avg. $	Senate Open Seat Avg. $	House Incumbents Avg. $	House Challengers Avg. $	House Open Seats Avg. $
1977–78	618,211	830,282	828,127	103,519	70,948	211,871
1979–80	1,355,660	557,006	1,188,903	158,010	93,313	180,312
1981–82	1,696,226	1,516,015	4,331,959	247,573	141,390	256,004
1983–84	1,755,004	1,515,412	5,797,131	279,203	124,508	350,804
1985–86	2,712,796	1,911,693	2,628,009	349,918	170,562	420,138
1987–88	3,457,145	2,160,770	3,197,528	358,260	143,785	446,959
1989–90	3,618,244	1,401,259	934,046	427,178	131,194	547,541
1991–92	2,851,102	2,551,654	3,145,940	621,890	143,935	480,375
1993–94	5,154,597	1,265,090	2,624,182	620,214	175,616	561,258

Sources: Norman J. Ornstein, Thomas E. Mann, and Michael J. Malbin, *Vital Statistics on Congress 1995–1996* (Washington, D.C.: CQ Press, 1996).

Table A.19
Average Campaign Disbursements, Republicans

Cycle	Senate Incumbents Avg. $	Senate Challengers Avg. $	Senate Open Seat Avg. $	House Incumbents Avg. $	House Challengers Avg. $	House Open Seats Avg. $
1977–78	2,065,674	551,999	812,835	126,022	77,012	189,205
1979–80	1,130,792	937,727	1,076,218	177,345	139,111	224,116
1981–82	2,123,089	1,034,324	3,953,415	287,543	162,354	314,547
1983–84	3,128,622	830,466	4,154,971	278,781	190,960	372,589
1985–86	3,688,089	1,874,864	3,648,555	379,917	141,356	440,830
1987–88	4,111,852	1,547,489	2,575,237	409,217	100,440	484,684
1989–90	3,541,212	1,988,680	2,265,538	414,222	133,889	538,037
1991–92	5,104,086	1,202,141	2,731,801	552,952	181,757	389,847
1993–94	3,934,799	508,494	3,377,844	473,135	275,867	616,724

Sources: Norman J. Ornstein, Thomas E. Mann, and Michael J. Malbin, *Vital Statistics on Congress 1995–1996* (Washington, D.C.: CQ Press, 1996).

Table A.20
Consumer Price Index (CPI) Conversion Factors (CF)

Year	CF	Year	CF	Year	CF	Year	CF
1840	0.06	1880	0.06	1920	0.127	1960	0.189
1841	0.07	1881	0.06	1921	0.114	1961	0.191
1842	0.06	1882	0.06	1922	0.107	1962	0.192
1843	0.06	1883	0.06	1923	0.109	1963	0.195
1844	0.06	1884	0.06	1924	0.109	1964	0.198
1845	0.06	1885	0.06	1925	0.112	1965	0.201
1846	0.06	1886	0.06	1926	0.113	1966	0.207
1847	0.06	1887	0.06	1927	0.111	1967	0.213
1848	0.06	1888	0.06	1928	0.109	1968	0.222
1849	0.05	1889	0.06	1929	0.109	1969	0.234
1850	0.05	1890	0.06	1930	0.106	1970	0.247
1851	0.05	1891	0.06	1931	0.097	1971	0.258
1852	0.05	1892	0.06	1932	0.087	1972	0.266
1853	0.05	1893	0.06	1933	0.083	1973	0.283
1854	0.06	1894	0.06	1934	0.085	1974	0.314
1855	0.06	1895	0.05	1935	0.087	1975	0.343
1856	0.06	1896	0.05	1936	0.089	1976	0.363
1857	0.06	1897	0.05	1937	0.092	1977	0.386
1858	0.06	1898	0.05	1938	0.090	1978	0.416
1859	0.06	1899	0.05	1939	0.089	1979	0.463
1860	0.06	1900	0.05	1940	0.089	1980	0.525
1861	0.06	1901	0.05	1941	0.094	1981	0.579
1862	0.06	1902	0.06	1942	0.104	1982	0.615
1863	0.08	1903	0.06	1943	0.110	1983	0.635
1864	0.10	1904	0.06	1944	0.112	1984	0.662
1865	0.10	1905	0.06	1945	0.115	1985	0.686
1866	0.09	1906	0.06	1946	0.124	1986	0.699
1867	0.09	1907	0.06	1947	0.142	1987	0.724
1868	0.09	1908	0.06	1948	0.154	1988	0.754
1869	0.09	1909	0.06	1949	0.152	1989	0.790
1870	0.08	1910	0.06	1950	0.154	1990	0.833
1871	0.08	1911	0.06	1951	0.166	1991	0.868
1872	0.08	1912	0.06	1952	0.169	1992	0.894
1873	0.08	1913	0.063	1953	0.170	1993	0.921
1874	0.07	1914	0.064	1954	0.171	1994	0 945
1875	0.07	1915	0.064	1955	0.171	1995	0.971
1876	0.07	1916	0.069	1956	0.173	1996	1.000
1877	0.07	1917	0.082	1957	0.179		
1878	0.06	1918	0.096	1958	0.184		
1879	0.06	1919	0.110	1959	0.185		

To convert dollars of a year to 1996 dollars, divide the dollar amount of that year by the conversion factor (CF) for that year. For example, $1,000 in 1930 = $9,434 in 1996 ($1,000 / 0.106). Updated conversion figures are available on the World Wide Web, http://www.orst.edu/Dept/pol_sci/sahr.html. Table by Robert Sahr. Reprinted by permission.

NOTES

Chapter 1

1. Senators were not directly elected nationwide until after 1913.

2. See Ralph M. Goldman, *The National Party Chairmen and Committees: Factionalism at the Top* (Armonk, N.Y.: M. E. Sharpe, 1990), chap. 2.

3. This point is very eloquently made by Leon Epstein, *Political Parties in the American Mold* (Madison: University of Wisconsin Press, 1986).

4. See David B. Truman, *The Congressional Party: A Case Study* (New York: John Wiley, 1959), and James MacGregor Burns, *The Deadlock of Democracy: Four-Party Politics in America* (Englewood Cliffs, N.J.: Prentice-Hall, 1963).

5. Epstein, *Political Parties in the American Mold*, chap. 2, contains an excellent exegesis of these ideas.

6. The classic example is Anthony Downs's definition of political party as "a coalition of men seeking to control the governing apparatus by legal means." Anthony Downs, *An Economic Theory of Democracy* (New York: Harper and Row, 1957), 24. Also, John Aldrich explains that politicians form political parties to provide economies of scale regarding voters, positing that all candidates of a certain party share some common fate. See John H. Aldrich, *Why Parties? The Origin*

and *Transformation of Political Parties in America* (Chicago: University of Chicago Press, 1995).

7. This point is expertly illustrated in David R. Mayhew's *Divided We Govern: Party Control, Lawmaking, and Investigations, 1946–1990* (New Haven: Yale University Press, 1991).

8. At times the highest congressional leaders have simply appointed CCC chairs. In other situations, the CCC chair has been elected by the entire party caucus. In either case, it is not possible for an individual to become CCC chair without the leadership's tacit or active consent.

9. For confirmation, one need only look at the defeat of DCCC chair Rep. James Corman in 1980, the defeat of NRCC chair Rep. Guy Vander Jagt in his 1990 primary election, and the defeat of Speaker Thomas Foley in 1994.

10. This idea is also developed by Gary C. Jacobson in "Party Organization and Distribution of Campaign Resources: Republicans and Democrats in 1982," *Political Science Quarterly* 100 (Winter 1985–86): 603–25.

11. There is a vast literature on this point. See, for example, Gary C. Jacobson, *The Politics of Congressional Elections*, 2d ed. (New York: HarperCollins, 1992), and Paul S. Herrnson, *Congressional Elections: Campaigning at Home and in Washington* (Washington, D.C.: CQ Press, 1995).

12. This emphasis on Washington resources is made by Paul S. Herrnson in both *Party Campaigning in the 1980s* (Cambridge, Mass.: Harvard University Press, 1988) and *Congressional Elections*.

13. This can include filming cable talk shows that are then sent back to the district, making taped statements on the day's issues for use on local radio programs, and a variety of other public relations assistance.

14. See David R. Mayhew, *Congress: The Electoral Connection* (New Haven: Yale University Press, 1974).

15. These may include a special election (in which the time frame is much shorter), an incumbent with a serious challenge (incumbents are always considered to be the CCCs' endorsed candidates), or a primary with a particularly odious candidate, such as David Duke in Louisiana.

16. This is the focus of Daniel M. Shea's *Transforming Democracy: Legislative Campaign Committees and Political Parties* (Albany: State University of New York Press, 1995).

17. For the reasons explained above, the national committees are not generally interested in the specific transactions of the CCCs.

18. See Mancur Olson, *The Logic of Collective Action* (Cambridge, Mass.: Harvard University Press, 1971).

19. See Herrnson, *Party Campaigning in the 1980s*.

20. In theory, each candidate could present a PAC with his or her version of a winning strategy to convince the PAC that a contribution to his or her campaign is a worthwhile investment, and in this way, each candidate would have an equal chance to solicit a contribution. In reality, PACs want to have a realistic assessment of candidate chances, and they rely on CCCs to tell them which races are most competitive, meaning that the least competitive candidates have the most to lose by cooperating with the CCC.

21. Herrnson, *Party Campaigning in the 1980s*, and Hugh A. Bone, *Party Committees and National Politics* (Seattle: University of Washington Press, 1958).

22. This tension is also explored by Frank J. Sorauf and Scott A. Wilson, "Campaigns and Money: A Changing Role for the Political Parties?" in L. Sandy Maisel, ed., *The Parties Respond* (Boulder, Colo.: Westview Press, 1990), 187–203.

23. See Thomas Mann, *Unsafe at Any Margin* (Washington, D.C.: American Enterprise Institute, 1978).

Chapter 2

1. The Seventeenth Amendment to the Constitution, which was ratified in 1913, provides for the direct election of senators, but it was not "to affect the election or term of any Senator chosen before it becomes valid as part of the constitution." Thus some appointed senators may not have sought election by direct means, which may account for the lack of interest in establishing a Senate CCC until 1919.

2. This is the modern name for the Republican House campaign committee. The committee has also gone by several other names: the Union Republican Congressional Committee, the Republican Congressional Committee, and the Republican Congressional Campaign Committee.

3. See Robert J. Dinkin, *Campaigning in America: A History of Election Practices* (New York: Greenwood Press, 1989).

4. Nelson W. Polsby's groundbreaking article, "The Institutionalization of the U.S. House of Representatives," *American Political*

Science Review 62 (1968): 144–68, testifies to the House's development through various empirical indicators.

5. See James G. March and Johan P. Olsen, *Rediscovering Institutions: The Organizational Basis of Politics* (New York: Free Press, 1989).

6. Letter from Zachariah Chandler to his wife, April 25, 1865, Container 3, Zachariah Chandler Papers, Manuscript Division, Library of Congress, Washington, D.C.

7. Richard Abbott, *The Republican Party and the South, 1855–77* (Chapel Hill: University of North Carolina Press, 1986), 47.

8. Ibid., 51.

9. Kenneth M. Stampp, *The Era of Reconstruction, 1865–77* (New York: Vintage Books, 1965), 61–62.

10. See James W. Ceaser, *Presidential Selection: Theory and Development* (Princeton: Princeton University Press, 1979), 112–21, for a fuller discussion.

11. James Sterling Young, *The Washington Community 1800–1828* (New York: Columbia University Press, 1966).

12. George Rothwell Brown, *The Leadership of Congress* (Indianapolis: Bobbs-Merrill, 1922), 69–70.

13. Woodrow Wilson, *Congressional Government* (Baltimore: Johns Hopkins University Press, 1981).

14. The Fourteenth Amendment provided for the application of constitutional protections to all individuals regardless of state desires; the Fifteenth provided the franchise without regard to race.

15. David J. Rothman, *Politics and Power: The United States Senate, 1869–1901* (Cambridge, Mass.: Harvard University Press, 1966), 3.

16. This point has been debated. Polsby, "Institutionalization," argues that the Congress began to institutionalize about that time. H. Douglas Price, "Congress and the Evolution of Legislative Professionalism," in Norman J. Ornstein, ed., *Congress in Change: Evolution and Reform* (New York: Praeger, 1975), 2–23, argues that although the number of members seeking reelection in the postbellum era increases substantially, the beginning of professionalized careers, in which members both seek reelection and achieve it, does not really begin until the realignment of 1896.

17. Rothman, *Politics and Power*, 155–56.

18. Abbott, *The Republican Party and the South*, 87; Jesse Macy, *Party Organization and Machinery* (New York: Century, 1904), 88; Bone, *Party Committees and National Politics*, 127–28; Gordon S. Kleeberg, *The*

Formation of the Republican Party as a National Political Organization (New York: Columbia University, 1911), 226; Republican Congressional Committee, "One Hundred Years: A History of the National Republican Congressional Committee" (Washington, D.C.: Judd and Detweiler, 1966), 13.

19. Bone, *Party Committees and National Politics*, 127.
20. Abbott, *The Republican Party and the South*, 87.
21. See Dinkin, *Campaigning in America*, chap. 4.
22. The Union party was the name adopted by the Northern Republicans during the war to signify their unity with Northern Democrats who also wished for quick restoration of the union. Documents found indicate that the RCC had the name Union attached to it until the late 1860s.
23. Very little is known about the position of "secretary" during these early years. It has most likely evolved into the two positions vice chairman and executive director, the latter being currently charged with oversight of the committee's daily affairs. In the case of Tullock and Schenck, it is clear that Tullock was an activist secretary, but Schenck's papers indicate that the general direction and planning for the specific CCC activities came from Schenck and other influential Republican representatives and senators.
24. Garrison Nelson, "Party Control Periods of the U.S. House of Representatives and the Recruitment of Its Leaders, 1789–1971" (Ph.D. dissertation, University of Iowa, 1973), 84.
25. General Fundraising Letter, Rooms of the Union Congressional Executive Committee, March 1, 1866, Reel 6, Frame 5757, Robert C. Schenck Papers, Microfilm, Hayes Library, Freemont, Ohio.
26. Schenck Papers, Reel 6, Frames 5912, 5980.
27. See the analysis of Andrew Johnson's rhetoric by Jeffrey Tulis, *The Rhetorical Presidency* (Princeton: Princeton University Press, 1987), 87–93.
28. Lawrence N. Powell, "Rejected Republican Incumbents in the 1866 Congressional Nominating Conventions: A Study in Reconstruction Politics," *Civil War History* 19, no. 3 (1973): 219–37.
29. Abbott, *The Republican Party and the South*, 87–109, gives a detailed accounting of these activities.
30. Ibid., 136.
31. Circular, Union Republican Congressional Executive Committee, July 20, 1867, Reel 6, Frame 6227, Schenck Papers.

32. Although as Richard Abbott points out, it was somewhat of a wasteful activity in 1867 since most of the blacks to whom the literature was targeted could not read.

33. Reel 6, Frames 6258–73, Schenck Papers.

34. Robert Booth Fowler and Allen D. Hertzke, *Religion and Politics in America: Faith, Culture, and Strategic Choices* (Boulder, Colo.: Westview Press, 1995), 156.

35. Letter, July 30, 1867, Reel 6, Frame 6240, Schenck Papers.

36. Circular, Executive Committee, January 29, 1868, Reel 6, Frame 6586, Schenck Papers.

37. Abbott, *The Republican Party and the South*, 165.

38. Stampp, *The Era of Reconstruction*, 173.

39. This was the name the committee was using in 1966 when it compiled this centennial booklet.

40. A document confirming a congressional recess in 1868 explains that Congress shall be out of session unless a session is called by "the Hon. Edwin D. Morgan, Chairman of the Union Rep. Cong. Com. on the part of the Senate and Hon. Robt. C. Schenck, Chairman of said Com. on the part of the House." Reel 7, Frame 7101, Schenck Papers. In other places, Morgan is listed as chairman of the full committee, Schenck of the executive committee.

41. Goldman, *The National Party Chairmen and Committees*, 49.

42. Stampp, *The Era of Reconstruction*, 187. The abuse of military heroes as party symbols is certainly nothing new in politics, but as will be shown later, there is a particularly high incidence of their use by the Republicans in the Reconstruction era.

43. The 40th Congress, convened following the 1866 elections, had 192 members; the 41st Congress, convened following the 1868 elections, had 243 members.

44. Abbott, *The Republican Party and the South*, 197.

45. Letter, July 20, 1867, Reel 6, Frame 6230, Schenck Papers.

46. Letter, Thomas Tullock to Robert Schenck, August 7, 1868, Reel 7, Frame 7113, Schenck Papers.

47. Abbott, *The Republican Party and the South*, 198.

48. Michael E. McGerr, *The Decline of Popular Politics: The American North, 1865–1928* (New York: Oxford University Press, 1986), 35.

49. Ibid., 25.

50. Dinkin, *Campaigning in America*, 60.

51. McGerr, *The Decline of Popular Politics*, 27.

52. Republican Congressional Committee, *One Hundred Years*, 22–25.
53. Kleeberg, *Formation of the Republican Party*, 230.
54. Sister Mary Carl George, R.S.M., *Zachariah Chandler: A Political Biography* (East Lansing: Michigan State University Press, 1969), 199.
55. Letter, J. M. Edmunds to Zachariah Chandler, October 14, 1870, Container 3, Chandler Papers.
56. Charles H. Coleman, *The Election of 1868: The Democratic Effort to Regain Control* (New York: Octagon Books, 1971; orig. 1933), 293.
57. Letter, John F. Willard to Samuel J. Randall, February 3, 1870, File: 1870—February 1–15, Box 3; also circular from Rooms of the National Democratic Executive Resident Committee 1870, File: 1870—December and undated, Box 4; both Samuel J. Randall Papers, Special Collections, Van Pelt Library, University of Pennsylvania, Philadelphia.
58. George, *Zachariah Chandler*, 223.
59. Logan's papers contain many appeals for Logan's speaking talents. See, for example, Letter, Charles Spencer to John Logan, February 12, 1868, Container 6, and Letter, Simon Cameron to Mary (Mrs. John) Logan, August 3, 1872, Container 2, both in the Papers of John A. Logan and Family, Manuscript Division, Library of Congress, Washington, D.C.
60. Erwin Stanley Bradley, *Simon Cameron: Lincoln's Secretary of War* (Philadelphia: University of Pennsylvania Press, 1966), 311.
61. Republican Congressional Committee, *One Hundred Years*, 27.
62. Ibid., 30.
63. Ibid., 33.
64. The latter argument has been given by the contemporary RNC as a reason for keeping the three committees separate.
65. McGerr, *The Decline of Popular Politics*, 70.
66. Polsby, "Institutionalization," 145.
67. This was especially true because of the continual growth of the country and the size of the House of Representatives.
68. Brown, *The Leadership of Congress*, 72.
69. For a full treatment of the Speakership, see Ronald M. Peters, Jr., *The American Speakership: The Office in Historical Perspective* (Baltimore: Johns Hopkins University Press, 1990).
70. In fact, at this time (the 51st Congress, 1875) the Rules Committee had five members. The three Republican members were Reed, William McKinley (chairman of the Ways and Means Committee,

which was also charged with floor leadership), and Joseph Cannon (chairman of the Appropriations Committee). Thus the three most powerful individual positions in the chamber were merged with another highly controlling institution.

71. Brown, *The Leadership of Congress*, 92.

72. The Seventeenth Amendment, adopted in May 1913, provides for the direct election of all senators.

73. George H. Haynes, *The Senate of the United States: Its History and Practice* (Boston: Houghton Mifflin, 1938), 83–95.

74. Ibid., 1003–4.

75. Frank Luther Mott, *American Journalism: A History, 1690–1960*, 3d ed. (New York: Macmillan, 1962), 507.

76. Letter, J. S. Clarkson to President Benjamin Harrison, September 19, 1890, September 28, 1890, Reel 29, Series 1, Benjamin Harrison Papers, Manuscript Division, Library of Congress, Washington, D.C.

77. "For Seats in Congress: Both Parties Sending out Information for Voters," *New York Times*, October 7, 1890, sec. 1, p. 1.

78. Ibid.

79. It is unclear what position Clarkson held, but there is correspondence from Clarkson to Harrison on RCC stationery in Harrison's papers.

80. Robert H. Wiebe, *The Search for Order, 1877–1929* (New York: Hill and Wang, 1967), 113–29.

81. McGerr, *The Decline of Popular Politics*, 138–60.

82. Ibid., 150.

83. Dinkin, *Campaigning in America*, 99.

84. McGerr, *The Decline of Popular Politics*, 144.

85. Herbert Croly, *Marcus Alonzo Hanna: His Life and Work* (New York: Macmillan, 1923), 217.

86. Republican Congressional Committee, *One Hundred Years*, 34.

87. Ibid., 35.

88. McGerr, *The Decline of Popular Politics*, 157.

89. Mott, *American Journalism*, 549.

90. H. F. Dodge, "Journal of Campaign Tour of Hon. Joseph G. Cannon, Speaker of the House of Representatives, United States Congress, September 15th to November 3rd 1904," File: Campaign Tour of Hon. Joseph G. Cannon and Party, Box 10, Joseph G. Cannon Collection, Illinois State Historical Society, Springfield.

91. McGerr, *The Decline of Popular Politics*, 146.

92. Letter, Henry De La Warr Flood to Col. Joseph Button, February 14, 1906, File: General Correspondence—Feb. 1906, Box 30, Papers of Henry D. Flood, Manuscript Division, Library of Congress, Washington, D.C.

93. This is the first instance of the use of Democratic Congressional *Campaign* Committee, the name I will use hereafter.

94. "Griggs to Run Campaign," *New York Times*, March 7, 1906, sec. 1, p. 6.

95. "Griggs in Williams' Place," newspaper clipping, December 25, 1907, File: Series 4—1908—#61, Box 5, James M. Griggs Papers, Southern Historical Collection, Library of the University of North Carolina at Chapel Hill.

96. Democratic Congressional Committee, *Democratic Campaign Book: Congressional Election*, Folder: 80, Vol. 7, Griggs Papers.

97. Ibid.

98. Samuel Kernell, "Toward Understanding 19th-Century Congressional Careers: Ambition, Competition, and Rotation," *American Journal of Political Science* 21 (1977): 671–72.

99. Michael Abram and Joseph Cooper, "The Rise of Seniority in the House of Representatives," *Polity* 1 (1968): 68.

100. John D. Baker, "The Character of the Congressional Revolution of 1910," *Journal of American History* 60 (1973): 680.

101. The Norris Resolution (named for its sponsor, George Norris) called for an expansion of Rules Committee membership from five members to ten members, elected by the House rather than appointed by the Speaker. Six would be members of the majority party, four of the minority. The Speaker would be denied membership on the committee. Brown, *The Leadership of Congress*, 165.

102. Baker, "Character of the Congressional Revolution," 683–86.

103. Randall B. Ripley, *Party Leaders in the House of Representatives* (Washington, D.C.: Brookings Institution, 1967), 25.

104. This refers to the system of rewards and punishments for deviant voting behavior that had previously been administered by the Speaker. Sanctions could include dismissal from powerful committee positions or the lack of recognition during floor debates.

105. James S. Fleming, "Re-establishing Leadership in the House of Representatives: The Case of Oscar W. Underwood," *Mid-America* 54 (1972): 244.

106. Seniority remained the primary determinant in powerful committee assignments through the mid-1970s, when party rules in Congress changed again to bypass seniority considerations when members desired this. In the 104th Congress the Republican majority in the House chose to return more power to the Speaker in the matters of committee assignments and selection of committee chairs.

107. Baker, "Character of the Congressional Revolution," 685.

108. This is the first occasion of the name change from RCC to NRCC: National Republican Congressional Committee.

109. McGerr, *The Decline of Popular Politics*, 161, comments on the NRCC's inactivity in 1912.

110. "Democratic Joint Plans," *New York Times*, May 18, 1913, sec. 1, p. 13.

111. "Harmony the Note of Republican Talk," *New York Times*, May 25, 1913, sec. 1, p. 1.

112. "Executive Committee Meeting, March 14, 1914," File: Republican National Congressional Committee Minutes, Box 53, William B. McKinley Papers, Syracuse University, Syracuse, New York.

113. Republican Congressional Committee, *One Hundred Years*, 39.

114. Ibid., 37–38.

115. Although the Democrats organized the House after 1916, it is because of the nine Independents who threw their support for Champ Clark's election as Speaker. The Democrats won 210 seats, the Republicans 216.

116. Republican Congressional Committee, *One Hundred Years*, 41.

117. Ibid., 42–43.

118. "Wilson's Campaign Plans," *New York Times*, October 1, 1914, sec. 1, p. 6.

119. Goldman, *National Party Chairmen and Committees*, 236–38.

120. McGerr, *The Decline of Popular Politics*, 162–64.

121. "Minutes—February 25, 1915," File: Republican National Congressional Committee Minutes, Box 53, McKinley Papers.

122. "Republicans Urged to Use New System," *New York Times*, December 24, 1916, sec. 1, p. 10.

123. Seward W. Livermore, *Politics Is Adjourned: Woodrow Wilson and the War Congress, 1916–1918* (Middletown, Conn.: Wesleyan University Press, 1966), 111.

124. That is, for the purposes of conducting the campaign. It does not appear that the organizations completely merged. It also appears

that the senatorial committee was already a separate entity at this time, but there is insufficient evidence to say this with certainty.

125. "McCormick to Fight for 1918 Congress," *New York Times*, November 22, 1916, sec. 1, p. 9.

126. Livermore, *Politics Is Adjourned*, 112.

127. Ibid., 114.

128. From time to time prominent former members have held high-level positions in the campaign committees.

129. Livermore, *Politics Is Adjourned*, 113.

130. Memo, Hays to Fess, October 18, 1918, (no file), Box 37, Simeon D. Fess Papers, Ohio Historical Society, Columbus.

131. "Notebook on Special Committee of the Republican National Congressional Committee, June 13, 1917," Box 37, Fess Papers.

132. Ibid., 111.

133. "Memorandum—Between Republican National Committee and National Republican Congressional Committee," Box 37, Fess Papers.

134. Letter, Simeon D. Fess to Will H. Hays, March 29, 1920, File: 4, Box 13, Fess Papers.

135. *Springfield Sun*, November 3, 1918, quoted in John Nethers, *Simeon D. Fess: Educator and Politician* (Brooklyn: Pageant-Poseidon, 1973), 177.

136. Campaign pamphlet, File 1: Box 34, Fess Papers.

137. Burton Ira Kaufman, "Henry De La Warr Flood: A Case Study of Organizational Politics in an Era of Reform" (Ph.D. dissertation, Rice University, 1966), 144.

138. Letter, Henry D. Flood to W. H. Steele, September 27, 1920, File: General Correspondence—September 1920, Box 56, Flood Papers.

Chapter 3

1. Walter J. Oleszek, "Party Whips in the United States Senate," *Journal of Politics* 33 (1971): 958.

2. Dinkin, *Campaigning in America*, chap. 6.

3. Republican Congressional Committee, *One Hundred Years*, 45.

4. Letter, Medill McCormick to Mrs. Mary Hight, July 17, 1922, File: Joseph Medill McCormick General Correspondence, July 1922, Box 7, Hanna-McCormick Family Papers, Manuscript Division, Library of Congress, Washington, D.C.

5. Various financial statements, File: Joseph Medill McCormick General Correspondence, October 26–31, 1922, Box 8, Hanna-McCormick Family Papers. The NRSC also made a loan to the NRCC.

6. Letter, Publicity Director to E. B. Clements, October 17, 1922, File: Joseph Medill McCormick General Correspondence, October 17–25, 1922, Box 8, Hanna-McCormick Family Papers; *The Truth, the Facts, the Record*, Republican Text Book–Campaign 1922, File: Speech File Joseph Medill McCormick 1922, Box 110, Hanna-McCormick Family Papers.

7. Letter, Medill McCormick to George H. Moses, February 26, 1923, File: Joseph Medill McCormick General Correspondence, February 1923, Box 8, Hanna-McCormick Family Papers.

8. Letter, Medill McCormick to George L. Meyer, May 6, 1922, File: Joseph Medill McCormick General Correspondence, May 1–6, 1922, Box 7, Hanna-McCormick Family Papers.

9. "The Democratic Senatorial Campaign Committee—Receipts and Expenditures 1918," Box 2, Series: Political Committees—Reports 1918, Records of Congress, National Archives, Washington, D.C.

10. Press Release, File: Maryland, Box 8, Papers of Edwin A. Halsey, Manuscript Division, Library of Congress, Washington, D.C.

11. Merrill A. Symonds, "George Higgins Moses of New Hampshire: The Man and the Era" (Ph.D. dissertation, Clark University, 1955), 201–6.

12. Ibid., 274.

13. Ibid., 286.

14. The practice of using employees of the House and Senate to staff the CCCs (thus saving the expense of staff salaries) carried on for both chambers until campaign finance reform law changes in the 1970s.

15. Letter, Claude Swanson to James P. Pope, September 1, 1932, File: Idaho, Box 6, Halsey Papers.

16. Letter, Claude Swanson to Walter Gleason, September 30, 1932, File: Oregon, Box 10, Halsey Papers.

17. Letter, Claude Swanson to Frederick Van Nuys, September 23, 1933, File: Indiana, Box 6, Halsey Papers.

18. Letter, Edwin Halsey to James Pope, August 26, 1932, File: Idaho, Box 6, Halsey Papers.

19. Letter, Edwin Halsey to Senator Carl Hatch, October 26, 1934, File: New Mexico, Box 9, Halsey Papers.

20. Joseph F. Guffey, *Seventy Years on the Red-Fire Wagon* (N.p.: Privately printed, 1952), 114, 150–52.

21. Memorandum to Democratic Senatorial Candidates, July 21, 1938, File: Indiana, Box 6, Halsey Papers.

22. "List of Pamphlets . . . ," 1938, File: 45, Box 3, Prentiss Marsh Brown Collection, Michigan Historical Collections, Bentley Historical Library, University of Michigan.

23. Letter, Halsey to Senator Prentiss Brown, July 28, 1938, File: 40, Box 3, Brown Collection.

24. Statement of the Democratic Senatorial Campaign Committee, June 10, 1939, File: 44, Box 3, Brown Collection.

25. G. Gould Lincoln, "Purge Efforts End in New York: After Tuesday Campaign Will Be Between G.O.P. and Democrats," source and date unknown, [September 1938], File: 44, Box 3, Brown Collection.

26. Letter, Halsey to Ernest McFarland, September 16, 1940, File: Arizona, Box 5, Halsey Papers.

27. Letter, Joseph Guffey to John McClellan, August 13, 1942, File: Arkansas, Box 5, Halsey Papers.

28. Letter, Joseph O'Mahoney to Hyman Guss, September 22, 1944, File: Utah, Box 12, Halsey Papers.

29. Letter, Scott W. Lucas to Adrian H. Scolten, August 31, 1948, Folder: 6, Box 123, Scott W. Lucas Papers, Illinois State Historical Society, Springfield; Letter, Scott W. Lucas to A. J. Sabath, October 11, 1948, File: Democratic Senatorial Campaign Committee, Box 123, Lucas Papers.

30. Press Release from the Office of Senator Scott W. Lucas, November 1, 1948, Folder: 6, Box 123, Lucas Papers.

31. Letter, Scott W. Lucas to Alben Barkley, May 22, 1945, Folder: 14, Box 207, Lucas Papers.

32. Letter, Clinton Anderson to William Boyle, February 10, 1950, File: Senatorial Campaign Committee 1950—Sen. Anderson Chairman, Box 1051, Clinton P. Anderson Papers, Manuscript Division, Library of Congress, Washington, D.C.

33. Letter, Kenneth Fry to Clinton Anderson, September 5, 1950, File: VEEP SPOT ENDORSEMENT: Senatorial Campaign Committee, 1950, Box 1050, Anderson Papers.

34. Letter, William Boyle to Clinton Anderson, February 24, 1950, File: Senatorial Campaign Committee, 1950—Sen. Anderson Chairman, Box 1051, Anderson Papers.

35. Memo, J. J. P. to Senator Anderson, August 28, 1950, File: Senatorial Campaign Committee, 1950—Sen. Anderson, Chairman, Box 1051, Anderson Papers.

36. Memorandum, Carol Graf to Senators, n.d., File: Maryland: Senatorial Campaign Committee, 1950, Box 1052, Anderson Papers.

37. Letter, Clinton Anderson to Bill Boyle, May 4, 1951, File: Democratic National Committee—Denver, Box 1051, Anderson Papers.

38. Often it appears the CCCs were not organized formally until the summer or fall of the upcoming election year.

39. "The Senate Picture," File: Political Series-Senatorial-Senate Campaign Workbook, Box 242, Earle C. Clements Collection, Special Collections, University Archives, University of Kentucky Libraries.

40. Letter, Earle Clements to Stephen Mitchell, November 7, 1952, File: Political Series-Senatorial-Senate Campaign Committee-Personnel 1952, Box 242, Clements Collection.

41. Memorandum to Senator Clements, November 12, 1952, File: Political Series-Senatorial-Senate Campaign Committee (Birkhead Memoranda), Box 241, Clements Collection.

42. Letter, Joseph M. Upchurch to Julian Henning, July 30, 1958, File: Post Senatorial Series-Subjects-DSCC Contributions-1958, Box 191, Clements Collection.

43. Senate Democratic Policy Committee, Press Release, April 22, 1953, File: Political Series-Senatorial-Senate Campaign Committee-General, 1952–54, Box 241, Clements Collection.

44. Letter, Ken Birkhead to Senator Clements, n.d., File: Political Series-Senatorial-Senate Campaign Committee (Finances 1952, 1953), Box 241, Clements Collection.

45. Letter, Stephen Mitchell to Earle Clements, September 22, 1953, File: Political Series-Senatorial-Senate Campaign Committee (Finances, 1952, 1953), Box 241, Clements Collection.

46. Letter, Stanley Woodward to Earle Clements, May 10, 1954, File: Political Series-Senatorial-Senate Campaign Committee (Campaign Expenditures, 1954, Folder 1), Box 241, Clements Collection.

47. Letter, Earle Clements to Lyndon Johnson, May 27, 1955, File: Political Series-Senatorial-Senate Campaign Committee (Report of Senator Clements on his resignation, 1955), Box 242, Clements Collection.

48. Letter, Earle Clements to Alan Bible, November 11, 1954, File: Political Series-Senatorial-Senate Campaign Committee (Campaign Expenditures, 1954, Folder 1), Box 241, Clements Collection.

NOTES TO PAGES 86–89 255

49. "Republican Conference Rules," File: 257, 1 EMD Leadership Series, Everett M. Dirksen Papers, Everett McKinley Dirksen Congressional Leadership Research Center, Pekin, Ill.
50. "Informal Views Regarding the Organization for the National Management of the Republican Party," March 16, 1951, File: 271, Dirksen Papers.
51. Report of Receipts and Disbursements made by the National Republican Senatorial Committee, January 1 to December 31, 1952, File: 196, Dirksen Papers.
52. Letter, Sinclair Weeks to Everett McKinley Dirksen, January 3, 1952, File: 88, Dirksen Papers.
53. "A Report to the Republican Conference by the Chairman of the National Republican Senatorial Committee," December 1952, File: 256, Dirksen Papers.
54. Form letter, Everett McKinley Dirksen to all committeemen, September 5, 1952, File: 95, Dirksen Papers.
55. Letter, Everett McKinley Dirksen to Styles Bridges, August 12, 1952, File: 106, Dirksen Papers.
56. Letter, Dirksen to Hobart Atkins, August 12, 1952, File: 94; Letter, Dirksen to Gore, undated, File: 100; both in Dirksen Papers.
57. Letter, Dirksen to Styles Bridges, August 12, 1952, File: 106; A Report to the Republican Conference by the Chairman of the NRSC, File: 256; both in Dirksen Papers.
58. Letter, Dirksen to Harold S. Taylor, October 19, 1951, File: 87, Dirksen Papers.
59. Letter, Dirksen to John W. Bricker, June 24, 1952, File: 105, Dirksen Papers.
60. "A Report to the Republican Conference . . ." December 1952, File: 256, Dirksen Papers.
61. Bulletin, "The Republican Senatorial Committee," File: 144, Dirksen Papers.
62. Letter, Everett Dirksen to All Candidates, August 27, 1954, File: 134, Dirksen Papers.
63. Letter, Dirksen to Clifford Case, July 6, 1954, File: 119, Dirksen Papers.
64. Glee Gomien (personal secretary to Everett Dirksen [and later NRSC staffer]), personal interview by author, Bethesda, Md., 7 December 1990.
65. Letter, Barry Goldwater to Everett Dirksen, February 8, 1955, File: 136, Dirksen Papers.

66. Barry M. Goldwater, with Jack Casserly, *Goldwater* (New York: Doubleday, 1988), 113.

67. Earlier in this chapter, the DSCC activities during the 1952 and 1954 cycles under Earle Clements were recounted, though the possibility of a DSCC shutdown was discussed. It is plausible that the DSCC was not active in 1955 and that Smathers's recollection could be based on this.

68. Letter, George Smathers to Editor, *Mobile Register*, November 3, 1960, File: 57c Dem. Sen. Camp. Comm. 1960, Box 27, George A. Smathers Collection, P. K. Yonge Library of Florida History, University of Florida.

69. Letter, George A. Smathers to Senator Vance Hartke, October 21, 1960, File: 57c Dem. Sen. Camp. Comm. 1960, Box 27, Smathers Collection.

70. A visit to the Smathers Papers at the University of Florida found nothing more than routine memos on DSCC matters. Archivists there said that Smathers personally went through the papers at the archive and pulled all material he deemed "sensitive."

71. Goldman, *National Party Chairmen and Committees*, 450–67.

72. Letter, George A. Smathers to Paul Butler, October 21, 1958, File: 57b, Box 17, Smathers Collection.

73. Letter, Everett McKinley Dirksen to Thruston B. Morton, January 29, 1963, File: Republican Senatorial Campaign Committee, 1963–65, Box 16, Thruston B. Morton Collection, Special Collections, University Archives, University of Kentucky Libraries.

74. Letter, Thruston B. Morton to Everett McKinley Dirksen, January 31, 1963, File: Republican Senatorial Campaign Committee, 1963–65, Box 16, Morton Collection.

75. See Sara Judith Smiley, "The Political Career of Thruston B. Morton: The Senate Years, 1956–1968" (Ph.D. dissertation, University of Kentucky, Lexington, 1975), 137–57.

76. Letter, Thruston B. Morton to Dean Burch, Chairman, RNC, December 3, 1964, File: Republican National Committee, 1963–68, Box 26, Morton Collection.

77. Letter, Thruston B. Morton to Hon. Donald Rumsfeld, April 14, 1965, File: Republican Senatorial Campaign Committee, 1963–65, Box 16, Morton Collection.

78. Ibid.

NOTES TO PAGES 94–96 257

79. Letter, Thruston B. Morton to Wirt A. Yerger, Chairman, Mississippi Republican Party, File: 1965–1968 Politics Misc., Box 19, Morton Collection.

80. Paul Hope, "Capitol GOP Battles Committee on Funds," *Evening Star* (Washington, D.C.), February 16, 1966.

81. Memo to Thruston B. Morton (sender unidentified), March 1, 1966, File: Republican Senatorial Campaign Committee, 1966, Box 16, Morton Collection.

82. Memos from Jessie Robertson to Warren Magnuson, October 12, 19, and 23, 1964, File: 1, Box 218, Warren G. Magnuson Papers, University of Washington Libraries.

83. Letter, Daniel K. Inouye to Warren Magnuson, February 3, 1964, File: 1, Box 218, Magnuson Papers.

84. Letter, Birch Bayh to Warren Magnuson, September 10, 1964, File: 1, Box 218, Magnuson Papers.

85. Letter, Warren G. Magnuson to Judge James Tunnell, August 24, 1966, File: 2, Box 218, Magnuson Papers.

86. Letter, Fred to Boss [Magnuson], January 9, 1964, File: 1, Box 218, Magnuson Papers.

87. Letter, George Murphy to Thruston Morton, December 13, 1966, File: Republican Senatorial Campaign Committee 1966–68, Box 26, Morton Collection.

88. Philip A. Klinkner, *The Losing Parties: Out-Party National Committees, 1956–1993* (New Haven: Yale University Press, 1994), 80.

89. Letter, George Murphy to Thruston Morton, May 9, 1967, File: Republican Senatorial Campaign Committee 1966–68, Box 26, Morton Collection.

90. Letter, George Murphy to Thruston Morton, May 23, 1967, File: Republican Senatorial Campaign Committee 1966–68, Box 26, Morton Collection.

91. Letter, George Murphy to Thruston Morton, September 7, 1967, File: Republican Senatorial Campaign Committee, 1966–68, Box 26, Morton Collection.

92. Letter, George Murphy to Thruston Morton, July 11, 1967, File: Republican Senatorial Campaign Committee, 1966–68, Box 26, Morton Collection.

93. Letter, George Murphy to Thruston Morton, February 15, 1968, File: Republican Senatorial Campaign Committee 1966–68, Box 26, Morton Collection.

94. David Menefee-Libey, "The Politics of National Party Organization: The Democrats from 1968 to 1986" (Ph.D. dissertation, University of Chicago, 1990), chap. 4, 33–44.

Chapter 4

1. Republican Congressional Committee, *One Hundred Years*, 46.
2. Ann B. Irish, "Joseph Wellington Byrns of Tennessee," manuscript.
3. Jewell M. Galloway, "Speaker Joseph W. Byrns: Party Leader in the New Deal," *Tennessee Historical Quarterly* 25 (1966): 67.
4. Ibid., 69.
5. Joseph W. Byrns, "Duties of Democratic Congressional Committee," in Floyd M. Riddick, *Congressional Procedure* (Boston: Chapman and Grimes, 1941), appendix, 345.
6. Associated Press, "Feelers Sent Out to Learn How F.D.R. Stands in Nation," June 28, 1934.
7. Irish, "Joseph Wellington Byrns."
8. For a full discussion of the concept of realignment, as well as information on the 1932 realignment in particular, see James L. Sundquist, *Dynamics of the Party System* (Washington, D.C.: Brookings Institution, 1983).
9. Republican Congressional Committee, *One Hundred Years*, 46–47.
10. Ibid., 47.
11. John L. Murphy, "Joseph M. Martin, Jr., 1924–1939" (M.A. thesis, Bridgewater State College, 1975), 73–74.
12. "National Affairs—The Congress," *Time* 31, no. 15, p. 13; File: 1938, Box 94, Joseph Martin Papers, Stonehill College, North Easton, Mass.
13. Martin alluded to the NRCC's money troubles (nothing new to the NRCC) in a letter to a member of Congress explaining why only a partial contribution was en route. See Letter, Martin to James W. Mott, July 19, 1938, File: 1938-17-LDR-G, Box 7, Martin Papers.
14. Letter, August H. Andresen to Joseph W. Martin, July 7, 1938, File: 1938-17-LDR-A, Box 7, Martin Papers.
15. Letter, Joseph W. Martin to All New Members, November 1938, Display Window, Martin Papers.
16. Robert A. Caro, *The Years of Lyndon Johnson: The Path to Power* (New York: Vintage Books, 1983), 608.

17. Ibid., 606–62.
18. Henry A. Scheele, *Charlie Halleck: A Political Biography* (New York: Exposition Press, 1966), 108.
19. Republican Congressional Committee, *One Hundred Years*, 49.
20. Scheele, *Charlie Halleck*, 108.
21. Ibid., 111–12.
22. Republican Congressional Committee, *One Hundred Years*, 51.
23. Ibid., 52.
24. Stanley Kelley, Jr., *Professional Public Relations and Political Power* (Baltimore: Johns Hopkins University Press, 1956), 35.
25. Republican Congressional Committee, "Blueprint for Victory": 1954 Campaign Services (pamphlet), File: 261, 1 EMD Leadership, Dirksen Papers.
26. Letter, Harold Slater to All Members, January 20, 1956, File: 218, Box 79, Martin Papers.
27. Bulletins from Harold Slater to All Members, February 20, 1957; August 1, 1957; June 20, 1957; all in File: 219, Box 79, Martin Papers.
28. Bulletin no. 6 by Richard M. Simpson, January 28, 1957, File: 219.1, Box 80, Martin Papers.
29. Bulletin no. 1, Committee Services, Harold Slater to Members, January 8, 1958, File: 220, Box 80, Martin Papers.
30. William R. Sweeney (former executive director of the DCCC), personal interview by author, Washington, D.C., 19 October 1989.
31. Menefee-Libey, "The Politics of National Party Organization," chap. 4, 7–10. The DSCC provided similar travel expense funds in the 1950s and 1960s; see chap. 3.
32. Michael J. Kirwan, with Jack Redding, *How to Succeed in Politics* (New York: MacFadden-Bartell, 1964), 10–22.
33. Letter, Michael J. Kirwan to Democratic Colleagues, February 13, 1964, File: Campaign 1964, Box 231, Thomas P. O'Neill Papers, Special Collections, Boston College.
34. Letter, Michael J. Kirwan to Democratic Colleagues, March 21, 1969, File: CCC 1969–70, Box 177, Ed Edmondson Collection, Northeastern State University, Talequah, Okla.
35. Unfortunately, Kirwan left no papers of substance, greatly hindering our knowledge of DCCC operations.
36. Letter, William E. Miller to Republican Colleagues, February 3, 1960; Letter, William E. Miller to Republican Colleagues, June 24,

1960; both in File: Political Affairs, Rep. Congressional Committee, Box 82, Robert C. Wilson Papers, San Diego State University, San Diego, Calif.

37. Letter, William E. Miller to Republican Colleagues, June 3, 1960, File: Political Affairs, Rep. Congressional Committee, Box 82, Wilson Papers.

38. "Republican Dinner Fact Sheet," n.d., File: Political Affairs (yellow label), Rep. Congressional Committee, Box 82, Wilson Papers.

39. Untitled press release, File: Election, Box 82; and UPI wire release, June 13, 1961, File: Election, Box 82; both in Wilson Papers.

40. Untitled press release, File: Election, Box 82, Wilson Papers.

41. Ibid., 3.

42. "Goldwater Backing Arizonan for Top House Campaign Job," press release, North American Newspaper Alliance, June 5, 1961, 1, File: Political Affairs, Rep. Congressional Committee, Box 82, Wilson Papers.

43. Republican Congressional Committee Personnel Lists, File: Congressional Committee, Staff, Box 81, Wilson Papers.

44. National Republican Congressional Committee Financial Report, File: Republican Congressional Committee Financial Reports, Box 74, Wilson Papers.

45. Letter, Bob Wilson to Charlie Halleck, April 10, 1962, File: Republican Congressional Committee Misc., Box 74, Wilson Papers.

46. Memo to RNC Chairman Ray C. Bliss from C. Langhorne Washburn, February 7, 1968, File: PA Congressional Committee January–February, Box 79, Wilson Papers.

47. Letter, Bob Wilson to John J. Schiff, March 12, 1968, File: PA Congressional Committee March–April, Box 79, Wilson Papers.

48. National Republican Congressional Committee Personnel List, November 14, 1968, File: PA Congressional Committee November–December, Box 79, Wilson Papers.

49. Chairman's Bulletin from Bob Wilson to Republican Colleagues, January 20, 1968, File: PA Congressional Committee January–February, Box 79, Wilson Papers.

50. Chairman's Bulletin from Bob Wilson to Republican Colleagues, February 14, 1968, File: PA Congressional Committee January–February, Box 79, Wilson Papers.

51. Memo, Bob Wilson to Lee Potter, April 11, 1968, File: PA Congressional Committee March–April, Box 79, Wilson Papers.

52. Letter, Charles E. Goodell to Bob Wilson, January 15, 1968, File: PA Congressional Committee January–February, Box 79, Wilson Papers.

53. Appointment Letter for Lee Bowman, June 13, 1969, File: PA Congressional Committee April–June, Box 78, Wilson Papers.

54. "1970 Marginal Congressional Seats," File: PA Congressional Committee November–December, Box 79; Letter, Bob Wilson to Hon. Seymour Halperm, July 15, 1969, File: PA Congressional Committee July–September, Box 78, Wilson Papers.

55. Letter, John T. Calkins, NRCC Executive Director to James Shue, June 2, 1970, File: PA Congressional Committee January–March, Box 81, Wilson Papers.

56. The Booster's Club was a separate fund-raising account for the exclusive use of challengers.

57. Letter, I. Lee Potter, NRCC Executive Director, to Hon. William McCulloch, November 18, 1969, File: PA Congressional Committee October–December, Box 78, Wilson Papers.

58. National Republican Congressional Committee Personnel List 2/19/70, File: PA Congressional Committee January–March, Box 81, Wilson Papers.

59. Pamphlet, "Nixon Needs House Power 1970," File: PA Congressional Committee January–March, Box 81, Wilson Papers.

60. Correspondence between Bob Wilson and I. Lee Potter, May 13–15, 1969, File: PA Congressional Committee April–June, Box 78, Wilson Papers.

61. Memorandum to Bob Wilson and I. Lee Potter from Ed Terrill, December 2, 1969, File: PA Congressional Committee October–December, Box 78, Wilson Papers.

62. Letter, Rogers C. B. Morton to Bob Wilson, July 23, 1969, File: PA Congressional Committee July–September, Box 78, Wilson Papers.

63. Letter, Bob Wilson to Mr. H. C. Fuller, August 13, 1969, File: PA Congressional Committee July–September, Box 78, Wilson Papers.

64. Republican Majority Dinner Report, April 8, 1970, File: PA Congressional Committee January–March, Box 81, Wilson Papers.

65. Letter, Bob Wilson to James Matthews, February 27, 1970, File: PA Congressional Committee January–March, Box 81, Wilson Papers.

66. Letter, Bob Wilson to Republican Colleagues, 1972, File: PA Congressional Committee January–March, Box 81, Wilson Papers.

67. Letter, Bob Wilson to Republican Colleagues, August 17, 1972, File: PA Congressional Committee August, Box 75, Wilson Papers.

68. Letter, Bob Wilson to William Ketchum, October 14, 1972, File: PA Congressional Committee October, Box 75, Wilson Papers.

69. Lester Bell, "Congressman Tells of Ford's Help: Haldeman Tried to Oust Him, Wilson Says," *San Diego Union*, August 13, 1974.

70. Menefee-Libey, "Politics of National Party Organization," chap. 4, 14.

71. "Democratic National Congressional Committee—Committee Report for Campaign 1972," March 20, 1973, File: DNC 1973, Box 201, O'Neill Papers.

Chapter 5

1. See Barbara Sinclair, *The Transformation of the U.S. Senate* (Baltimore: Johns Hopkins University Press, 1989).

2. Herrnson, *Party Campaigning in the 1980s*.

3. See John J. Coleman, "Resurgent or Just Busy? Party Organizations in Contemporary America," in *The State of the Parties*, 2d ed., ed. John C. Green and Daniel Shea (Lanham, Md.: Rowman and Littlefield, 1996), 367–84.

4. For a thorough treatment of campaign finance before 1970, see George Thayer, *Who Shakes the Money Tree?* (New York: Simon and Schuster, 1973).

5. Jeffrey M. Berry and Jerry Goldman, "Congress and Public Policy: A Study of the Federal Election Campaign Act of 1971," *Harvard Journal on Legislation* 10 (1973): 336.

6. This topic is discussed at length in Robert L. Peabody et al., *To Enact a Law: Congress and Campaign Financing* (New York: Praeger, 1972).

7. The Federal Corrupt Practices Act of 1925 was rarely enforced rigorously, especially since it was administered by the clerk of the House and the secretary of the Senate, employees of the regulated.

8. Sweeney, interview..

9. Robert L. Peabody, *Leadership in Congress: Stability, Succession, and Change* (Boston: Little, Brown, 1976), 211–12, 242.

10. Berry and Goldman, "Congress and Public Policy," 354.

11. Ibid., 361.

12. For a colorful discussion of his tenure at the DCCC, see Tip O'Neill, with William Novak, *Man of the House: The Life and Political Memoirs of Speaker Tip O'Neill* (New York: Random House, 1987), 207–10.

13. Susan B. King and Robert L. Peabody, "Control of Presidential Campaign Financing," in Harvey C. Mansfield, ed., *Congress Against the President, Proceedings of the Academy of Political Science* 32, no. 1 (1975): 181.

14. Brooks Jackson, *Broken Promise: Why the Federal Election Commission Failed* (New York: Priority Press Publications, 1990), 27.

15. Peabody, *Leadership in Congress*, 242.

16. Sweeney, interview.

17. Memorandum from Democratic Associates to Wayne Hays, May 7, 1973, File: DNC 1973, Box 201, O'Neill Papers.

18. Memorandum from Edmund L. Henshaw, Jr. (Executive Director, DCCC), to all Democratic Congressmen, March 19, 1973, File: DNC 1973, Box 201, O'Neill Papers.

19. Letter, Bob Michel to All Republican Colleagues, June 6, 1973, File: Political Affairs—Congressional Committee, Box 75, Wilson Papers.

20. Memorandum from Senator Lloyd Bentsen to Senators, Administrative Assistants, Legislative Assistants, December 5, 1973, File: 21, Box 201, Magnuson Papers.

21. Though for the times the spending limits were not considered to be particularly restrictive. Although many complained about the principle of spending limits, few were materially affected by the cap.

22. Buckley v. Valeo 424 U.S. 1 (1976).

23. Ford nominated the same people who had been serving as governors under the old arrangement.

24. Menefee-Libey, " Politics of National Party Organization," chap. 6, p. 5.

25. For more discussion of this event, see chapter 7.

26. Steven Stockmeyer (former executive director, NRCC), personal interview by author, Washington, D.C., 26 October 1989.

27. Stockmeyer, interview.

28. Rep. Guy Vander Jagt, personal interview by author, Washington, D.C., 12 December 1990.

29. James R. Wagner, "Big Government: All-Purpose Issue of 1976," *Congressional Quarterly Weekly Reports*, October 23, 1976, pp. 3036–37.

30. Stockmeyer, interview.

31. Included in these amendments was the provision that congressmen could not keep surplus campaign contributions for personal expenses once they left office as had been the tradition. The sitting congressmen were "grandfathered." Later, the provision was modified to apply only to members who were elected prior to 1980 and left Congress by 1993.

32. Congressional Quarterly, *1978 Congressional Quarterly Almanac* (Washington, D.C.: CQ Press, 1979), 769.

33. Stockmeyer, interview.

34. Nancy Sinnott Dwight (former executive director, NRCC), telephone interview by author, 7 August 1990.

35. Paul E. Ried, *The Orator: Guy Vander Jagt on the Hustings*. (Ottawa, Ill.: Green Hill, 1984), 12.

36. Rhodes Cook, "1976 Election Showed Erosion of GOP Base," *Congressional Quarterly Weekly Reports*, March 19, 1977, 488–90.

37. "Origins of the NRSC," General Release, File: Rep. Natl. Comm., Box 174, O'Neill Papers.

38. Menefee-Libey, "Politics of National Party Organization," chap. 6, 12–38.

39. "Democrats in '78: Protecting What They've Got," *Congressional Quarterly Weekly Reports*, January 14, 1978, 62.

40. The limits on contributions to candidates are $1,000 per election per year from individuals, $5,000 per election per year from multicandidate committees, and $5,000 per election for party committees (except in the case of Senate elections, when the limits are $17,500 combined). See Frank J. Sorauf, *Money in American Elections* (Glenview, Ill.: Scott, Foresman, 1988), app. B.

41. The formula is state VAP x $0.02, plus the latest cost-of-living increase (based on the consumer price index).

42. Dwight, interview.

43. Remember that the main source of CCC fund-raising was subscriptions from members plus a few direct mail efforts and a House-Senate dinner—clearly not enough to meet the new financial needs of incumbents.

44. Klinkner, *The Losing Parties*, shows how decimated the RNC was after Watergate and how consumed the DNC was over delegate selection rules. Neither organization was having outstanding fund-raising success on its own, and both were more immediately concerned with debts from past presidential elections.

45. *FEC v. Democratic Senatorial Campaign Committee et al.* 454 U.S. 27 (1981).

46. The number of elections can range from one to four (or even more in extraordinary circumstances) since the following each count as a separate election: general, primary, run-off, and special.

47. See Richard S. Katz and Robin Kolodny, "The USA: The 1990 Congressional Campaign," in *Electoral Strategies and Political Marketing*, ed. Shaun Bowler and David Farrell, 183–203 (London: Macmillan, 1992), for a detailed analysis of one election cycle.

48. For states with more than one House seat, the coordinated expenditure limit is $10,000 x COLA. For states with only one House seat, the limit is $20,000 x COLA. For Senate seats, the limit is the greater of $0.02 x VAP x COLA or $20,000 x COLA.

49. NRCC Press Release, September 28, 1981, File: Rep. Natl. Comm., box 174, O'Neill Papers; Bob Benenson, "Once a Key Force in Elections, House Is Now Just a Sideshow," *Congressional Quarterly Weekly Reports*, October 3, 1987, 2379–82.

50. According to key inside sources, Ford was allowed to run the DSCC while he was up for reelection in 1980 and to serve for an unusual three consecutive terms because of the laissez-faire attitude of the majority leader, Robert Byrd and because the only other senator who was actively interested in the job was Howard Metzenbaum (D-OH) who was unacceptable to the leadership.

51. Anita Dunn (communications director, DSCC), personal interview by author, Washington, D.C., 29 September 1989.

52. For an excellent treatment of the Coelho years, see Brooks Jackson, *Honest Graft: Big Money and the American Political Process* (New York: Knopf, 1988).

53. Herrnson, *Party Campaigning in the 1980s*, chap. 2.

54. Ibid., 81.

55. See especially Frank I. Luntz, *Candidates, Consultants and Campaigns: The Style and Substance of American Electioneering* (New York: B. Blackwell, 1988), for corroboration on the unfocused nature of CCC technical services.

56. The dates for these transitions vary by committee: NRCC, 1980; NRSC, 1980; DCCC, 1982; DSCC, 1984.

57. Eddie Mahe (former field director, NRCC and NRSC, former executive director, NRCC), personal interview by author, Washington, D.C., 7 July 1990.

58. Joseph Gaylord (former executive director, NRCC), personal interview by author, Washington, D.C., 2 August 1990.

59. No politician likes to ask for money, but the FECA put members of Congress in the uncomfortable position of having to ask for a large number of small contributions from ordinary individuals rather than a few wealthy backers or interest groups.

60. In the 1988 cycle the Incumbent Review Panel had five members.

61. Dwight, interview.

62. Martin Franks (former executive director, DCCC) personal interview by author, Washington, D.C., 8 August 1990.

63. Vander Jagt–Coelho Press Conference, "How Will the House Go in November?" National Press Club, Washington, D.C., September 30, 1982; quoted in Ried, *The Orator*, 13.

64. See Jackson, *Honest Graft*, chap. 9.

65. The Hon. Tony Coelho, personal interview by author, Washington, D.C., 24 May 1996.

66. Chuck Alston, "Senate GOP Has a Big Problem: How to Spend All that Cash," *Congressional Quarterly Weekly Reports*, September 29, 1990, 3087–92.

67. Diana Dwyre, "Spinning Straw into Gold: Soft Money and U.S. House Elections," *Legislative Studies Quarterly* 21 (1996): 409–24.

68. Dunn, interview.

69. Jackson, *Honest Graft*; Franks, interview.

70. Gaylord, interview.

71. Deb Amend (assistant campaign director, NRCC), personal interview by author, Washington, D.C., 28 September 1989.

72. Richard E. Cohen, "Party Help," *National Journal*, August 16, 1986, 2001.

73. Franks, interview.

74. Jacobson, "Party Organization and Distribution of Campaign Resources."

Chapter 6

1. See Arturo Vega and Ronald M. Peters, Jr., "Principal-Agent Theories of Party Leadership under Preference Heterogeneity: The Case of Simpson-Mazzoli," *Congress and the Presidency* 23 (Spring 1996):15–32.

2. The notable exception to this trend is Gary W. Cox and Mathew D. McCubbins, *Legislative Leviathan: Party Government in the House* (Berkeley: University of California Press, 1993).

3. See, for example, Barbara Sinclair, *Majority Leadership in the U.S. House* (Baltimore: Johns Hopkins University Press, 1983), and David W. Rohde, *Parties and Leaders in the Postreform House* (Chicago: University of Chicago Press, 1991).

4. I do not mean to imply that passing legislation is easy or straightforward, just that it has clearer signposts of progress. The budget process has several "must meet" deadlines.

5. That is, Washington-based leaders have no way of knowing whether their actions will result in a net increase, a net decrease, or a zero sum of seats. What may help one set of members secure reelection may hurt another set of members or candidates. The extreme uncertainty makes some leaders less likely to devote their time to these efforts.

6. Jacobson, "Party Organization and Distribution of Campaign Resources."

7. This is David Mayhew's argument in *Congress: The Electoral Connection.*

8. See Peabody, *Leadership in Congress*, for a fuller treatment of these issues.

9. DCCC chair Tony Coelho was instrumental in getting the caucus to change its policy and in doing so became the caucus's first elected whip.

10. Ripley, *Party Leaders*, 36–37.

11. Lawrence C. Dodd, "The Expanded Roles of the House Democratic Whip System: The 93rd and 94th Congresses," *Congressional Studies* 7 (1977): 31.

12. Sinclair, *Majority Leadership*, 68.

13. For an extensive treatment of this phenomenon, see Rohde, *Parties and Leaders.*

14. Ripley, *Party Leaders*, 25.

15. Ibid., 109.

16. Oleszek, "Party Whips in the United States Senate," 958.

17. Peabody, *Leadership in Congress*, 332.

18. Oleszek, "Party Whips in the United States Senate," 959.

19. Ibid., 965–67.

20. Charles O. Jones, *The Minority Party in Congress* (Boston: Little, Brown, 1970), 46.

21. The Speaker appointed Bill Paxon (who had been elected by the Republican Conference to head the NRCC for the 1994 election cycle) to a second term for the 1996 election cycle. This strategy was told to the author by Maria Cino (executive director of the NRCC), personal interview, Washington, D.C., 13 November 1995. Speaker Gingrich appointed John Linder (R-GA) NRCC chair for the 1998 election cycle.

22. This is a point of contention in the small literature on the CCCs. The argument for primarily electoral considerations by the CCCs is made when considering the CCCs as national party organizations instead of congressional party organizations.

23. Coelho mentions his surprise at this in Jackson, *Honest Graft*.

24. See Truman, *The Congressional Party*, for more on the requirements for good leaders. See also Burdett A. Loomis, "Congressional Careers and Party Leadership in the Contemporary House of Representatives," *American Journal of Political Science* 28 (1984): 180–202.

25. See tables A.2–A.5.

26. This figure is not necessarily equivalent to the number of years served in Congress. When discontinuous service is used for a total, a footnote has been made to that effect. However, congressmen who then served in the Senate and chaired their senatorial committee do not have the House service reflected in their totals.

27. See Joseph Schlesinger, *Ambition and Politics* (Chicago: Rand McNally, 1966), 194–211.

28. David T. Canon, "The Institutionalization of Leadership in the United States Congress," *Legislative Studies Quarterly* 14 (1989): 437.

29. Polsby, "Institutionalization."

30. Canon, "Institutionalization of Leadership," 421–22.

31. Ibid., 421–22.

32. For example, Senator Moses (R-NH) was accused of being too conservative (see chap. 3), Rep. Guffey (D-PA) complained of having to fund conservative Democrats (see chap. 4), and Senator Packwood was accused of being too liberal (see below).

33. Loomis, "Congressional Careers," 191.

34. Peabody, *Leadership in Congress*.

35. Truman, *Congressional Party*; William E. Sullivan, "Criteria for Selecting Party Leadership in Congress," *American Politics Quarterly* 3 (1975): 25–44.

36. This may simply be a result of incomplete information gathered by the author rather than an indication of a more recent

phnomenon. Also, Rep. Guy Vander Jagt did return to CCC service after his failed leadership bid—the only one of the five to do so. Vander Jagt ended his CCC service when he lost his own reelection bid in 1992.

37. See Susan Webb Hammond, "Committee and Informal Leaders in the U.S. House of Representatives," 57–69, and Steven S. Smith, "Informal Leadership in the Senate: Opportunities, Resources, and Motivations," 71–83, both in John J. Kornacki, ed., *Leading Congress: New Styles, New Strategies* (Washington, D.C.: CQ Press, 1990).

38. This is because the Senate Democratic leader also wears many hats. He is chair of the Policy Committee, the Democratic Steering Committee, and the Democratic Conference.

39. Recent chairs such as Vander Jagt (NRCC), Paxon (NRCC), and Coelho (DCCC) were under the age of forty-five when they became CCC chairs.

40. Vander Jagt, interview 1990.

41. Mike Johnson (former administrative assistant to Rep. Robert Michel), personal interview by author, Washington, D.C., 10 October 1995.

42. The Hon. Guy Vander Jagt, personal interview by author, Washington, D.C., 4 October 1995.

43. Johnson, interview.

44. In addition to the 1975 contest, there was the 1961 race won by Bob Wilson (see chap. 4).

45. Kim Mattingly, "GOP Strategists Advise Hill Republicans in Tight Races to Run Against the President," *Roll Call*, October 15, 1990, 1, 34.

46. Dan Balz, "Bush Seeks Firing of Party Official: White House Turns to Damage Control over Handling of Budget," *Washington Post*, October 26, 1990, A1.

47. Ibid.

48. Vander Jagt, interview.

49. Marjorie Williams, "Ed Rollins, in the Worst of Times: The GOP Strategist on the Brink of the Elections," *Washington Post*, October 20, 1990, D1.

50. This is mostly because Speaker O'Neill had been DCCC chair in 1970 and 1972 and continued to oversee staff matters and general operations.

51. The loss of Democrats, combined with the staying power of Southern Democrats (boll weevils) who agreed with the Reagan agenda, caused this alarm. Coelho, interview.

52. Jackson, *Honest Graft*, 51; Coelho, interview.

53. Coelho, interview.

54. Jackson, *Honest Graft*; also Jake Seher (former DCCC fundraiser), personal interview by author, Washington, D.C., 10 October 1995.

55. Coelho, interview.

56. Lynne P. Brown and Robert L. Peabody, "Patterns of Succession in House Democratic Leadership: The Choices of Wright, Foley, and Coelho, 1986," paper presented at the Annual Meeting of the American Political Science Association, Chicago, September 3–6, 1987.

57. Capitol Boxscore, *Congressional Quarterly Weekly Reports*, December 20, 1986, 3134.

58. Jennifer Pharaoh (former DCCC fund-raiser), personal interview by author, Washington, D.C., 30 November 1995.

59. Janet Hook, "Key House Democrats Balk at Taking Campaign Job," *Congressional Quarterly Weekly Reports*, February 10, 1990, 371–73.

60. *Roll Call*, December 13, 1990, 1.

61. Congressional Quarterly, *Congressional Quarterly Almanac*, 3.

62. Ibid.

63. Associated Press, "GOP Solicitation Featuring Packwood Halted," *Washington Post*, April 1, 1982, A13.

64. Bill Peterson, "Rift over Fund Letter Costs GOP $2 Million," *Washington Post*, April 16, 1982, A3.

65. Rowland Evans and Robert Novak, "Punish Packwood?" *Washington Post*, March 8, 1982, A13; Rowland Evans and Robert Novak, "Shoving Packwood from the Pack," *Washington Post*, April 19, 1982, A11.

66. Lou Cannon, "Reagan Planning Summit," *Washington Post*, May 3, 1982, A3.

67. "Packwood Ousted as Campaign Head," *Congressional Quarterly Weekly Reports*, December 4, 1982, 2973.

68. Diane Granat, "Dole Elected Majority Leader," *Congressional Quarterly Weekly Reports*, December 1, 1984, 3021.

69. Paul Curcio (former political director, NRSC), personal interview by author, Alexandria, Va., 15 November 1995.

70. David Gasson (former leadership liaison, DSCC), personal interview by author, Washington, D.C., 23 October 1995.

71. Janet Hook, "Democrats Moving Swiftly to Organize Senate," *Congressional Quarterly Weekly Reports*, November 22, 1986, 2935.

72. Don Schimanski (former fund-raiser, DSCC and DCCC), personal interview by author, Washington, D.C., 10 November 1995.

73. In a parliamentary party, material steps such as "real" candidate recruitment would be conducted by a central party organ as a way to prevent numerical losses. In the congressional party, such action would be considered far too intrusive. Instead, the congressional party expects its electoral arm to monitor electoral prospects and warn members about potential problems. They should make their information universally available as well.

Chapter 7

1. For a detailed account of the disposition of Contract items during the one hundred days, see Robin Kolodny, "The Contract with America in the 104th Congress," in John C. Green and Daniel M. Shea, eds., *The State of the Parties*, 2d ed. (Lanham, Md.: Rowman and Littlefield, 1996), 314–27.

2. See William F. Connelly, Jr., and John J. Pitney, Jr., *Congress' Permanent Minority?* (Lanham, Md.: Rowman and Littlefield, 1994), chap. 2.

3. Richard E. Cohen, "Taking the Very Long View, the Parties Begin Planning for the 1992 House Elections," *National Journal*, April 13, 1985, 794.

4. For fuller information on this period, see Robin Kolodny, "Congressional Party Politics and the Congressional Campaign Committees: The 1990 Leadership Challenge to Rep. Guy Vander Jagt," paper presented at the Annual Meeting of the American Political Science Association, Washington, D.C., August 29–September 1, 1991.

5. Herrnson, *Congressional Elections*, 23.

6. Cino, interview.

7. Cino, interview.

8. This has been institutionalized for the 1996 cycle by requiring "dues" from all members for the NRCC's Incumbent Support Fund. The amounts required differ by the position held by House Republicans: $2,500, freshman; $5,000, regular; $6,500, subcommittee chairs; $7,500, party leaders and committee chairs. (Cino interview.)

9. Republican National Committee, *1993 Chairman's Report to the Members of the Republican National Committee* (Washington, D.C.: Republican National Committee, 1993), 9.

10. Ibid., 12.

11. Federal Election Commission, "FEC Reports on Political Party Activity for 1993-94," April 13, 1995.

12. Janet A. Barnes, "Haley's Comet," *National Journal*, February 25, 1995, 474–78.

13. Don Fierce, RNC communications director, and Cece Hall Boyer, Hill liaison in the Office of Congressional Affairs, were both actively involved in the Contract's development.

14. Cece Hall Boyer (congressional liaison, RNC), personal interview by author, Washington, D.C., 4 October 1995.

15. Ed Gillespie (Communications Division, RNC), telephone interview by author, 21 February 1996.

16. Three Republican incumbents, Lincoln Diaz-Balart (R-FL), Ileana Ros-Lehtinen (R-FL), and Don Young (R-AK), did not sign the Contract or participate in the September event. Diaz-Balart and Ros-Lehtinen took issue with the anti-immigrant provisions in the proposals.

17. Alan I. Abramowitz, "The End of the Democratic Era? 1994 and the Future of Congressional Election Research," *Political Research Quarterly* 48 (1995): 882.

18. According to Ornstein and Schenkenberg, only 53 percent of House freshmen previously held elective office. Norman J. Ornstein and Amy L. Schenkenberg, "The 1995 Congress: The First Hundred Days and Beyond," *Political Science Quarterly* 110 (1995): 183–206.

19. Gary C. Jacobson, "The 1994 House Elections in Perspective," paper presented at the Annual Meeting of the Midwest Political Science Association, Chicago, April 6–8, 1995.

20. Cino, interview; Johnson, interview.

21. See Diana Dwyre and Robin Kolodny, "Strategic Advancements toward Collective Party Goals: National Party Organizations and House Elections, 1993–96," paper presented at the Annual Meeting of the American Political Science Association, San Francisco, August 29–September 1, 1996.

22. Abramowitz, "The End of the Democratic Era?," 874; Ornstein and Schenkenberg, "The 1995 Congress," 184.

23. Barbara A. Bardes, Mack C. Shelley II, and Steffen W. Schmidt, *American Government and Politics Today: The Essentials 1996–1997 Edition* (St. Paul, Minn.: West Publishing, 1996), 269.

24. "Republicans Now Dominate Ranks of Best-Funded House Challengers," *Roll Call*, October 27, 1994, 1, 14.

25. Jacobson, "1994 House Elections in Perspective," 7.

26. Ornstein and Schenkenberg, "The 1995 Congress," 205, state that the first hundred days resembled a parliamentary style of legislating rather than a transformative style. Also, they show that among the public, support for the Contract as a concept exceeds support for any of its individual items.

27. Cino, interview.

28. Jackie Koszczuk, "Democrats Aiming Moderation at Revolution-Weary Voters," *Congressional Quarterly Weekly Reports*, June 29, 1996, 1859.

29. Benjamin Sheffner, "Dems 'Agenda' Takes Back Seat to Bashing Newt," *Roll Call*, June 27, 1996, 15.

30. Morton M. Kondracke, "Democrats Embrace the Center, but Is It Just a Campaign Ploy?" *Roll Call*, June 27, 1996, 8.

31. See Herrnson, *Party Campaigning in the 1980s*.

32. Klinkner, *The Losing Parties*.

BIBLIOGRAPHY

Manuscript Collections

Anderson, Clinton.
    Clinton P. Anderson Papers, Manuscript Division, Library of Congress, Washington, D.C.

Brown, Prentiss.
    Prentiss Marsh Brown Collection, Michigan Historical Collections, Bentley Historical Library, University of Michigan, Ann Arbor.

Cannon, Joseph.
    Joseph G. Cannon Collection, Illinois State Historical Society, Springfield.

Chandler, Zachariah.
    Zachariah Chandler Papers, Manuscript Division, Library of Congress, Washington, D.C.

Clements, Earle.
    Earle C. Clements Collection, Special Collections, University Archives, University of Kentucky Libraries, Lexington.

Dirksen, Everett.
    Everett McKinley Dirksen Papers, Everett McKinley Dirksen Congressional Leadership Research Center, Pekin, Illinois.

Edmondson, Ed.
    Ed Edmondson Collection, Northeastern State University, Talequah, Oklahoma.

Fess, Simeon.
   Simeon D. Fess Papers, Ohio Historical Society, Columbus.
Flood, Henry De La Warr.
   Papers of Henry D. Flood, Manuscript Division, Library of Congress, Washington, D.C.
Griggs, James Matthews.
   James Matthews Griggs Papers, Southern Historical Collection, Library of the University of North Carolina at Chapel Hill.
Halsey, Edwin.
   Papers of Edwin A. Halsey, Manuscript Division, Library of Congress, Washington, D.C.
Harrison, Benjamin.
   Benjamin Harrison Papers, Manuscript Division, Library of Congress, Washington, D.C.
Logan, John.
   Papers of John A. Logan and Family, Manuscript Division, Library of Congress, Washington, D.C.
Lucas, Scott.
   Scott W. Lucas Papers, Illinois State Historical Society, Springfield.
McCormick, (Joseph) Medill.
   Hanna-McCormick Family Papers, Manuscript Division, Library of Congress, Washington, D.C.
McKinley, William.
   William B. McKinley Papers, Syracuse University, Syracuse, New York.
Magnuson, Warren.
   Warren G. Magnuson Papers, University of Washington Libraries, Seattle.
Martin, Joseph.
   Joseph W. Martin Papers, Stonehill College, North Easton, Massachusetts.
Morton, Thruston.
   Thruston B. Morton Collection, Special Collections, University Archives, University of Kentucky Libraries, Lexington.
O'Neill, Thomas P.
   Thomas P. O'Neill Papers, Special Collections, Boston College, Boston, Massachusetts.
Randall, Samuel.
   Samuel J. Randall Papers, Special Collections, Van Pelt Library, University of Pennsylvania, Philadelphia.

Schenck, Robert.
  Robert C. Schenck Papers, Microfilm Reels, Rutherford B. Hayes Library, Freemont, Ohio.
Smathers, George.
  George A. Smathers Collection, P. K. Yonge Library of Florida History, University of Florida, Gainesville.
U.S. Congress.
  Records of Congress, National Archives, Washington, D.C.
Wilson, Robert.
  Robert C. Wilson Papers, San Diego State University, San Diego, California.

Books and Articles

Abbott, Richard. *The Republican Party and the South, 1855–77*. Chapel Hill: University of North Carolina Press, 1986.

Abram, Michael, and Joseph Cooper. "The Rise of Seniority in the House of Representatives." *Polity* 1 (1968): 52–85.

Abramowitz, Alan I. "The End of the Democratic Era? 1994 and the Future of Congressional Election Research." *Political Research Quarterly* 48 (1995): 873–89.

Aldrich, John H. *Why Parties? The Origin and Transformation of Political Parties in America*. Chicago: University of Chicago Press, 1995.

Alston, Chuck. "Senate GOP Has a Big Problem: How to Spend All that Cash." *Congressional Quarterly Weekly Reports*, September 29, 1990, 3087–92.

Associated Press. "GOP Solicitation Featuring Packwood Halted." *Washington Post*, April 1, 1982, A13.

Baker, John D. "The Character of the Congressional Revolution of 1910." *Journal of American History* 60 (1973): 679–91.

Balz, Dan. "Bush Seeks Firing of Party Official: White House Turns to Damage Control over Handling of Budget." *Washington Post*, October 26, 1990, A1.

Bardes, Barbara A., Mack C. Shelley II, and Steffen W. Schmidt. *American Government and Politics Today: The Essentials 1996–1997 Edition*. St. Paul, Minn.: West Publishing, 1996.

Barnes, Janet A. "Haley's Comet." *National Journal*, February 25, 1995, 474–78.

Bell, Lester. "Congressman Tells of Ford's Help: Haldeman Tried to Oust Him, Wilson Says." *San Diego Union*, August 13, 1974.

Benenson, Bob. "Once a Key Force in Elections, House Is Now Just a Sideshow." *Congressional Quarterly Weekly Reports*, October 3, 1987, 2379–82.
Berry, Jeffrey M., and Jerry Goldman. "Congress and Public Policy: A Study of the Federal Election Campaign Act of 1971." *Harvard Journal on Legislation* 10 (1973): 331–65.
Bone, Hugh A. *Party Committees and National Politics.* Seattle: University of Washington Press, 1958.
Bradley, Erwin Stanley. *Simon Cameron: Lincoln's Secretary of War.* Philadelphia: University of Pennsylvania Press, 1966.
Brown, George Rothwell. *The Leadership of Congress.* Indianapolis: Bobbs-Merrill, 1922.
Brown, Lynne P., and Robert L. Peabody. "Patterns of Succession in Democratic Leadership: The Choices of Wright, Foley, Coelho, 1986." Paper presented at the Annual Meeting of the American Political Science Association, Chicago, September 3–6, 1987.
Burns, James MacGregor. *The Deadlock of Democracy: Four-Party Politics in America.* Englewood Cliffs, N.J.: Prentice-Hall, 1963.
Byrns, Joseph W. "Duties of Democratic Congressional Committee." In Floyd M. Riddick, *Congressional Procedure.* Boston: Chapman and Grimes, 1941.
Cannon, Lou. "Reagan Planning Summit." *Washington Post*, May 3, 1982, A3.
Canon, David T. "The Institutionalization of Leadership in the United States Congress." *Legislative Studies Quarterly* 14 (1989): 415–33.
Caro, Robert A. *The Years of Lyndon Johnson: The Path to Power.* New York: Vintage Books, 1983.
Ceaser, James W. *Presidential Selection: Theory and Development.* Princeton: Princeton University Press, 1979.
Cohen, Richard E. "Party Help." *National Journal*, August 16, 1986, 1998–2004.
———. "Taking the Very Long View, the Parties Begin Planning for the 1992 House Elections." *National Journal*, April 13, 1985, 794–97.
Coleman, Charles H. *The Election of 1868: The Democratic Effort to Regain Control.* New York: Octagon Books, 1971. Originally published 1933.
Coleman, John J. "Resurgent or Just Busy? Party Organizations in Contemporary America." In John C. Green and Daniel M. Shea, eds., *The State of the Parties*, 2d ed. Lanham, Md.: Rowman and Littlefield, 1996. Pp. 367–84.

BIBLIOGRAPHY

Congressional Quarterly. *1978 Congressional Quarterly Almanac.* Washington, D.C.: Congressional Quarterly, 1979.

———. *1980 Congressional Quarterly Almanac.* Washington, D.C.: Congressional Quarterly, 1981.

Connelly, William F., Jr., and John J. Pitney, Jr. *Congress' Permanent Minority?* Lanham, Md.: Rowman and Littlefield, 1994.

Cook, Rhodes. "1976 Election Showed Erosion of GOP Base." *Congressional Quarterly Weekly Reports*, March 19, 1977, 488–90.

Cox, Gary W., and Mathew D. McCubbins. *Legislative Leviathan: Party Government in the House.* Berkeley: University of California Press, 1993.

Croly, Herbert. *Marcus Alonzo Hanna: His Life and Work.* New York: Macmillan, 1923.

Dinkin, Robert J. *Campaigning in America: A History of Election Practices.* New York: Greenwood Press, 1989.

Dodd, Lawrence C. "The Expanded Roles of the House Democratic Whip System: The 93rd and 94th Congresses." *Congressional Studies* 7 (1977): 31–40.

Downs, Anthony. *An Economic Theory of Democracy.* New York: Harper and Row, 1957.

Dwyre, Diana. "Spinning Straw into Gold: Soft Money and U.S. House Elections." *Legislative Studies Quarterly* 21 (1996): 409–24.

Dwyre, Diana, and Robin Kolodny. "Strategic Advancements toward Collective Party Goals: National Party Organizations and House Elections, 1993–96." Paper presented at the Annual Meeting of the American Political Science Association, San Francisco, August 29–September 1, 1996.

Epstein, Leon. *Political Parties in the American Mold.* Madison: University of Wisconsin Press, 1986.

Evans, Rowland, and Robert Novak. "Punish Packwood?" *Washington Post*, March 8, 1982, A13.

———. "Shoving Packwood from the Pack." *Washington Post*, April 19, 1982, A11.

Federal Election Commission. "FEC Reports on Political Party Activity for 1993–94." April 13, 1995.

Fleming, James S. "Re-establishing Leadership in the House of Representatives: The Case of Oscar W. Underwood." *Mid-America* 54 (1972): 234–50.

Fowler, Robert Booth, and Allen D. Hertzke. *Religion and Politics in America: Faith, Culture, and Strategic Choices.* Boulder, Colo.: Westview Press, 1995.

Galloway, Jewell M. "Speaker Joseph W. Byrns: Party Leader in the New Deal." *Tennessee Historical Quarterly* 26 (1966): 63–76.

George, Sister Mary Carl, R.S.M. *Zachariah Chandler: A Political Biography.* East Lansing: Michigan State University Press, 1969.

Goldman, Ralph M. *The National Party Chairmen and Committees: Factionalism at the Top.* Armonk, N.Y.: M. E. Sharpe, 1990.

Goldwater, Barry M., with Jack Casserly. *Goldwater.* New York: Doubleday, 1988.

Granat, Diane. "Dole Elected Majority Leader." *Congressional Quarterly Weekly Reports*, December 1, 1984, 3021.

Guffey, Joseph F. *Seventy Years on the Red-Fire Wagon.* N.p.: Privately printed, 1952.

Hammond, Susan Webb. "Committee and Informal Leaders in the U.S. House of Representatives." In John J. Kornacki, ed., *Leading Congress: New Styles, New Strategies.* Washington, D.C.: CQ Press, 1990. Pp. 57–69.

Haynes, George H. *The Senate of the United States: Its History and Practice.* Boston: Houghton Mifflin, 1938.

Herrnson, Paul S. *Congressional Elections: Campaigning at Home and in Washington.* Washington, D.C.: CQ Press, 1995.

———. *Party Campaigning in the 1980s.* Cambridge, Mass.: Harvard University Press, 1988.

Hook, Janet. "Democrats Moving Swiftly to Organize Senate." *Congressional Quarterly Weekly Reports*, November 22, 1986, 2935.

———. "Key House Democrats Balk at Taking Campaign Job." *Congressional Quarterly Weekly Reports*, February 10, 1990, 371–73.

Hope, Paul. "Capitol GOP Battles Committee on Funds." *Evening Star* (Washington, D.C.), February 16, 1966.

Irish, Ann B. "Joseph Wellington Byrns of Tennessee." Manuscript.

Jackson, Brooks. *Broken Promise: Why the Federal Election Commission Failed.* New York: Priority Press Publications, 1990.

———. *Honest Graft: Big Money and the American Political Process.* New York: Knopf, 1988.

Jacobson, Gary C. "The 1994 House Elections in Perspective." Paper presented at the Annual Meeting of the Midwest Political Science Association, Chicago, April 6–8, 1995.

———. "Party Organization and Distribution of Campaign Resources: Republicans and Democrats in 1982." *Political Science Quarterly* 100 (Winter 1985–86): 603–25.

———. *The Politics of Congressional Elections*, 2d ed. New York: HarperCollins, 1992.

Jones, Charles O. *The Minority Party in Congress*. Boston: Little, Brown, 1970.

Katz, Richard S., and Robin Kolodny. "The USA: The 1990 Congressional Campaign." In Shaun Bowler and David M. Farrell, eds., *Electoral Strategies and Political Marketing*. London: Macmillan, 1992. Pp. 183–203.

Kaufman, Burton Ira. "Henry De La Warr Flood: A Case Study of Organization Politics in an Era of Reform." Ph.D. dissertation, Rice University, 1966.

Kelley, Stanley, Jr. *Professional Public Relations and Political Power*. Baltimore: Johns Hopkins University Press, 1956.

Kernell, Samuel. "Toward Understanding 19th-Century Congressional Careers: Ambition, Competition, and Rotation." *American Journal of Political Science* 21 (1977): 669–93.

King, Susan B., and Robert L. Peabody. "Control of Presidential Campaign Financing." In Harvey C. Mansfield, ed., *Congress Against the President, Proceedings of the Academy of Political Science* 32 (1975): 180–95.

Kirwan, Michael J., with Jack Redding. *How to Succeed in Politics*. New York: MacFadden-Bartell, 1964.

Kleeberg, Gordon S. *The Formation of the Republican Party as a National Political Organization*. New York: Columbia University, 1911.

Klinkner, Philip A. *The Losing Parties: Out-Party National Committees, 1956–1993*. New Haven: Yale University Press, 1994.

Kolodny, Robin. "Congressional Party Politics and the Congressional Campaign Committees: The 1990 Leadership Challenge to Rep. Guy Vander Jagt." Paper presented at the Annual Meeting of the American Political Science Association, Washington, D.C., August 29–September 1, 1991.

———. "The Contract with America in the 104th Congress." In John C. Green and Daniel M. Shea, eds., *The State of the Parties*, 2d ed. Lanham, Md.: Rowman and Littlefield, 1996. Pp. 314–27.

Kondracke, Morton M. "Democrats Embrace the Center, but Is It Just a Campaign Ploy?" *Roll Call*, June 27, 1996, 8.

Koszczuk, Jackie. "Democrats Aiming Moderation at Revolution-Weary Voters." *Congressional Quarterly Weekly Reports*, June 29, 1996, 1859.

Livermore, Seward W. *Politics Is Adjourned: Woodrow Wilson and the War Congress, 1916–1918.* Middletown, Conn.: Wesleyan University Press, 1966.

Loomis, Burdett A. "Congressional Careers and Party Leadership in the Contemporary House of Representatives." *American Journal of Political Science* 28 (1984): 180–202.

Luntz, Frank I. *Candidates, Consultants and Campaigns: The Style and Substance of American Electioneering.* New York: B. Blackwell, 1988.

McGerr, Michael E. *The Decline of Popular Politics: The American North, 1865–1928.* New York: Oxford University Press, 1986.

Macy, Jesse. *Party Organization and Machinery.* New York: Century, 1904.

Mann, Thomas. *Unsafe at Any Margin.* Washington, D.C.: American Enterprise Institute, 1978.

March, James G., and Johan P. Olsen. *Rediscovering Institutions: The Organizational Basis of Politics.* New York: Free Press, 1989.

Mattingly, Kim. "GOP Strategists Advise Hill Republicans in Tight Races to Run Against the President." *Roll Call*, October 15, 1990, 1, 34.

Mayhew, David R. *Congress: The Electoral Connection.* New Haven: Yale University Press, 1974.

———. *Divided We Govern: Party Control, Lawmaking, and Investigations, 1946–1990.* New Haven: Yale University Press, 1991.

Menefee-Libey, David. "The Politics of National Party Organization: The Democrats from 1968 to 1986." Ph.D. dissertation, University of Chicago, 1990.

Mott, Frank Luther. *American Journalism: A History, 1690–1960*, 3d ed. New York: Macmillan, 1962.

Murphy, John L. "Joseph M. Martin, Jr., 1924–1939." Master's thesis, Bridgewater State College, 1975.

Nelson, Garrison. "Party Control Periods of the U.S. House of Representatives and the Recruitment of Its Leaders, 1789–1971." Ph.D. dissertation, University of Iowa, 1973.

Nethers, John. *Simeon D. Fess: Educator and Politician.* Brooklyn: Pageant-Poseidon, 1973.

Oleszek, Walter J. "Party Whips in the United States Senate." *Journal of Politics* 33 (1971): 955–79.

Olson, Mancur. *The Logic of Collective Action.* Cambridge, Mass.: Harvard University Press, 1971.
O'Neill, Tip, with William Novak. *Man of the House: The Life and Political Memoirs of Speaker Tip O'Neill.* New York: Random House, 1987.
Ornstein, Norman J., and Amy L. Schenkenberg. "The 1995 Congress: The First Hundred Days and Beyond." *Political Science Quarterly* 110 (1995): 183–206.
Peabody, Robert L. *Leadership in Congress: Stability, Succession, and Change.* Boston: Little, Brown, 1976.
Peabody, Robert L., Jeffrey M. Berry, William G. Frasure, and Jerry Goldman. *To Enact a Law: Congress and Campaign Financing.* New York: Praeger, 1972.
Peters, Ronald M., Jr. *The American Speakership: The Office in Historical Perspective.* Baltimore: Johns Hopkins University Press, 1990.
Peterson, Bill. "Rift over Fund Letter Costs GOP $2 Million." *Washington Post*, April 16, 1982, A3.
Polsby, Nelson W. "The Institutionalization of the U.S. House of Representatives." *American Political Science Review* 62 (1968): 144–68.
Powell, Lawrence N. "Rejected Republican Incumbents in the 1866 Congressional Nominating Conventions: A Study in Reconstruction Politics." *Civil War History* 19, no. 3 (1973):219–37.
Price, H. Douglas. "Congress and the Evolution of Legislative Professionalism." In Norman J. Ornstein, ed., *Congress in Change: Evolution and Reform.* New York: Praeger, 1975. Pp. 2–23.
Republican Congressional Committee. *One Hundred Years: A History of the National Republican Congressional Committee.* Washington, D.C.: Judd and Detweiler, 1966.
Republican National Committee. *1993 Chairman's Report to the Members of the Republican National Committee.* Washington, D.C.: Republican National Committee.
Ried, Paul E. *The Orator: Guy Vander Jagt on the Hustings.* Ottawa, Ill.: Green Hill, 1984.
Ripley, Randall B. *Party Leaders in the House of Representatives.* Washington, D.C.: Brookings Institution, 1967.
Rohde, David W. *Parties and Leaders in the Postreform House.* Chicago: University of Chicago Press, 1991.
Rothman, David J. *Politics and Power: The United States Senate, 1869–1901.* Cambridge, Mass.: Harvard University Press, 1966.

Scheele, Henry A. *Charlie Halleck: A Political Biography.* New York: Exposition Press, 1966.
Schlesinger, Joseph. *Ambition and Politics.* Chicago: Rand McNally, 1966.
Shea, Daniel M. *Transforming Democracy: Legislative Campaign Committees and Political Parties.* Albany: State University of New York Press, 1995.
Sheffner, Benjamin. "Dems 'Agenda' Takes Back Seat to Bashing Newt." *Roll Call,* June 27, 1996, 15.
Sinclair, Barbara. *Majority Leadership in the U.S. House.* Baltimore: Johns Hopkins University Press, 1983.
———. *The Transformation of the U.S. Senate.* Baltimore: Johns Hopkins University Press, 1989.
Smiley, Sara Judith. "The Political Career of Thruston B. Morton: The Senate Years, 1956–1968." Ph.D. dissertation, University of Kentucky, 1975.
Smith, Steven S. "Informal Leadership in the Senate: Opportunities, Resources, and Motivations." In John J. Kornacki, ed., *Leading Congress: New Styles, New Strategies.* Washington, D.C.: CQ Press, 1990. Pp. 71–83.
Sorauf, Frank J. *Money in American Elections.* Glenview, Ill.: Scott, Foresman, 1988.
Sorauf, Frank J., and Scott A. Wilson. "Campaigns and Money: A Changing Role for the Political Parties?" In L. Sandy Maisel, ed., *The Parties Respond.* Boulder, Colo.: Westview Press, 1990. Pp. 187–203.
Stampp, Kenneth M. *The Era of Reconstruction, 1865–77.* New York: Vintage Books, 1965.
Sullivan, William E. "Criteria for Selecting Party Leadership in Congress." *American Politics Quarterly* 3 (1975): 25–44.
Sundquist, James L. *Dynamics of the Party System.* Washington, D.C.: Brookings Institution, 1983.
Symonds, Merrill A. "George Higgins Moses of New Hampshire: The Man and the Era." Ph.D. dissertation, Clark University, 1955.
Thayer, George. *Who Shakes the Money Tree?* New York: Simon and Schuster, 1973.
Truman, David B. *The Congressional Party: A Case Study.* New York: John Wiley, 1959.
Tulis, Jeffrey. *The Rhetorical Presidency.* Princeton: Princeton University Press, 1987.

Vega, Arturo, and Ronald M. Peters, Jr. "Principal-Agent Theories of Party Leadership under Preference Heterogeneity: The Case of Simpson-Mazzoli." *Congress and the Presidency* 23 (Spring 1996): 15–32.

Wagner, James R. "Big Government: All-Purpose Issue of 1976." *Congressional Quarterly Weekly Reports*, October 23, 1976, 3036–37.

Wiebe, Robert H. *The Search for Order, 1877–1929*. New York: Hill and Wang, 1967.

Williams, Marjorie. "Ed Rollins, in the Worst of Times: The GOP Strategist on the Brink of the Elections." *Washington Post*, October 20, 1990, D1.

Wilson, Woodrow. *Congressional Government*. Baltimore: Johns Hopkins University Press, 1981.

Young, James Sterling. *The Washington Community, 1800–1828*. New York: Columbia University Press, 1966.

Legal Cases

Buckley v. Valeo 424 U.S. 1 (1976).

FEC v. Democratic Senatorial Campaign Committee et al. 454 U.S. 27 (1981).

Unattributed Newspaper Articles

"Capitol Boxscore." *Congressional Quarterly Weekly Reports*, December 20, 1986, 3134.

"Democrats in '78: Protecting What They've Got." *Congressional Quarterly Weekly Reports*, January 14, 1978, 62.

"Democratic Joint Plans." *New York Times*, May 18, 1913, sec. 1, p. 13.

"For Seats in Congress: Both Parties Sending Out Information for Voters." *New York Times*, October 7, 1890, sec. 1, p. 1.

"Griggs to Run Campaign." *New York Times*, March 7, 1906, sec. 1, p. 6.

"Harmony the Note of Republican Talk." *New York Times*, May 25, 1913, sec. 1, p. 1.

"McCormick to Fight for 1918 Congress." *New York Times*, November 22, 1916, sec. 1, p. 9.

"Packwood Ousted as Campaign Head." *Congressional Quarterly Weekly Reports*, December 4, 1982, 2973.

"Republicans Now Dominate Ranks of Best-Funded House Challengers." *Roll Call*, October 27, 1994, 1, 14.

"Republicans Urged to Use New System." New York Times, December 24, 1916, sec. 1, p. 10.

Untitled. *Roll Call*, December 13, 1990.
"Wilson's Campaign Plans." *New York Times*, October 1, 1914, sec. 1, p. 1.

Interviews

Amend, Deb. Personal interview, September 28, 1989.
Boyer, Cece Hall. Personal interview, October 4, 1995.
Cino, Maria. Personal interview, November 13, 1995.
Coelho, Tony. Personal interview, May 24, 1996.
Curcio, Paul. Personal interview, November 15, 1995.
Dunn, Anita. Personal interview, September 29, 1989.
Dwight, Nancy Sinnott. Telephone interview, August 7, 1990.
Franks, Martin. Personal interview, August 8, 1990.
Gasson, David. Personal interview, October 23, 1995.
Gaylord, Joseph. Personal interview, August 2, 1990.
Gillespie, Ed. Telephone interview, February 21, 1996.
Gomien, Glee. Personal interview, December 7, 1990.
Johnson, Mike. Personal interview, October 10, 1995.
Mahe, Eddie. Personal interview, July 1990.
Pharaoh, Jennifer. Personal interview, November 30, 1995.
Schimanski, Don. Personal interview, November 10, 1995.
Seher, Jake. Personal interview, October 10, 1995.
Stockmeyer, Steven. Personal interview, October 26, 1989.
Sweeney, William R. Personal interview, October 19, 1989.
Vander Jagt, Guy. Personal interview, December 12, 1990; October 4, 1995.

INDEX

Abbott, Richard, 22–23, 28
Agency agreements. *See*
 Campaign finance reform;
 Congressional campaign
 committee; Federal Election
 Campaign Act Amendments of
 1974; NRSC
Albert, Carl, 132
Aldrich, Nelson, 40
Allison, William, 40
Anderson, Clinton, 80–83
Andresen, August, 105
Anthony, Beryl, 190
Arends, Les, 132

Babcock, Joseph Weeks, 44, 47, 50
Baker, Howard, 192–93
Baker, James, 192
Baran, Jan, 133
Barbour, Haley, 201–203; creation of congressional liaison at RNC, 202
Barkley, Alben, 80–81

Belden, J. J., 42
Bentsen, Lloyd, 131, 144, 152, 194
Blaine, James G., 35
Boggs, Hale, 128, 130
Bolton, Chester, 103–104
Bone, Hugh, 23
Boschwitz, Rudy, 193
Boyle, Bill, 82
Breaux, John, 177, 181, 194
Bridges, Styles, 88
Brock, William, 131, 134, 139
Brown, George Rothwell, 21, 39–40
Brown, Prentiss, 76–78
Bryan, William Jennings, 45
Buckley, James, 131
Buckley v. Valeo, 131–33
Burns, James MacGregor, 4
Bush, George, 184–86, 202
Butler, Paul, 91
Byrd, Robert, 164, 194, 265n.50
Byrns, Joseph Wellington, 101; as candidate for Speaker from DCCC chair, 101–102; elected

Speaker, 102; majority leader while DCCC chair, 102

Cameron, Simon, 35
Campaigns, overall cost of, 153–54
Campaign activities: allocation of funds to candidates, 12, 80, 86, 101, 111, 116, 143, 146–50; appearances with congressional leaders, 121; art services, 110, 119; candidate recruitment, 147; cartoons produced for newspaper ads, 77, 103; by CCCs, 11, 65–66; *Congressional Record* used for speech reproduction, 46, 77; films on Washington matters, subsidized rates for, 110, 116, 130; general media services, 83, 96, 104, 117, 130; issue books and papers, 36, 41, 49, 56, 71, 87, 110, 121, 131, 138, 198; legal advice, 109, 121; letters of endorsement from chair, 102; literature, 28, 31, 34, 41–42, 44, 46–47, 56, 58, 60–61, 78, 80–81, 86, 103, 108, 110, 112, 119, 121; marching companies, 32; modern campaign technologies used, 146; money channeling/earmarking, 70, 74–75, 79–80, 85–86, 88–90, 94, 106, 119, 124, 128, 130–31, 138; newspaper ads, copy for, 89, 93, 108; news services, 96, 119; opposition research, 75, 80, 83, 86, 93, 96, 103, 111, 138; paid advertising, 58, 76, 109; photographic services, 88, 93, 110, 111–12, 119, 121; press releases for newspapers, 41, 44, 46, 56–57, 60, 77, 101–103, 107, 109–10, 116, 119; radio speeches for national networks, 103; radio spots—production, 89, 93, 96, 109–10, 112, 119; recommendation of consultants to candidates, 97; seminars on campaign techniques, 130, 134, 136, 138, 153; speakers employed, 27, 28, 31, 47, 56, 60–61, 70–71, 83, 88–89, 95, 116, 121, 138; speeches and speech materials, 25, 27, 31, 34, 75, 77, 81, 87, 95–96, 103–104, 108–10, 121, 131, 134; television coach provided, 116; television spots—production, 80, 88–89, 93, 96, 109–10, 112, 116, 119; transitional services for new members, 85, 152–53; travel credit card, 93, 96; TV and radio production allowance, 97, 110, 112, 116, 119; visual aids provided, 109, 117; voting records compiled, 57, 75, 83, 134. *See also* Fund-raising; Washington resources
Campaign finance reform: agency agreements, 139; contribution limits, 142; contributions by party committees, 134, 136–37, 138, 141; coordinated expenditures by party committees, 134, 136–37, 138, 141, 142–43; coordinated expenditures, formula for

INDEX

calculating, 142; fund-raising practices before and after, 124; independent expenditures, 137; relevance of reforms to CCC operations, 126–36; role of Watergate in, 129; voting age population (VAP), 137
Campaigning: army style, 15–16, 38; connection to governing, 158; educational style, 38, 43–44; local nature of, 212; merchandised style, 16, 70; techniques in late nineteenth century, 23
Cannon, Joseph (Speaker), 16, 40; revolt against, 51–55; speaking tour for NRCC, 46–47
Canon, David T., 170–73
Carter, Jimmy, 139, 143, 188
CCC. *See* Congressional Campaign Committees
Chandler, Zachariah, 18, 33; as head of RNC, 34–35
Civil War: congressional struggle with president during, 21; symbols of in campaigns, 32–33
Clark, Champ, 64, 250n.115
Clarkson, James, 42
Clay, Henry, 20
Clay, Lucius, 96
Clements, Earle, 92, 98, 176, 256n.67; as DSCC chair 83–84; as DSCC executive director, 85; whip while DSCC chair, 83–84
Clinton, Bill, 209
Coelho, Anthony (Tony), 144, 147–52, 154, 176, 187–90, 213, 269n.39

Colorado Republican Federal Campaign Committee v. Federal Election Commission, 137. *See also* Campaign finance reform
Congress, institutionalization of, 38–40, 99–100, 244n
Congressional campaign committees (CCCs), 8–9; adaptation to campaign environment, 211–16; campaign activities for House CCCs, (1866–1890) 22–29, (1890–1908) 41–49, (1910–1920) 54–64, (1922–1932) 100–102, (1932–1952) 103–108, (1952–1972) 108–122; campaign activities for Senate CCCs, (1919–1950), 70–80, (1950–1972), 80–97; campaign activities by all, 138, 142, 146, 150–54; clerk-hire allowance used for staff salaries, 84, 127–28; comparison of House and Senate CCCs, 122–23; composition of, 167; coordinated expenditures, exclusion from, 138; divisions, 145; dual agency agreements, use of, 141; electoral outcomes, impact on, 154, 182; field force use of, 103; goals of, 9, 11–12; information gathering on races, 130; location on federal property, 135, 144–45; relationship with congressional leaders, 8, 47, 125, 214; relationship with national committees, 50, 55–56, 66, 137–39, 213, 215; role of

ideology in, 118; Senatorial campaign committees, origin of, 68–69; staff, 144–45
Congressional campaign committee (CCC) chair: career analysis of, 169–75; careers after CCC tenure, 175–81; competition for position, 159; incentives to seek in House, 13, 48, 126, 168; incentives to seek in Senate, 13, 69, 126, 167–68, 177–81; institutionalization of, 171–75; interaction with leadership, 12–13, 97, 146, 159–60, 195–96; leadership role in selecting, 13, 158–59, 167, 242n.8; in leadership structure, 24, 66, 67, 98, 166–68; as leadership training ground, 12–14, 48–49, 80, 98, 122–23, 159, 169, 175–77, 182, 195–96, 214; performance judged by leadership, 173–74, 181–82; presidential bids from, 169, 177; requirements for selection, 173; rotation of chairs in Senate, 167; shift away from Senate leadership of House CCCs, 35. *See also* Congressional leadership; DCCC chair; DSCC chair; NRCC chair; NRSC chair
Congressional careers, institutionalization of, 16, 52, 99–100
Congressional leadership: evolution of House Speakership, 39–41; institutionalization of, 99–100, 170–71; leadership activities, 156–59; recruitment of future leaders, 174; role in CCC operation, 158–60; role in selecting CCC chair, 158–60; role in selecting CCC staff, 158; structure in the House, 48, 52–54; structure of leadership in the House, 160–64; structure of leadership in the Senate, 69, 164–66. *See also* CCC chair
Conservative Opportunity Society (COS), 199
Contract with America, 197–98, 202–10; development of, 203; use by candidates in 1994 election, 204–205; use by candidates in 1996 election, 207–10. *See also* NRCC
Contribution strategies of CCCs. *See* Campaign activities, allocation of funds to candidates; Campaign finance reform
Corman, James, 132, 136, 144, 187–88, 242n.9
COS. *See* Conservative Opportunity Society
Cranston, Alan, 144, 152

D'Amato, Alfonse, 193
DCCC. *See* Democratic Congressional Campaign Committee
Democratic Congressional Committee (DCC). *See* Democratic Congressional Campaign Committee
Democratic Congressional Campaign Committee (DCCC): allocation decisions,

INDEX

111, 142; budget, 111, 135; campaign activities, 42, 47–48, 58, 60, 105–106, 110–12, 120–22, 130–32; emulation of NRCC activities, 149; events at DNC convention, 121; *Families First* in 1996 election, 208–10; fund-raising dinner with DCCC, 90, 111; fund-raising through member subscriptions, 101, 106; origins, 23; relationship with DNC, 58, 105, 111, 209; relationship with PAC community, 149–50; special elections, 101; staff, 121, 130, 136; use of Speaker to promote candidates, 111. *See also* PAC

Democratic Congressional Campaign Committee (DCCC) chair: desirability of, 48, 132; in House Democratic leadership circle, 152, 187–91; promotion from, 48–49, 150

Democratic National Committee (DNC): coordination with DCCC, 58, 105, 111, 209; coordination with DSCC, 74–76, 78, 80, 83, 84, 90; coordination with DCCC and DSCC, 56, 60

Democratic party: fund-raising from PACs, 150; fund-raising from wealthy individuals, 150; Harriman Communications Center, 151; leadership in the House, 160–63; leadership structure in the Senate, 164–65

Democratic Senatorial Campaign Committee (DSCC): allocation decisions by, 142; budget, 77, 84, 97; campaign activities, 74–79, 80–81, 83–85, 90–92, 94–97, 101–102, 136, 152; coordination with DNC, 74–76, 78, 80, 83, 84, 90; coordination with DNC and DCCC, 95; divisions of, 152; fund-raising, 77–78, 84, 90; full-time operation after 1953, 83; origins, 72; plans to disband in 1952, 83; staff, 80, 83–85, 96, 136, 152

Democratic Senatorial Campaign Committee (DSCC) chair: desirability of, 82; evaluation of performance as, 84; in leadership structure, 78, 193–95; as leadership training ground, 80, 92, 152, 193–95

Derwinski, Ed, 117

Dinkin, Robert J., 15, 32

Dirksen, Everett McKinley, 87–89, 97; interest in NRSC as minority leader, 92; use of NRSC chair as leadership training ground, 89, 176

Ditter, William, 106

DNC. *See* Democratic National Committee

Dole, Robert (Bob), 120, 191, 193

Dominick, Peter, 129

Doremus, Frank, 57–58

Drewry, Patrick Henry, 106, 110

DSCC. *See* Democratic Senatorial Campaign Committee

du Pont, Pierre, 132, 182

Dwight, Nancy Sinnott, 135, 139, 148

Dwyre, Diana, 151–52

Earmarking. *See* Campaign activities
Eckart, Dennis, 190
Edmondson, Ed, 120–21
Eisenhower, Dwight, 88, 91, 108
Election: of 1866, 17; of 1867, 27; of 1868, 28–29; of 1870, 34; of 1872, 34; of 1874, 34–35; of 1876, 35; of 1880, 36; of 1882, 36; of 1884, 35; of 1888, 38; of 1890, 41–43; of 1892, 42; of 1894, 44–45; of 1896, 45; of 1898, 45; of 1900, 45–46; of 1902, 46, 48; of 1904, 46, 48; of 1906, 48–49; of 1908, 54–55; of 1910, 53–55; of 1912, 51, 55; of 1914, 55, 57; of 1916, 57–60; of 1918, 59–60, 62–63; of 1920, 62–64; of 1922, 70–71, 100; of 1924, 71, 72, 73, 101; of 1926, 73, 101; of 1928, 100–101; of 1930, 72, 73, 100–101, 103; of 1932, 73, 75, 101; of 1934, 75, 102–103; of 1936, 73, 76, 103, 106; of 1938, 76, 104–105; of 1940, 78, 106; of 1942, 77–78, 106; of 1944, 106; of 1946, 78–79, 106–107; of 1948, 78–79, 108, 111; of 1950, 80, 82, 86, 108; of 1952, 82–83, 86, 108; of 1954, 83–85, 88, 108; of 1956, 85, 89–90, 108–109; of 1958, 85, 90–91, 93, 108, 110; of 1960, 89–90, 93, 110, 112–113; of 1962, 89, 92, 114; of 1964, 92–94; of 1966, 92–94; of 1968, 95–96, 115, 117, 127; of 1970, 96, 116, 117, 120; of 1972, 97, 114, 119, 121, 128; of 1974, 121, 128, 131, 133–34; of 1976, 128, 132–35; of 1978, 135–36, 183, 191, 193; of 1980, 143–46, 148, 183, 187–88, 193; of 1982, 141, 149, 188–89, 191, 192–93; of 1984, 184, 188, 192, 194; of 1986, 188–89, 194; of 1988, 184, 193–94; of 1990, 185–86, 193–94, 199; of 1992, 190, 193–95, 199–200, 202; of 1994, 147, 190, 193, 195, 198, 199, 201–202, 204–205, 207, 210, 212, 216; of 1996, 147, 187, 191, 193, 195, 201, 207–10; of 1998, 187, 191, 193, 195, 210, 213

Families First. See DCCC
Faulkner, Charles J., 45
Fazio, Vic, 176, 214; as DCCC and Democratic Caucus chair, 190–92
FEC. *See* Federal Election Commission
Federal Corrupt Practices Act of 1925, 87, 125, 127, 129, 262n.7
Federal Election Campaign Act of 1971, 127–29, 138–39
Federal Election Campaign Act Amendments of 1974, 107, 128–29, 131, 133, 134, 137, 138; and agency agreements, 139, 148; effect on campaign industry, 154; effect on CCC operations, 153–54, 182, 197; and section 441a(d), 137–43, 148
Federal Election Campaign Act Amendments of 1979, 134, 136
Federal Election Commission (FEC), 129–30, 132–33, 151

INDEX 293

Federal Election Commission v. Democratic Senatorial Campaign Committee, et al., 139–41
Ferris, Scott, 60
Fess, Simeon, 23, 61, 62, 63–64, 100
Fifteenth Amendment, 21, 244n.14
Flood, Henry De La Warr, 48, 64
Foley, Thomas (Tom), 189–90, 242n.9
Ford, Gerald, 120, 132–33
Ford, Wendell, 144, 176, 193, 265n.50
Fourteenth Amendment, 19, 21, 244n.14
Franks, Martin, 154
Frost, Martin, 191
Fund-raising, 25, 57, 61, 77–78, 80, 84, 88, 94, 104, 106, 121; bundling, 151; creation of agents, 151; direct mail, 146, 150; high dollar, 146, 150; from member subscriptions, 31, 264nn.43,44; soft money, 150–52; transfers to state parties, 151. *See also* Campaign finance reform; DCCC; DSCC; NRCC; NRSC

Garner, John Nance, 101
Gaylord, Joseph, 152
Gillett, Frederick, 63
Gingrich, Newt, 184, 186–87, 199–203, 205–207, 209
Goldwater, Barry, 89, 92–93, 113–14, 177
Goodell, Charles, 116
Graham, Bob, 181, 195
Gramm, Phil, 177, 193
Grant, Ulysses S., 29, 30, 33, 34, 37

Green, Theodore Francis, 78
Griggs, James Matthews, 48, 50; promotion from DCCC to Ways and Means Chair, 48–49
Guffey, Joseph, 76, 78

Hall, Leonard, 108, 112
Halleck, Charles (Charlie), 93, 106, 107, 112, 114, 122, 176
Halsey, Edwin A., 74, 76, 77
Hanna, Mark, 45, 71
Harding, Warren G., 63
Harrison, Benjamin, 38, 41–42
Hartke, Vance, 92
Hatfield, Henry, 73
Hayes, Rutherford B., 35
Hays, Wayne, 128, 130, 132, 176
Hays, Will, 61, 62
Hefner, Bill, 189
Heinz, John, 143, 152, 191, 193
Henderson, David, 40
Herrnson, Paul, 144–45
Hill, Ebenezer, 59
Hollings, Ernest, 129
Hoover, Herbert, 73, 103
House of Representatives: institutionalization of, 51–54; political parties in, 6; power of 22; Republican party in before Contract with America, 199–202. *See also* Congressional careers; Congressional leadership; DCCC; Institutional party interest; NRCC
Hubbell, Jay, 35–36
Hughes, Charles Evans, 59

Ickes, Harold, 210
Incumbency advantage, 146

Incumbent protection, as CCC strategy, 147–48, 155, 205
Inouye, Daniel, 96
Institutional party interest, 4–14, 64–67, 125, 196, 211–16; of Democrats in the House, 102; of Republicans in the House, 37, 115, 118–99, 199. See also Incumbent protection; Majority status
Issue research, books and papers. See Campaign activities

Jackson, Andrew, and presidential nominating convention, 20
Jacobson, Gary, 155, 158, 206
Johnson, Andrew: allies of in 1868, 30; attempted impeachment of, 21, 28, 33, 37; and campaign in 1866, 25; as catalyst for NRCC formation, 37; Reconstruction policy, 18–19; vice presidential candidate on 1864 ticket, 17
Johnson, Lyndon Baines, 84–85, 91–92, 106
Johnson, Vic, 88
Johnston, J. Bennett, 132, 194

Kelley, Stanley, 108
Kernell, Samuel, 51
Kerrey, Robert (Bob), 177, 195
Kerry, John, 152, 194
King, Susan, 129
Kirwan, Michael, 82, 95, 110–12, 120, 171
Klinkner, Philip A., 215

Landon, Alfred, 104
Leadership. See also CCC chair; Congressional leadership
Legislative Reorganization Act of 1946, 85, 100, 107
Lewis, James Hamilton, 75, 98
Lincoln, Abraham: assassination of, 17; and Reconstruction plans, 19
Linder, John, 187
Livermore, Seward, 60
Lloyd, James Tilghman, as DCCC Chair and minority whip, 55
Logan, John, 34
Loomis, Burdett, 174
Lucas, Scott, 78–80, 98; request to resign DSCC chair, 79
Lugar, Richard, 152, 192–93

Magnuson, Warren G., 94–95
Majority status (pursuit of), 5–12, 155, 158–59, 168, 197, 205, 208
March, James G., 16
Martin, Joseph, 104, 108, 112, 176; use of NRCC chair as leadership training ground, 105, 106, 107, 122, 176
Mayhew, David, 9
McCain, John, 193
McCarthy, Joseph, condemnation of, 81–82
McClure, James, 191
McConnell, Mitch, 193
McCormick, John, 121
McCormick, Medill, 70, 71, 72
McCormick, Vance, 60
McCreary, Jim, 185
McCulloch, William, 112–14
McFarland, Ernest, 82–83

McGerr, Michael, 31–33, 44, 58
McKinley, William, 40, 45, 71
McKinley, William Brown, 55, 57
McKinley Tariff, 43
McNary, Charles L., 70, 72
Michel, Bob, 131–32, 182, 186, 199, 214; leadership challenge from Vander Jagt, 183–84
Miller, William, 93, 112–13, 122
Mitchell, George, 152, 164–66, 176; importance of DSCC in becoming Assistant Leader, 194
Money channeling. *See* Campaign activities
Morgan, Edwin, 29
Morton, Rogers C. B., 117
Morton, Thruston, 92–96, 176
Moses, George Higgins, 71, 72; talk of removal as NRSC chair, 73
Mott, Frank Luther, 41
Murphy, George, 95–96, 116
Muskie, Edmund, 96

National committees (NCs): CCCs as Washington base for, 50; coordinated expenditures by, 141; national party as intermediary, 144; relationship with CCCs, 7, 50, 55–56; relationship with presidential candidate, 8; structure of 8–9
National Republican Congressional Committee (NRCC): agency agreements with RNC, 201, 210; allocation decisions, 61, 117, 142, 148, 201; becomes full-time operation, 114; budget, 118, 119, 135; campaign activities, 25, 27, 30, 31, 34, 44, 56–57, 61, 100, 103–105, 106–10, 112–20, 132–35, 148–49, 197–210; candidate conference, 112, 117; candidate recruitment, 117, 135; coordinated expenditures by, 201, 210; coordination with NRSC, 113; coordination with RNC, 31, 35, 36, 56, 59, 60–62, 104, 119, 201–202, 209; coordination with RNC and NRSC, 106–107, 115, 117–18, 143; divisions of, 115; encourage incumbent donations to candidates, 201–202; film production center, construction of, 109; fund-raising through House-Senate dinner, 113, 115, 118; fund-raising through member assessments, 31; fund-raising scandal of 1916, 57, 61; Incumbent Review Panel, 148–50, 207–208; Incumbent Support Fund, 207; leadership involvement in, 116; and Literary Bureau, 44–45; offices of in Washington, D.C., 33, 45; offices of in New York City, 46; origins, 15–20, 23; party-building in the South, 23; period of hibernation, 36; plan to shut down 1975, 133; and Southern constitutional conventions, 26–27; and Speaker's Bureau, 44; staff, 103–104, 107, 109, 114–15, 117, 133, 135, 201, 245n.23

National Republican Congressional Committee (NRCC) chair: 1914 contest for, 57; 1916 contest for, 57; 1959 contest for, 112; 1961 contest for, 113; 1972 contest, role of White House in, 120; 1974 contest for, 132; 1975 contest for, 182–83; 1990 contest for, 184–87; evolution of 1975–present, 182–87; as leadership training ground, 63, 105, 107, 112

National Republican Senatorial Committee (NRSC): agency agreements, invention of, 139, 143; allocation decisions, 142; budget, 86, 94, 96, 143; campaign activities, 70–71, 86–90, 92–94, 96, 134, 143; coordination with RNC, 73, 86, 93, 94; coordination with RNC and NRCC, 70–71, 88, 143; fund-raising innovations, 151; fund-raising solicitation of Senators, 96; leadership involvement in, 92; origins, 70; Republican Senatorial Inner Circle, 151; staff, 86, 89, 93, 134, 136

National Republican Senatorial Committee (NRSC) chair: contests for, 95–96, 191–93; in leadership structure, 71–72; as leadership training ground, 89, 191–93; utility in presidential bids, 89–90, 191–93

NC. *See* National committees

Nelson, Garrison, 24

Nickles, Don, 151, 193

Nixon, Richard, 88, 96, 112–13, 119–20, 127, 129

Nofziger, Lyn, 192

NRCC. *See* National Republican Congressional Committee

NRSC. *See* National Republican Senatorial Committee

O'Brien, Larry, 95

Oldfield, William, DCCC chair while minority whip, 101

Olsen, Johan P., 16

O'Mahoney, Joseph, 78

O'Neill, Thomas, 120–21, 128–30, 132, 188–89

Opposition research. *See* Campaign activities

PAC. *See* Political action committees

Packwood, Robert (Bob), 135–36, 152, 191–92

Party resurgence, 125

Paxon, Bill, 187, 200–203, 207, 210, 213, 269n.39

Payne-Aldrich Tariff, and 1910 election, 54

Peabody, Robert L., 129, 174, 189

Phipps, Lawrence, 73

Pittman, Key, 72

Political action committees (PACs): contribution strategies, 137; relationship with parties, 145

Political Broadcasting Act, 127

Political parties in the House of Representatives. *See* CCCs; Democratic party; House of

INDEX 297

Representatives, political parties in; Republican party
Political parties in the United States Senate. *See* CCCs; Democratic party; Republican party; Senate, political parties in
Polsby, Nelson, 39, 170
Pre-primary endorsements, prohibition on by CCCs, 10, 87, 147
Presidency, decline of in 1866–1896, 21
Presidential party, 6; relationship with House and Senate parties, 6–10
Progressive movement, influence on campaign activity, 50

Radical Republicans, 17, 18, 30; and use of Union Congressional Committee, 24; views of Andrew Johnson, 18
Radical rule during, 29
Rainey, Henry, 102
Randall, Samuel, 34
Rangel, Charles, 189
Rayburn, Sam, 76, 91, 106
Reagan, Ronald, 135, 143, 184, 199; tensions with Packwood at NRSC, 191–92
Recession of 1893, 43
Reconstruction: length of, 28; radical views of, 18–19, 26–27
Redding, Jack, 111
Reed, Thomas, 39, 40, 42, 51
Republican Congressional Committee. *See* National Republican Congressional Committee (NRCC)

Republican National Committee (RNC), 29; coordination with NRCC, 30, 31, 35, 36, 59; coordination with NRSC, 31, 35, 36, 56, 59, 60–62, 104, 119, 201–202, 209; coordination with NRCC and NRSC, 143; offices in New York, 33; use of RCC headquarters in Washington, 45
Republican National Finance Committee (RNFC), 93, 96, 113, 115, 119
Republican party: fund-raising successes with small donors, 150; leadership structure in the House, 163–64; leadership structure in the Senate, 166; split in 1910—NRCC role in, 55; split in 1912, 51, 57. *See also* Radical Republicans
Rhodes, John, 113–14, 183
Richardson, James, 45; made minority leader after RCC service, 46, 48
RNC. *See* Republican National Committee
RNFC. *See* Republican National Finance Committee
Robb, Charles (Chuck), 177, 194; DSCC and presidential bid, 194–95
Rollins, Ed, as NRCC co-chair, 184–87
Roosevelt, Franklin Delano, 101, 103
Roosevelt, Theodore, 46, 50, 54–55
Rothman, David, 21–22
Rousselot, John, 132, 182–83

Schenck, Robert Cumming, 24, 27, 29
Schoeppel, Andrew, 90
Senate: institutionalization of, 69; patronage, 22; political parties in, 6; relationship with House parties 22, 40–41. *See also* Congressional careers; Congressional leadership; DSCC; Institutional party interest; NRSC
Senatorial campaign committees. *See* Congressional campaign committees
Senators: method of election, 40–41, 54–55, 69, 241n.1; power of in nineteenth century, 21–22, 41
Seniority in Congress, 250n.106. *See also* Congressional careers
Seventeenth Amendment, 41, 55, 243n.1
Sherman, James Schoolcraft, 49
Simpson, Richard, 108, 110, 112, 122
Sisk, B. F., 188
Slater, Harold, 109
Smathers, George, 90–91, 98, 256n.70
Snell, Bertrand, 104–105
Soft money: defined, 150–51; disclosure of, 151–52; as used by DCCC, 150–51
Speaker of the House. *See* Congressional leadership
Speakers. *See* Campaign activities
Speaker's Advisory Group, 210
Speeches or speech materials. *See* campaign activities

Springer, William, 112
Stampp, Kenneth M., 19
Stevens, Ted, 134
Stevenson, Adlai, 91
Stewart, Wyatt, 133
Stockmeyer, Steven, 133
Sullivan, William, 174
Sundquist, Donald, 184, 186
Swanson, Claude, 74, 75

Taft, William Howard, 49, 50, 54–55
Tower, John, challenge to Murphy for NRSC chair, 95–96; 116, 118
Townsend, John, 73
Truman, David, 4, 174
Tullock, Thomas, 24, 27
Tydings, Millard, 72, 82

Underwood, Oscar, 53
Union Congressional Committee, 17. *See also* NRCC

Valeo, Francis, 131
Vander Jagt, Guy, 132–33, 139, 148–49, 182–83, 189, 190, 200; 1990 challenge, 184–87
Voting records used in campaigns. *See* Campaign activities

Wallace, William, 36
Wallop, Malcolm, 193
Walsh, David, 72
Washington resources: defined, 9, 10, 11; used to assist campaigns, 13, 71, 80, 95, 97, 110, 146–47, 211–16, 242n.12

Westland, Jack, 113
White, Justice Byron, 140
Wiebe, Robert, 43
Williams, John Sharp, 48
Wilson, Robert (Bob), 92, 94, 112–15, 116, 118–20, 129, 131
Wilson, Woodrow, 21, 51, 54; and 1916 elections, 59–60; work for DCCC in 1914 elections, 58
Wood, William, 100–101, 103
Woods, Frank, 57
Wright, Jim, 188, 190